ENGLISH G

HIGHLIGHT

1

Cornelsen

English G · Highlight · Band 1

Im Auftrag des Verlages herausgegeben von
Frank Donoghue, Nenagh, Irland

Konzepterarbeitung von
Susan Abbey, Nenagh, Irland
Wolfgang Biederstädt, Köln
Frank Donoghue, Nenagh, Irland

Erarbeitet von
Sydney Thorne, York
Susan Abbey, Nenagh, Irland
Frank Donoghue, Nenagh, Irland

in Zusammenarbeit mit der Englischredaktion
Susanne Döpper (Projektleitung); Silvia Wiedemann
(koordinierende Redakteurin); Britta Bensmann,
Christine Maxwell (Bildredaktion) sowie Stefanie
Dahlhoff, Jenny Dames, Michael Dunkel, Sandhya
Gupta, Karin Wedepohl, Ralph Williams

Vokabelanhang
Ingrid Raspe, Düsseldorf

Beratende Mitwirkung
Armin Düpmeier, Warendorf; Anke Jauß, Wallhausen;
Petra Klein, Villmar; Christa Lüdemann, Hannover;
Tobias Pfeifer, Dossenheim; Stefan Royl, Lörrach;
Dagmar Wengh, Ankum; Ellen Wiegard-Kaiser,
Bielefeld sowie Herbert Willms, Herford

Illustrationen
Steffen Wolff, Brohl-Lützing sowie
Christian Görke, Berlin; Jeongsook Lee, Heidelberg;
David Norman, Meerbusch; Elwood Smith,
Rhinebeck, USA

Layoutkonzept und technische Umsetzung
Klein & Halm Grafikdesign, Berlin

Umschlaggestaltung
Cornelsen Schulverlage Design unter Verwendung
der Entwürfe von Klein & Halm Grafikdesign, Berlin
und kleiner und bold GmbH, Berlin

Für die freundliche Unterstützung danken wir dem
Eggbuckland Community College, Plymouth.

www.cornelsen.de

Die Webseiten Dritter, deren Internetadressen
in diesem Lehrwerk angegeben sind, wurden
vor Drucklegung sorgfältig geprüft. Der Verlag
übernimmt keine Gewähr für die Aktualität und
den Inhalt dieser Seiten oder solcher, die mit ihnen
verlinkt sind.

Dieses Werk berücksichtigt die Regeln der
reformierten Rechtschreibung und Zeichensetzung.

Alle Drucke dieser Auflage sind inhaltlich unverändert
und können im Unterricht nebeneinander verwendet
werden.

Druck und Bindung: Livonia Print, Riga

1. Auflage, 2. Druck 2017
broschiert
ISBN 978-3-06-032571-9

1. Auflage, 3. Druck 2022
gebunden
ISBN 978-3-06-032572-6

ISBN 978-3-06-032798-0 (E-Book)

PEFC zertifiziert
Dieses Produkt stammt aus nachhaltig
bewirtschafteten Wäldern und kontrollierten
Quellen.
www.pefc.de

PEFC/12-31-006

Dein Englischbuch enthält folgende Teile:

Unit 1 bis 5	Die fünf Kapitel des Buches
Summer is here!	Ein fakultatives, kurzes Kapitel zum Abschluss
Diff-Bank	Weitere Aufgaben – unterschiedlich schwer
Wordbank	Zusätzliche Wörter zu bestimmten Themen
Text file TF	Weitere Lesetexte, passend zu den Units
Skills file SF	Beschreibung wichtiger Lern- und Arbeitstechniken
Language file LF	Zusammenfassung wichtiger Sprachregeln
Vocabulary	Wörterverzeichnis zum Lernen der neuen Wörter
Dictionary	Alphabetisches Wörterverzeichnis zum Nachschlagen (*English-German* und *German-English*)

Die Units bestehen aus diesen Teilen:

Lead-in	Einstieg in die neue Unit
Theme 1 / Theme 2	Neue Themen mit vielen Aktivitäten und Übungen
Story	Eine Geschichte zum Lesen
Skills training	Hören|Listening (L) – Lesen|Reading (R) – Sprechen|Speaking (S) – Schreiben|Writing (W) – Sprachmittlung|Mediation (M) – Hör-Sehverstehen|Viewing (V)
Focus on language	Texte und Aufgaben zum Entdecken von Regeln und Üben wichtiger Strukturen
Practice / Test	Üben, Vertiefen, Lernfortschritt feststellen

In den Units findest du diese Symbole:

🎧	Hörtexte / Buchtexte auf CD
🎥	Filme auf der DVD
MK	Aufgaben zur Schulung von Medienkompetenz
○ ●	leichtere Übungen/schwierigere Übungen
○ //●	Bei dieser Aufgabe gibt es zur leichteren Variante in der Unit eine schwierigere in der Diff-Bank.
More practice 1 p.123	Weitere Übungen in der Diff-Bank

Hi! What's your name?

Unit 1 · Welcome to our school

Unit 2 · At home with Ellie

Unit 3 · Luca's birthday

INHALT

Unit 4 · Berry's farm

Unit 5 · All about Adam

* Summer is here!

Anhang

L	*Listening*
R	*Reading*
S	*Speaking*
W	*Writing*
V	*Viewing*
M	*Mediation*
I	*Intercultural competence*
ST	*Study skills*
*	*Fakultativ*

Hi! What's your name?

Hi, I'm Cyril the crab. What's your name?

I'm four. What about you?

I'm from Plymouth in England. What about you?

1 Cyril

a) Listen and repeat.
1.2

b) Listen and answer Cyril's questions.
1.3

Hi, I'm Sabina.

I'm ten.

I'm from Leimen in Germany.

2 Partners in your class.

Talk to four partners in your class.

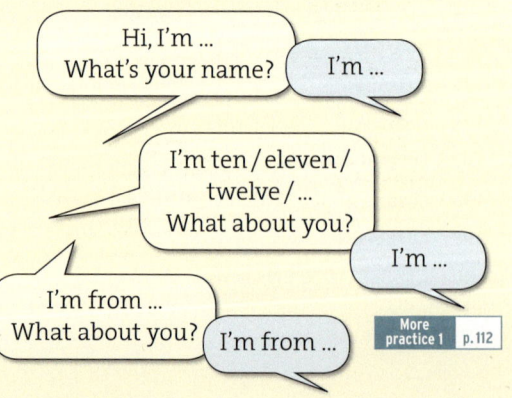

Hi, I'm ...
What's your name?

I'm ...

I'm ten / eleven / twelve / ...
What about you?

I'm ...

I'm from ...
What about you?

I'm from ...

More practice 1 p. 112

► Workbook 1, p. 2

3 GAME   I can see …

a) What can you see? Find five things in the picture.

b) Play the game.
– I can see Cyril.
– I can see Cyril and a beach.
– I can see Cyril and a beach and …

4   SONG

1.4
1.5

CYRIL'S SONG

I'm Cyril the crab
And I like the sea.
I love water
All around me.

I run and I hide,
I dive in the sand.
Don't pick me up
Or I'll pinch your hand.

Colours

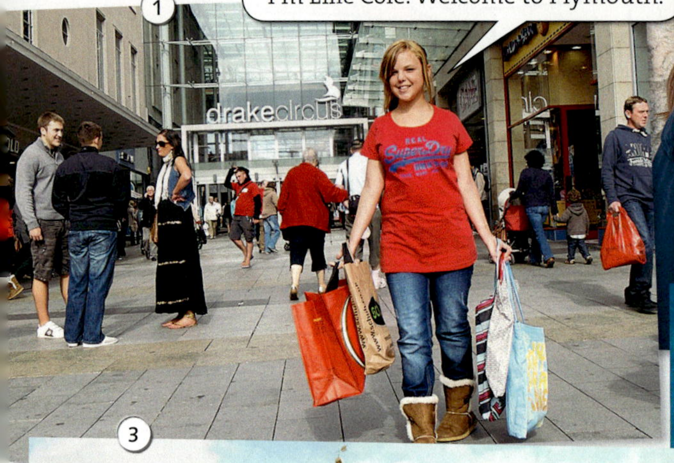

1
I'm Ellie Cole. Welcome to Plymouth.

2

3

4

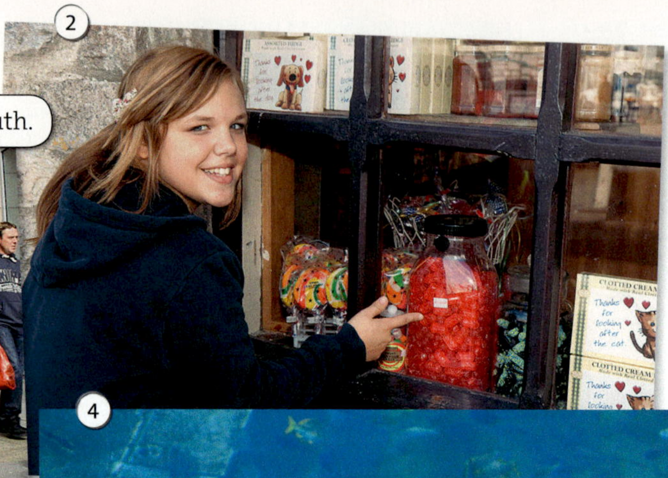

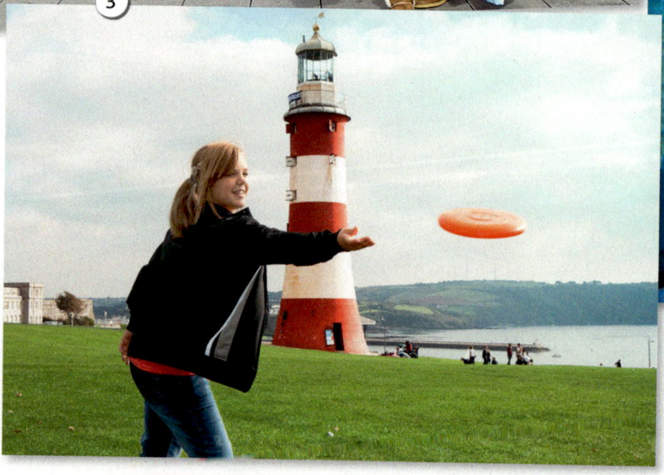

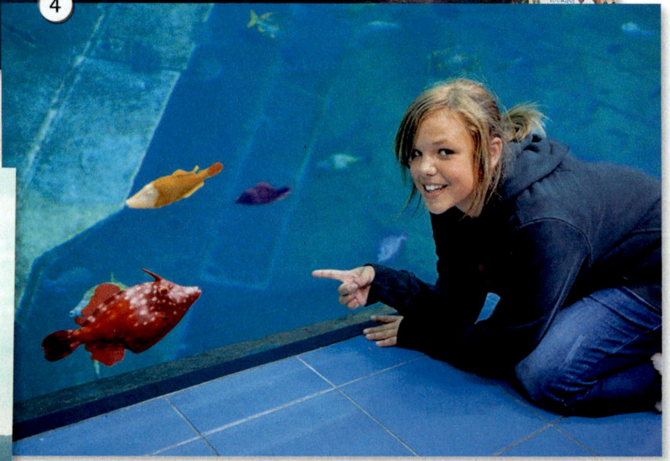

1 Colours

a) Make colour cards.

green red yellow

brown black blue

white pink orange

green

b) Listen to Ellie. (1.6)
What colours can you hear?

c) Listen again. What's right?
Ellie says:

1 I like pink sweets.
2 I like yellow sweets.
3 I don't like black sweets.

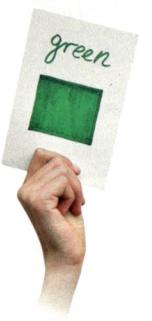

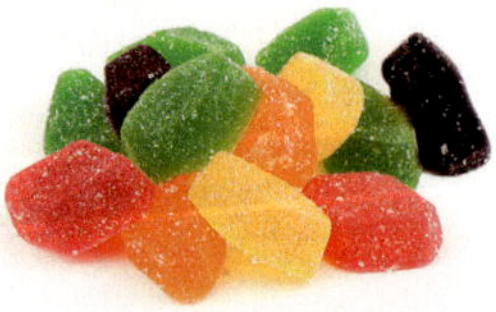

2 What about you?

a) Talk to two or three partners.

A I like green. What about you?
B I like ...

A I don't like ... What about you?
B I don't like ...

b) Write about you.

I like ...
I don't like ...

More practice 2 p. 112

Hast du alles richtig geschrieben? Gib deine Sätze einem Partner oder einer Partnerin zur Kontrolle.

► Workbook 2–4, p. 3

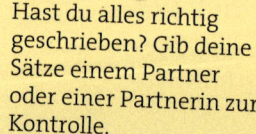

Sports and hobbies

1 playing football

I'm Adam Osmanovic. I like playing football. And I like watching TV too.

2 swimming

3 watching TV

4 dancing

5 skateboarding

6 reading

7 riding

8 playing games

1 What are the sports and hobbies?

a) Listen to Adam. What are the six right pictures – one, two, three, four, five, six, seven, eight?

1.7

b) Listen and repeat what Adam says.

1.8

2 What about you?

Talk to three or more partners.
- I like ... What about you?
- I like ... too.
  I don't like ...

▶ Wordbank 1, p. 150

3 A sports and hobbies poster

Make a class poster.

Sports and hobbies in class 5a

reading

skateboarding

swimming

Animals

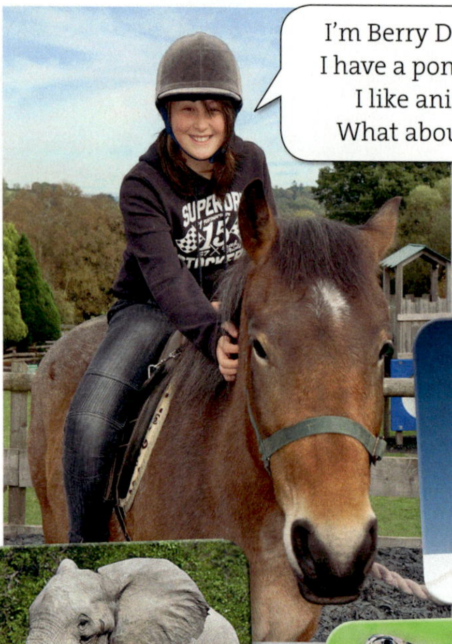
I'm Berry Donovan.
I have a pony, Harry.
I like animals.
What about you?

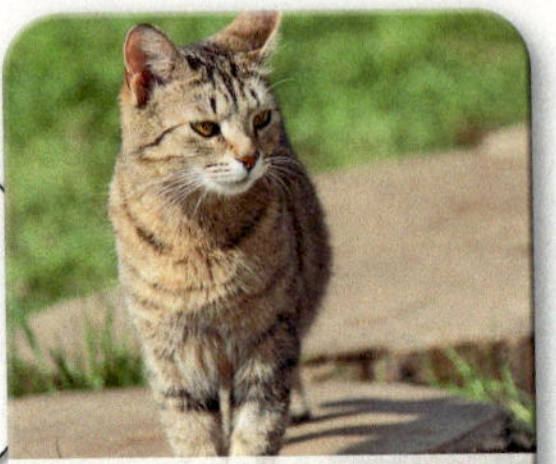
a cat

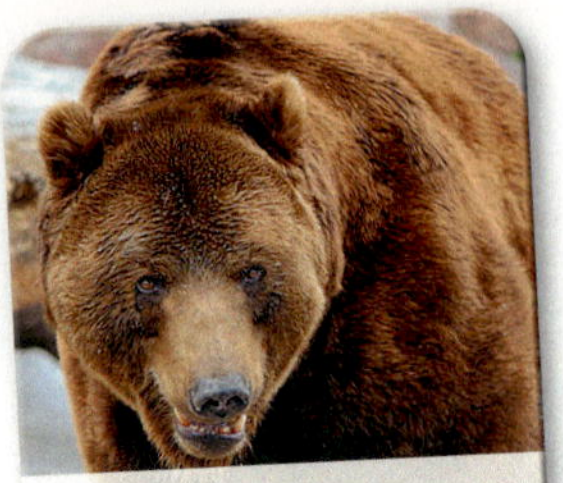
a bear

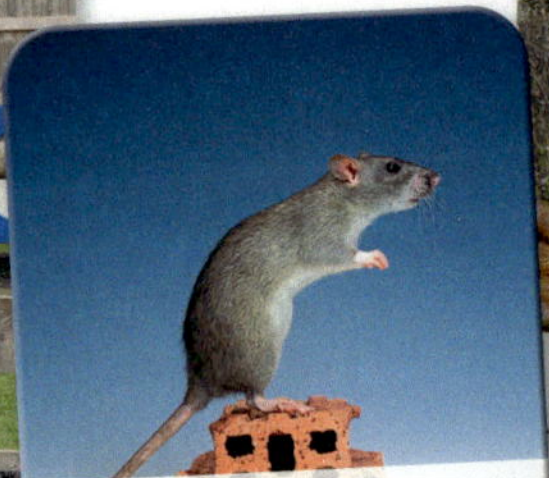
a rat

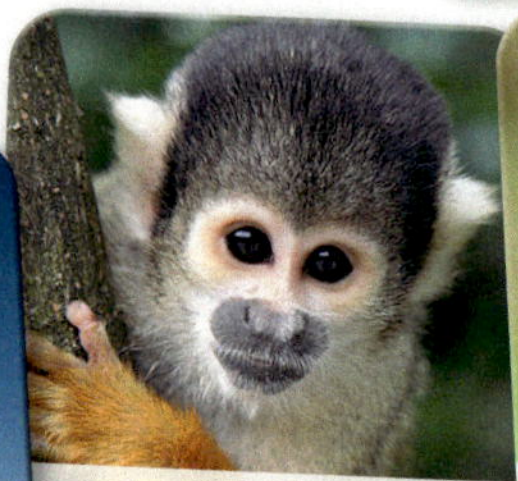
a monkey

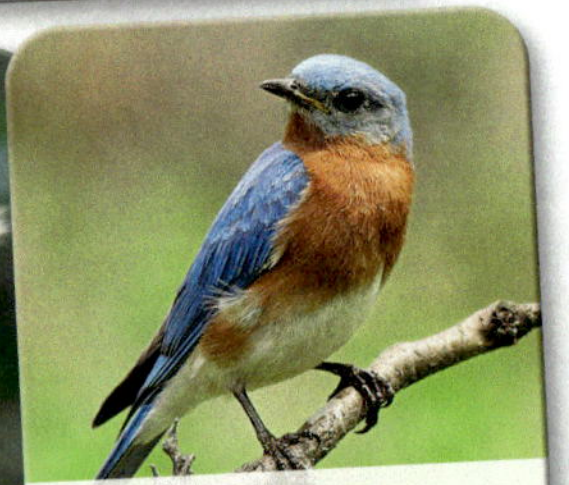
a bird

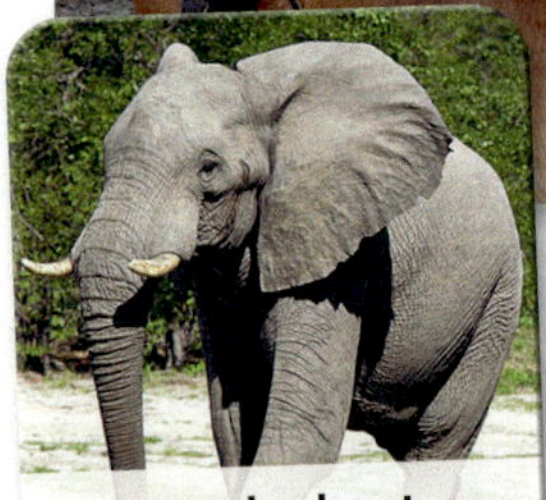
an elephant

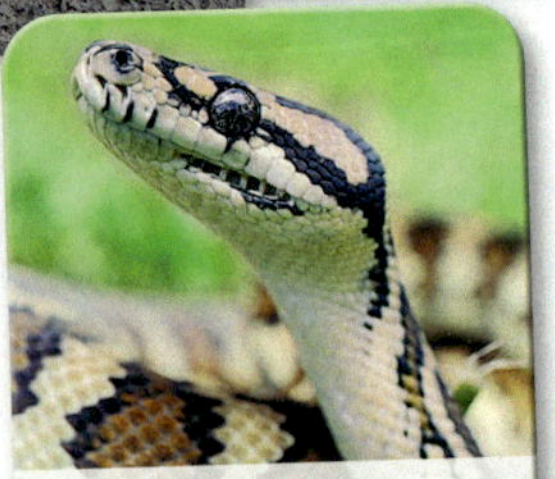
a snake

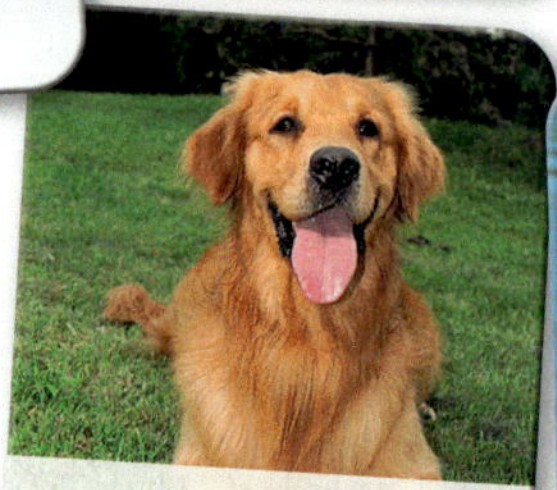
a dog

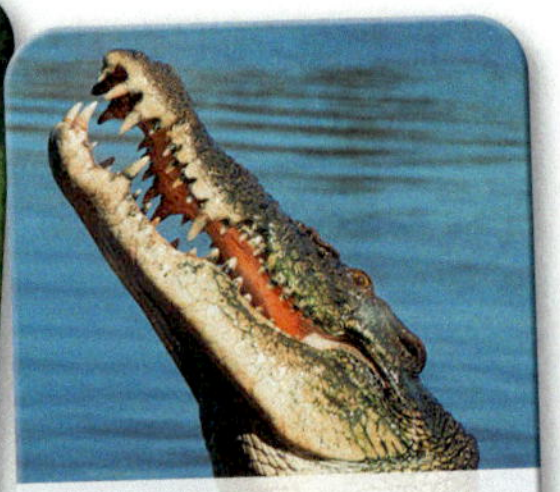
a crocodile

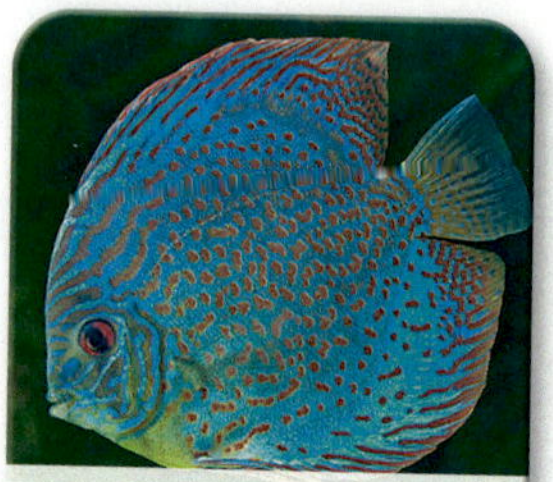
a fish

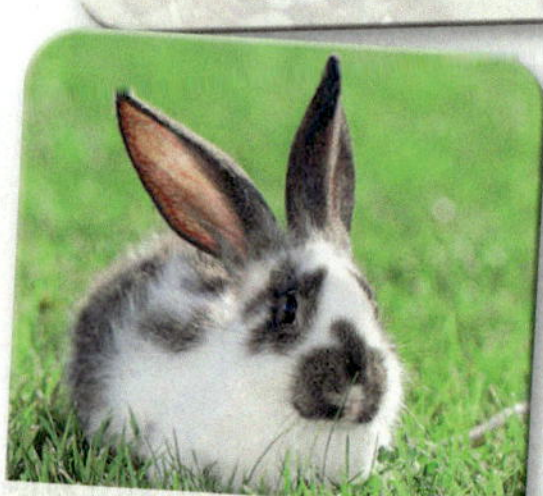
a rabbit

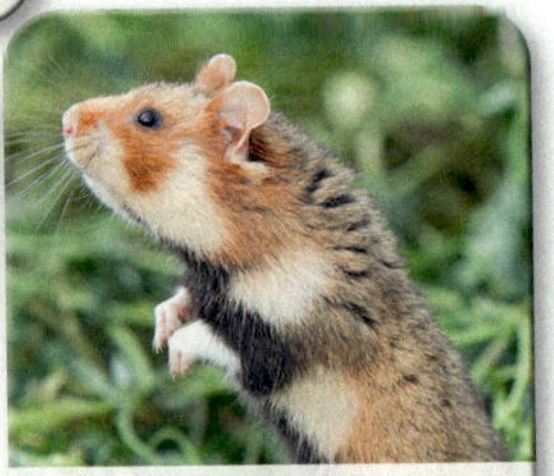
a hamster

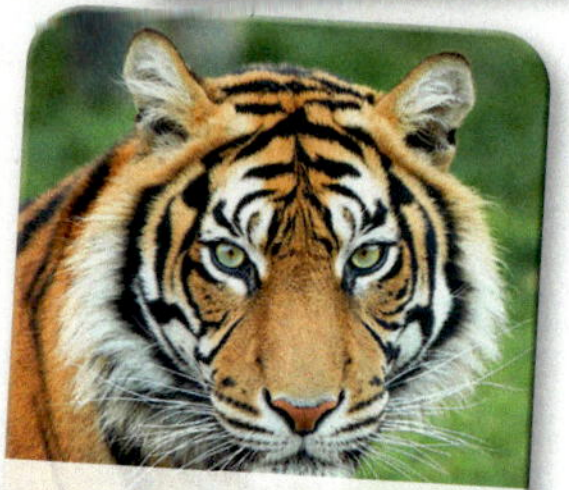
a tiger

1.9

1 Different animals

Listen. What animal can you hear?

1 a cat, 2 a ...

2 Partner work

Look at the animals for one minute. Then close your book. Can you say nine animals? Can you write nine animals?

3 GAME

Make animal cards. You can ask your teacher too. Play the *Animal pairs* game.

a dog

▸ *Workbook 6, p. 4*

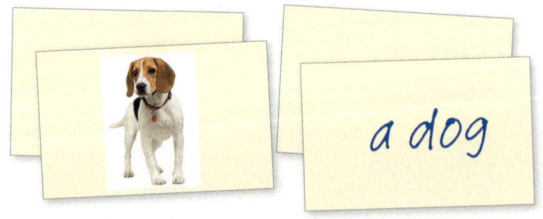

My favourite thing

1 I like my bike

a) Listen and read.

I'm Luca Boateng.

Ellie —— What's your favourite thing, Luca?

Luca —— My favourite thing? My favourite thing is my bike. It's great. It's blue and black. It's small and it's old, but I like my bike.

b) Listen again and repeat.

2 Your favourite thing

a) What's your favourite thing?

my camera

my computer

my mobile

my football

b) Write about your favourite thing.

My favourite thing is my ...
It's old / new.
It's red / green / black / ...
It's big / small.
I like my ...
It's great.

▶ Wordbank 2, p. 151

c) Talk to the class about your favourite thing.

My favourite thing is ...
It's ... and it's ...
I like my ...

3 Group work

a) Ask three or more partners about favourite colours, animals and hobbies.

– What's your favourite colour, Anna?
– Blue! What's your favourite animal?
– A tiger! What's ... hobby?
– ...

b) Write the answers on the board.

Favourite colours	Favourite animals	Favourite hobbies
blue ‖‖‖	tiger │	...
red ‖‖	...	...
...	...	...

The last day of the holidays

1 **A story**

a) Look at the pictures. Cyril is in pictures A and F. And Luca? Ellie? Berry? Adam? Sandy?

b) Listen to part one of the story. Put the pictures (A–F) in the right order.

1.11

c) Listen to part two of the story. Put the pictures (A–E) in the right order.

A

B

C

D

E

The last day of the holidays – yippee!

2 SONG
1.13
1.14

1 2 3   No more swimming in the sea
4 and 5   Summer holidays – goodbye!
6 7 8   Last day of the holidays.
9 and 10   Oh no! Back to school again.

Welcome to our school

A
B

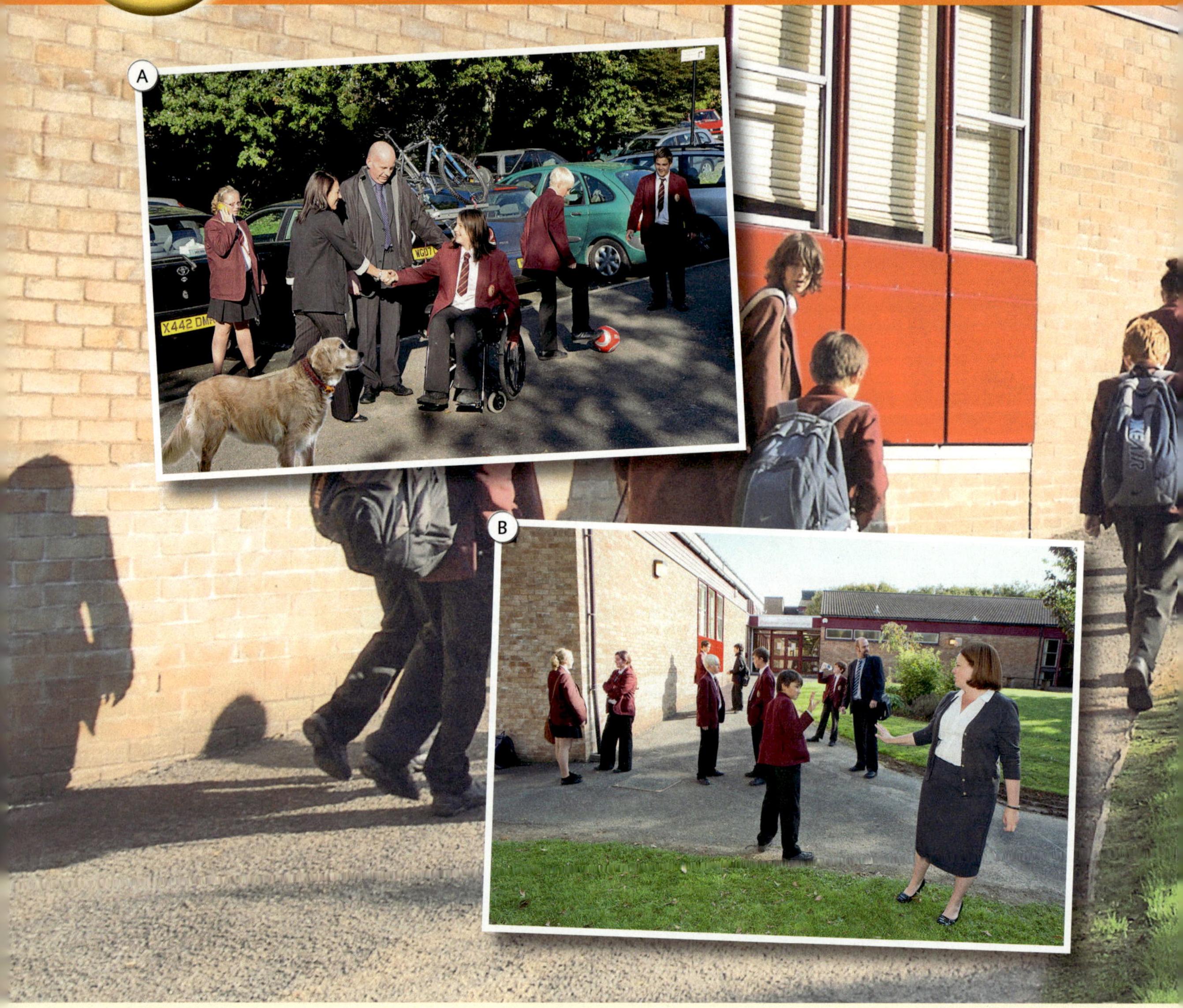

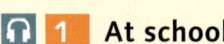

1 At school

1.15

Listen. What can you hear? Point at the right pictures.

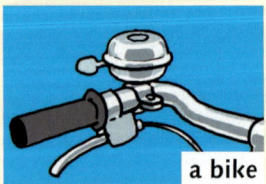

a bike

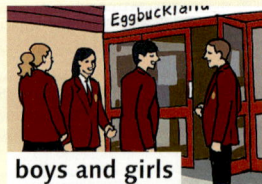

boys and girls

a teacher

a bird

a car

a mobile

a dog

a football

▸ Workbook 1, p. 7

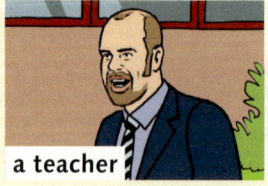

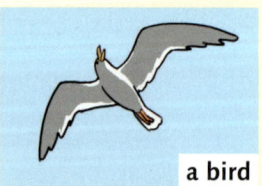

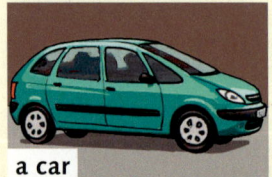

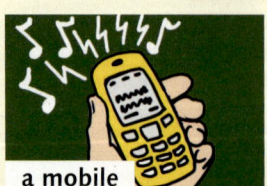

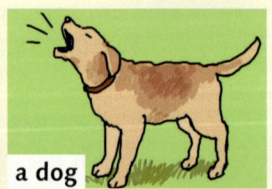

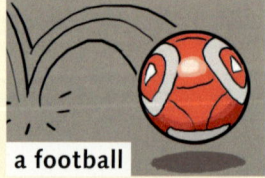

2 The first day

a) Listen. Put the pictures (A–D) in the right order.

1.16

b) Listen and repeat.

1.17

c) Read one card with a partner. Then read a new card with a new partner.

1
A: Hello, I'm ...
   What's your name?
B: Hi, I'm ...
A: How are you?
B: I'm OK.

2
A: Hi, ...
B: Hi, ... How are you?
A: I'm fine, thanks.
   How are you?
B: OK, thanks.

3
A: Goodbye, ...
B: Bye, ...
A: Have a good day.
B: You too. See you.
A: OK, see you.

In my class

1 Good morning, class 7Y

a) Who's in class 7Y? Who's the English teacher?

1.18

> Good morning, class 7Y. I'm Ms Lee – your English teacher. And who are you?

> Hi, I'm Berry. I'm eleven. I have no brothers and sisters.

> I'm Ellie. I'm twelve. I have two brothers and one sister. We're from Plymouth. My best friends are Ruby and Charlie. They're in class 7X.

> Hi, I'm Luca. I'm ten. I have one brother – Jack. He's fourteen. And I have one sister – Grace. She's six.

b) Copy and complete the table.

Name	How old?	Brothers	Sisters
Berry	11	no	...
Luca	...	...	...
Ellie	...	...	...

c) Listen to Adam. Is the right picture 1 or 2?

1.19

d) Listen again. Complete the table in 1b) for Adam.

▶ *Workbook 4, p. 8*

2 Ms Lee, Ellie and Luca

Copy and complete what they say.

he • I • she • they •
we • you

Ms Lee ___ Good morning class 7Y. ...'m Ms Lee. And who are ...?

Luca ___ Hi, I'm Luca. I have one brother – Jack. ...'s fourteen.
And I have one sister – Grace. ...'s six.

Ellie ___ I'm Ellie. I have two brothers and one sister. ...'re from Plymouth.
My best friends are Ruby and Charlie. ...'re in class 7X.

More
practice 1 | p. 112

3 What about you?

a) Write notes. Start like this:

I'm ... *(name)*

I'm ... *(how old?)*

I'm from ...

I'm in class ...

I'm at ... school.

My class teacher is Mr / Mrs / Ms ...

My English teacher is Mr / Mrs / Ms ...

⬤ Can you write more?

My favourite hobby / sport / colour is ...

I have ... brother(s). I have ... sister(s).

👤 Ms Smith **or** Mrs Smith

👤 Mr Smith

b) Use the notes in 3a) and talk to your group.

Hi. I'm Lukas. I'm ...

Das Dossier ist eine Mappe,
in der du deine wichtigen
und schönen Arbeiten
sammeln kannst. Es gehört
zum Portfolio.

c) Write about you for your class.

The text is for your DOSSIER too.

Hello. I'm ...

I'm Vanessa.
I'm eleven.
I'm at Erich
Kästner School.
I'm in class 5a.
My class teacher
is Mrs Schmidt.

Hello, I'm Tim. I'm from
Düsseldorf in Germany.
I'm at Erich Kästner School.
My favourite teacher is
Mr Jahn.

I have two sisters
and one dog .

My best friends are
Samir and Patrick.

My favourite sport is
playing football and my
favourite colours are red
and white.

The first day at school

🎧 1 A tour of the school
1.20

a) Class 7Y is on a tour of the school with Ms Lee.
Listen and point at the pictures in the right order.

C

You have ICT here.

A

You have English, maths and geography here.

D

You have art here.

B

You have science here.

E

We have PE here.

b) Listen again. Match 1–5 with the pictures A–E.

1 picture B, 2 ..., 3 ...

1 Where's Ellie? She isn't here.

2 Welcome to Eggy!

3 This isn't a PE lesson now!

4 Hello, Mr Brown.

5 It's OK. I'm here!

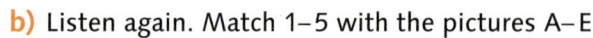

2 School rap
1.21
1.22

All my teachers say,
Work hard every day!
Music, French and ICT,
Drama and technology.

Work on Monday,
Work on Tuesday,
Work on Wednesday,
Thursday, Friday.

All my teachers say,
Work hard every day!

3 The new timetable

Eggbuckland Community College
Class 7Y timetable

Lesson	Time	Monday	Tuesday	Wednesday	Thursday	Friday
1	9.00–10.00	English	music	technology	geography	PE
2	10.00–11.00	maths	English	history	French	PE
	11.00–11.25	BREAK				
3	11.25–12.25	art	history	English	science	geography
4	12.25–1.25	art	science	maths	science	English
	1.25–2.05	LUNCH				
5	2.05–3.05	French	drama	science	ICT	technology

a) Look at the Eggy timetable. What are the names of the lessons?

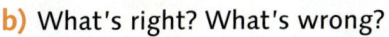

More practice 2   p. 113

b) **What's right? What's wrong?**
1 Lesson one on Monday is French.
2 Lesson two on Tuesday is music.
3 Lesson three on Wednesday is English.
4 Lesson four on Thursday is science.
5 Lesson five on Friday is PE.

c) **Listen to Ellie and Adam.**
1.23   **What's right? What's wrong?**

More practice 3   p. 113

Right.

Wrong.

1 Before you read

What can you see?

I can see (1) a blue and white tie, (2) a …

> green • red • yellow • brown • black •
> blue • white • pink • orange

Ellie has no tie

1.24

It's Tuesday morning at Eggy.

Miss B — Good morning, boys and girls.
I'm Miss Borowski, the school
principal. Welcome to Eggy.
Please remember – the uniform
is important here in our school!

Ellie ___ Oh no! My tie!

Before the English lesson

Miss B — Hello. What's your name?

Ellie ___ Hello, Miss Borowski. I'm Ellie Cole.

Miss B — Where's your tie, Ellie?

Ellie ___ Sorry. It's at home.

Miss B — That isn't good, Ellie. Remember
– the uniform is important!

In the English lesson

Luca ___ Where's your tie, Ellie?

Ellie ___ It's at home.

Luca ___ The uniform is important!

Ellie ___ I know, I know.

In the science lesson

Berry ___ Where's your tie, Ellie?

Ellie ___ It's at home.

Berry ___ Oh, but the uniform is …

Ellie ___ … important! I know, I know.

5

6

In the art lesson
Ellie ___ Look Adam – no tie. It's at home.
Adam _ That's bad, Ellie.
Ellie ___ I know, I know.
The uniform is important!
Luca ___ Hey, I have an idea.

In the canteen
Berry ___ Great tie, Ellie!
Luca ___ Cool colours.
Ellie ___ Thanks!
Miss B _ I like your tie, Ellie.
Ellie ___ Thanks, Miss Borowski.
Miss B _ But it isn't the school tie.
L/B/A ___ The uniform is important!
Miss B _ Yes, that's right.

2 People in the story

1 Who has no tie?
2 Who has a good idea?
3 Who has a cool tie?
4 Who says, "Where's your tie?"
5 Who says, "The uniform is important!"

> More practice 4 p. 113

3 Uniforms: Good or bad?

1 I think uniforms are a good/bad idea.
2 I like/don't like the Eggy uniform.
3 Our school has no uniform.
That's good/bad.
4 I think a tie is/isn't cool.
5 I like/don't like Ellie's tie.

4 School words

Write the words in the right lists.

> principal • tie • art • girls •
> science • boys • English

Lessons	People	Uniform
art	...	...
...	...	...

5 THEATRE TIME

a) Make groups of six students: Ellie, Luca, Adam, Berry, Miss Borowski and a narrator. Read the scenes.

b) Act the scenes for the class. What's the best group?

> More practice 5 p. 114

A brochure

1 Before you read

What can you buy at Martins?   Things for Ⓐ riding?   Ⓑ school?   Ⓒ dancing?

WELCOME TO MARTINS

Buy **2** for **£1**

Rubber

Pencil sharpener

Ruler

Help for boys and girls in Africa

- Give Martins your old pencil case with good pens and pencils.
- We will send your pencil cases to schools in Africa.
- Buy your new school things at Martins and we will give you £1.

Special offers

10 pens £3.89 £1.94   10 pencils £3.89 £1.94

Pencil case £7.99 £3.90   Calculator £5.19 £2.50

Exercise book £1.95   Digicomp laptop £327 £299

Buy your school things at MARTINS

2 ○ School things at Martins
Look at the brochure.
What can you buy for …
a) maths lessons? → *a pencil, …*
b) £1?

3 Your school things
a) Make a list of the things in your pencil case: *a ruler, …*

b) You can buy your school things at Martins. You have £10.
Write a shopping list.

4 ● MEDIATION   Help for boys and girls in Africa
Wie hilft ein Einkauf bei Martins Mädchen und Jungen aus Afrika? Wähle Ⓐ, Ⓑ oder Ⓒ.
Ⓐ Die Federmäppchen von Martins werden von einer Schule in Afrika hergestellt.
Ⓑ Bei jedem Einkauf bei Martins spendet das Geschäft ein Pfund für eine Schule in Afrika.
Ⓒ Martins schickt dein altes Federmäppchen an eine Schule in Afrika.

1 Networks

a) 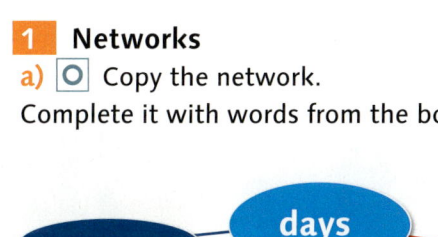 Copy the network.
Complete it with words from the box.

> Friday • Monday •
> school days •
> Thursday • Tuesday •
> weekend

> Besonders gut behält man Vokabeln, wenn man sie aufschreibt, zum Beispiel in einem *network* (Aufgabe 1) oder auf kleinen Kärtchen (Aufgabe 2).

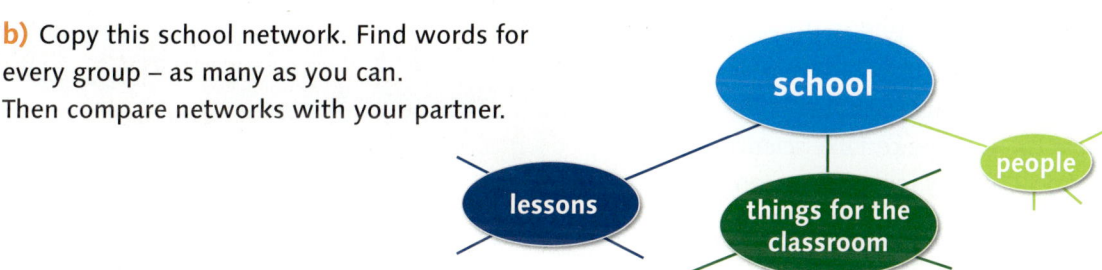

Saturday   Sunday   Wednesday

b) Copy this school network. Find words for
every group – as many as you can.
Then compare networks with your partner.

school

people

lessons

things for the
classroom

2 Word and phrase cards

a) Make cards with phrases from the green box.

> Welcome to
> our school.

> Have a good day.
> How are you?
> Where's Ms Lee?
> See you.
> Good morning.
> I'm in class 5.
> Sorry!
> Welcome to our school.
> Thanks.
> I'm from Germany.
> We're best friends.
> What's your name?
> That's right.

b) Write the German phrase on the back of the card.

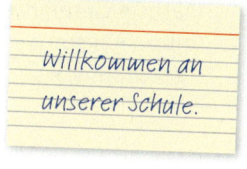

> Willkommen an
> unserer Schule.

Word and phrase box

c) Put the cards in a box.

d) Work with a partner. First your partner checks you.
Then check your partner.
– What's 'Willkommen an unserer Schule' in English?
– Welcome to our school.
– Right.

> Lerne Vokabeln regelmäßig – lieber jeden Tag 5–10 Minuten als einmal die Woche zwei Stunden.
>
> Mehr Tipps zum Wörterlernen findest du im Skills file.

▶ Skills file 1, pp. 140–141

Speaking to friends at school

1 Hi, Berry!

a) Read the dialogue.
1.25

Ellie ___	Hi, Berry! How are you?
Berry ___	Hi, Ellie. I'm fine, thanks. What about you?
Ellie ___	I'm fine too, thanks. Can I borrow a pen, please?
Berry ___	Sure, here you are.
Ellie ___	Thanks. What's the next lesson?
Berry ___	It's PE. I like PE. What's your favourite lesson?
Ellie ___	It's science. I like science. It's my favourite lesson.

b) Practise the dialogue with a partner – and then again with a new partner.

2  NOW YOU // ● p.114

Write the dialogue with a partner. Then practise with your partner.

> Your name and your partner's name →

A Hi, ...! How ... you?
B Hi, ... I'm fine. What about you?
A I'm fine too, thanks.
  Can I borrow a ..., please?
B Sure, here you are.
A Thanks. What's the next lesson?
B It's ... I like ...
  It's my favourite lesson.

> pen • pencil • ruler • rubber • ...

> English • science • maths • German • music • history • geography • ...

3 Interviews

a) Copy the table.
● Write a question 5.

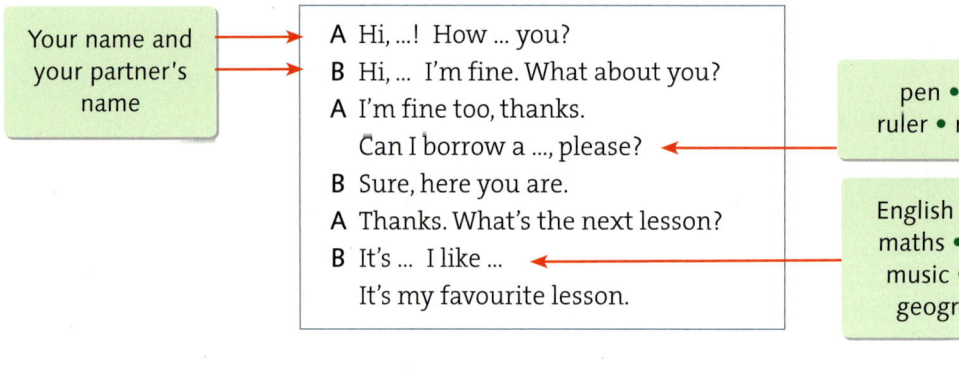

	NAME: ...	NAME: ...	NAME: ...	NAME: ...
1 Who's your favourite teacher?				
2 Who's your best friend in our class?				
3 What's your favourite hobby?				
4 What's your favourite animal?				

> Who's ...? = Wer ist ...?
> What's ...? = Was ist ...?

b) Walk around: Ask four partners.
Write the names and answers in the table.

1 The kids from Harbour Road¹:

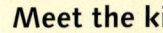

Meet the kids²!

a) Watch the film. Who are the kids?
Talk to a partner.

Photo A is …   Photo B is …   Photo C is …

Sarah
Paul
Anna

b) Where are the kids in the film?

1 They're in Harbour Road.   3 Then they're in …   5 And then they …
2 Then³ they're in …   4 Then …

assembly⁴

the canteen

Harbour Road

c) Talk to your partner:

Anna is cool.

Paul is OK.

I don't like …

a maths lesson

I like Sarah. She's great.

the sports hall

2 People and places: Eggbuckland Community College

a) Watch the film. What's in the film:

What rooms⁵?

art room • canteen • classroom •
computer room • music room • sports hall

What lessons?

drama • French • German • ICT • music •
PE • science • technology

b) Talk to your partner:

– I think the school is old / new / big / small / …
– I think the film is cool / great / OK / stupid / …
– I like / I don't like the music.

---

¹ Harbour Road *Hafenstraße*   ² Meet the kids! *Lerne die Jugendlichen kennen!*   ³ then *dann*
⁴ assembly *Morgenversammlung in der Schule*   ⁵ What rooms? *Welche Räume?*

1 The unit quiz

Can you answer questions 1–8?
Work with a partner. Write your answers.
Check your answers on page 129.

1 It's a lesson. It isn't in a class-room. It starts with P. What is it?

2 We're two girls in class 7Y. We aren't sisters. Who are we?

3 He's a boy at Eggy. He isn't Luca. Who is he?

4 They're brothers. They aren't Adam and Zack. Who are they?

5 I'm at Eggy. I'm not a student, I'm the 7Y class teacher. Who am I?

6 She's a girl. She's six. She isn't at Eggy. Who is she?

7 I'm a girl in class 7Y. I'm not Ellie. Who am I?

8 You're a student. You aren't at Eggy. What's your name?

2 'm   's   're = Yes

a) Copy and complete the sentences.

1 I... at Eggy. (Card 5)
2 You... a student. (8)
3 He... a boy. (3)
4 She... six. (6)
5 It... a lesson. (1)
6 We... two girls in class 7Y. (2)
7 They... brothers. (4)

Look at the quiz cards!

b) Make the rule with: 'm • 's • 're

> FOCUS   Yes
>
> I + ...
> he/she/it + ...
> we/you/they + ...

▶ *Language file 1+2, p. 146*

3 Berry, Harry, Connie and William

Copy and complete with: 'm • 's • 're

1 Hi. I... Berry. Remember Harry?
2 He... my pony. Connie and William are our ponies too.
3 They... great.
4 Connie is old. She... seventeen.
5 Harry is twelve. He... my favourite pony.
6 I love my ponies. We... friends!

4 `'m not` `isn't` `aren't` = **No**

a) Complete the sentences.
1 I... a student. (Card 5)
2 You ... at Eggy. (8)
3 He ... Luca. (3)
4 She ... at Eggy. (6)
5 It ... in a classroom. (1)
6 We ... sisters. (2)
7 They ... Adam and Zack. (4)

b) Make the rule with: *'m not • isn't • aren't*

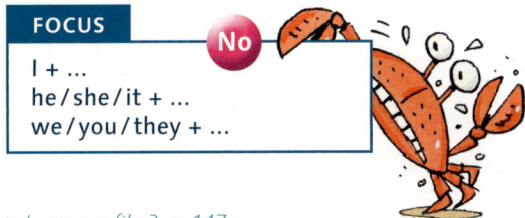

> **FOCUS**   **No**
>
> I + ...
> he / she / it + ...
> we / you / they + ...

▶ *Language file 3, p. 147*

5   **Hi! I'm Prince William**
Write: *'m not • isn't • aren't*
1 Hi! I... Daniel. I'm William.
2 Harry is my brother. He ... bad. He's OK.
3 We ... from Berlin. We're from London.
4 London ... small. It's big.
5 My hobbies ... skateboarding and swimming. They're riding and football.
6 I... a teacher. I'm a prince.

6 O **What's right?** `//●` p. 115
Write the six sentences.

Eggy is	a boy."
Eggy isn't	students at Eggy.
Cyril and Sandy are	a girl."
Cyril and Sandy aren't	a school in Plymouth.
Berry: "I'm	in Germany.
Berry: "I'm not	animals.

7 O **At Eggy** `//●` p. 115
Write the sentences with: *He • She • It • They*
1 Eggy is my new school. *(My school)* is big.
2 Ellie is a new girl at Eggy. *(Ellie)* is great.
3 Mr Brown is at Eggy. *(Mr Brown)* isn't our art teacher. *(Mr Brown)* is our ICT teacher.
4 Mrs Ford is a teacher too. *(Mrs Ford)* isn't the school principal. *(Mrs Ford)* is our maths teacher.
5 Ms Lee, Mrs Ford and Mr Brown are my new teachers. *(My new teachers)* aren't bad.

> *He, she, it* und *they* sind Pronomen.
> Ein Pronomen ersetzt ein Nomen (*Luca, school*), damit man das gleiche Wort nicht zweimal sagen muss:
>
> Luca is ten.   My school is OK.
> He's ten.   It's OK.
>
> Berry isn't ten.   The ponies aren't here.
> She isn't ten.   They aren't here.

More practice 6 p. 115

▶ *Language file 1, p. 146*

1 ◯ WORDS   Two animals in one
Can you write the ten animals in pictures 1–5?

Picture 1: a ... and a ...   Picture 2: ...

2 ◯ LANGUAGE   Cyril
What is Cyril saying?
Pick the right words from the box.
1 "I'... a crab."
2 "I'... at Eggy."
3 "I'... from Plymouth."
4 "I'... from Germany."
5 "I'... a bird."
6 "I'... orange."

> I'm
> I'm not

3 ◯ LANGUAGE   Ellie and Berry
Pick the right words.
1 "We're / We aren't girls."
2 "We're / We aren't from London."
3 "We're / We aren't students."
4 "We're / We aren't in class 7Y."
5 "We're / We aren't 13."
6 "We're / We aren't German."

4 LANGUAGE   Write sentences.

My	camera mobile computer pencil case	is isn't	old / new. big / small. red / green / ...

5 LANGUAGE   Remember Sandy?
Put in: *'m • 's • 're • is • are*

Hi, I... (1) Sandy.

This ... (2) Cyril. He... (3) my friend.

Benny and Babe ... (4) my friends too. They... (5) cool.

We... (6) from Kingsand.

Kingsand ... (7) near Plymouth. It... (8) great!

6 READING Cyril

a) ◯ Read the text. Put the pictures (A–D) in the right order.

Hi, I'm Cyril. I'm from Kingsand beach. It's near Plymouth. Benny and Babe are my friends. They're from Kingsand too. We're crabs! Look. This is Sandy. She isn't a crab. She's a bird.

Oh no! Mr Johnson is here. I don't like Mr Johnson. He likes crabs!

b) Right or wrong?

1 Cyril isn't from London.
2 Kingsand is near Plymouth.
3 Benny and Babe are students.
4 They're crabs.
5 Sandy is a crab too.
6 Mr Johnson is OK.
7 Mr Johnson and Cyril aren't friends.

7 LISTENING Adam and Luca

a) ◯ Listen. Adam and Luca talk about things. What things? Write 1–10.

b) Match Adam's and Luca's questions and answers. Then listen and check.

1 How are you?
2 I like the Kaiser Chiefs. What about you?
3 What's your hobby?
4 Who's your favourite teacher?
5 What's the next lesson?
6 Can I borrow your calculator, please?

A I like football.
B Sorry, it's at home.
C French.
D I'm fine, thanks.
E They're OK.
F Ms Lee. She's great.

PRACTICE

8 SPEAKING What lessons on Monday?

a) Partner B: Look at page 110.
Partner A: Copy the Monday timetable into your exercise book.
Ask partner B. Complete the Monday timetable.
Answer partner B's questions about Tuesday.

Lesson	Monday
1	....
2	....
3	....
4	....
5	....

Lesson	Tuesday
1	English
2	science
3	maths
4	French
5	art

> What's lesson one on Monday?

> It's ... What's lesson one on Tuesday?

> It's English.

> Check your answers with your partner's timetable.

b) ● Write your timetable in English. ▶ *Wordbank 3, p. 151*

9 My learner log

Write your learner log. You can put it in your DOSSIER.

My learner log for Unit 1

Im *learner log* schreibst du auf, was du gelernt hast, was du jetzt gut kannst und was noch nicht so gut geht.
Führe dein *learner log* regelmäßig.
Wichtig: Versuche immer ehrlich zu antworten!

I THINK ENGLISH IS:
– Ok.

MY FAVOURITE BOY/GIRL
– Berry

MY FAVOURITE PHRASES
– That's cool!
– See you.
– Have a good day!
– How are you?

MY FAVOURITE WORDS:
– timetable
– lunch
– Eggy
– pony

DIFFICULT WORDS:
– calculator
– they're
– remember
– science

I REMEMBER:
Lessons: French, German, English, history, ...
School things: pens, pencils, exercise books, ...
Hobbies: swimming, reading, football, ...
Animals: dog, cat, snake, ...
Colours: red, black, green, ...

I'M GOOD AT:
– Listening, reading

I'M OK AT:
– Words, language

I'M NOT GOOD AT:
– Speaking, writing

▶ *Workbook 1–3, p. 17*

1 WORDS   School, hobbies, colours, …

a) What's the wrong word?

1 pen, pencil, tie, rubber
2 maths, Monday, French, science
3 swimming, canteen, dancing, reading
4 yellow, brown, lesson, black
5 brother, school, lesson, classroom
6 art, twelve, eleven, fourteen

> First **test** yourself. Then **check** your answers on page 193.

b) Find six more right words for 1–6 in a).
1 ruler   2 …

c) Copy and complete the sentences.

1 My favourite school day is …
2 My favourite lesson is …

2 WORDS   **Talking to friends**
Put in the right word.

> class • good • How • lesson • She's • to • you • your

1 Hi. … are you? – I'm OK, thanks.
2 Have a … day. – You too!
3 Welcome … our school. – Thanks!
4 See …! – OK, bye!

5 I like … uniform. – Oh, thanks!
6 I'm in … 7A. – Me too!
7 This is Emma. … in my class.
8 What's the next …? – It's maths.

3 LANGUAGE   **Pictures on Ellie's mobile**

a) Pick the right words.

b) ⬤ Copy and complete the sentences.

Look, this is Eggy. It's / isn't (1) my school. Here are two teachers. They's / 're (2) OK. This is Ms Lee. No, she isn't / 'm not (3) my PE teacher – she 'm / 's (4) my English teacher.

Here's Adam. He… (5) OK. And here are my friends, Ruby and Charlie. But they … (6) in my class. They… (7) in 7X. I… (8) in 7X – I… (9) in 7Y!

4 WRITING   **Tamara – a new student**
Read Berry's questions and put Tamara's sentences in the right order. Write the dialogue.

Berry	Tamara
– Hi, I'm Berry. What's your name?	– I'm in class 7X. What's your favourite lesson?
– Are you from Plymouth?	– OK. Bye.
– I'm from Woolwell. I'm in class 7Y. What about you?	– Hi, I'm Tamara.
– I like science. What about you?	– I like history.
– See you Tamara.	– No, I'm from London. What about you?

At home with Ellie

1

a house

Hill Road

CITY OF PLYMOUTH

2

a flat

Greatfield Street

5

a small kitchen

6

a room in a new flat

1 A house and a flat

a) Look at photos 1–10.
Talk to a partner.

> What can you see?

In photo 1/2 … I can see a	big small pink yellow new nice	house. flat. kitchen. bedroom. garden. living room. toilet. bathroom. room.

b) Listen. Ellie is with Berry.
What photos show Ellie's house?
Write the numbers.
1.27

c) Listen again.
What's right (✓)? What's wrong (✗)?
1.27
1 Ellie's mum has a flat.
2 Ellie lives in Hill Road.
3 Ellie lives with her dad.
4 Ellie's kitchen is big.
5 Ellie has a garden.
6 Ellie's bedroom is small.

a bedroom for two girls

a small living room with TV

a garden

a kitchen and living room

a bathroom

a toilet

2 Dad's new flat
1.28
a) Listen to Ellie and her dad.
Point at the right photos.

b) Listen again.
Pick the right answer **A** or **B** .

1 Dad's flat is in   **A** Greatfield Street.
                       B London Road.

2 The flat has   **A** one bedroom.
                       B two bedrooms.

3 Ellie's bedroom is **A** pink.
                       B green.

3 Right or wrong?
1.29
a) Look at the photos.
Listen and say *Right*! or *Wrong*!
– Photo 9 is a bathroom. Right or wrong?
– Right!

b) Practise with a partner.

4 ○ ACTIVITY   Rooms in a house
Find photos of the rooms in a house.
Make a collage and write the names.

More practice 1 p. 115

Ellie's family

🎧 1 At Ellie's house
1.30

a) Look at the pictures: who's Ellie's
a) mum? b) dad? c) sister? d) brother?
Guess and point. Then read and check.

Ellie ___ Hi, Mum, this is Berry.

Mum ___ Hi, Berry. I'm Jackie.

Berry ___ Hello.

Ellie ___ Is Zoe upstairs?

Mum ___ Yes, she is. But here's Conor.
Conor, this is Berry, Ellie's new
friend. Conor is Ellie's brother.

Conor ___ Hi, Berry. Are you at Eggbuckland?

Berry ___ Yes, I am. What about you?

Conor ___ I'm at Plymouth High School.

Mum ___ And here's Zoe, Ellie's big sister.

Zoe ___ Hi, welcome to the madhouse!

Berry and Ellie are in the living room.

Berry ___ Your family is great.

Ellie ___ They're OK.

Berry ___ What about your stepdad?
Is he OK?

Ellie ___ Yes, but I miss my real dad. He lives
with his new partner and his baby
– a boy. Look, I have a photo of the
baby.

Berry ___ Oh, he's cute! You're lucky. I'd like
a brother or a sister.

Ellie ___ You're lucky. You live with your
mum and your dad. That's cool.

b) Finish the sentences.
1 Berry is …
2 Jackie is …
3 Conor is …
4 Zoe is …
5 Eggbuckland is …
6 The baby is …

> Ellie's big brother.
> Ellie's friend.
> Ellie's school.
> Ellie's sister.
> Ellie's brother too.
> Ellie's mum.

c) 🔘 *His* or *her*? ⬛ p. 116
1 Ellie lives with his / her mum, her brother
Conor and her sister Zoe.
2 Conor lives with his / her two sisters,
Zoe and Ellie.
3 Berry lives with his / her mum and dad.
4 Ellie's dad lives with his / her new
partner.
5 Ellie's mum lives with his / her new
partner and Ellie, Zoe and Conor.

2 **Ellie's family tree**

Work with a partner. Pick the right words for Ellie.

1 Pete is my stepdad / real dad.

2 Pete has one boy / two boys.

3 Zoe is my stepmum / stepsister.

4 Conor is my baby brother / stepbrother.

5 My dad has a new partner.
  Her name is Alisha / Jackie.

6 Finn is my baby brother / big brother.

7 Grandpa Fox is my mum's / dad's dad.

3 **ACTIVITY** **Your family tree**

a) Draw your family tree or make a family tree with photos. You can put it in your DOSSIER.
Talk with a partner about the family tree:

This is my mum / dad / grandma / ...   His / Her name is ...

▶ Wordbank 4, p. 152

b) 🔵 Write about your family.

I live with my dad / grandma / ... My dad's name is ...
I have a brother / sister / ... His / Her name is ... He's / She's OK.
I have two stepsisters, Mara and ... They're ...

Problems at home

 1 What's your problem?
1.31

a) Read and find out: Is Zoe happy?

Yes, she is. / No, she isn't.

Ellie is in her bedroom with her stepsister, Zoe.

Zoe ___ Ellie, look at the room!

Ellie ___ What's your problem?

Zoe ___ Is this your pullover?

Ellie ___ Yes, it is. What's your problem?

Zoe ___ And are they your shoes?

Ellie ___ Yes, they are. What's your problem?

Zoe ___ The room is messy!

Ellie ___ It isn't your room now, Zoe.
It's my room too!

 b) Now Ellie is in the kitchen. Is she happy?
1.32

Yes, she is. / No, she isn't.

Mum ___ Are you OK, Ellie?

Ellie ___ No, I'm not. Zoe is bossy, Mum.
Our bedroom is too small.
And I have no table. Where can
I do my homework?

Mum ___ Oh, Ellie! The kitchen is a good
place for homework.

Ellie ___ No, it isn't. It's too noisy!

Mum ___ What about the living room?

Ellie ___ It's noisy too!

Mum ___ Oh, Ellie!

2 Ellie isn't happy

a) Find the right sentences
for the pictures.

1 Zoe isn't happy.

2 Are they your shoes?

3 The room is messy.

4 Zoe is bossy.

5 I have no table.

6 The kitchen is noisy.

A

B

C

D

E

F

b) 🔘 Read the dialogues again. Copy and complete the answers with *yes* or *no*.  p. 116

1 Is Zoe happy? – ..., she isn't.

2 Are Ellie's shoes in the room?
– ..., they are.

3 Are Ellie and her mum in the kitchen?
– ..., they are.

4 Is the kitchen noisy?
– ..., it is.

5 Is Ellie OK? – ..., she isn't.

6 Is the kitchen a good place for
homework? – ..., it isn't.

3 New things for a room

Ellie is with her friends at Eggy. She has a brochure.

a) Listen to Ellie.
1.33 Write what she likes.

b) Then listen to Luca.
1.34 Write what he likes.

c) NOW YOU

Compare with a partner.

A ___ I like / I don't like the lamp.
What about you?

B ___ I like / I don't like it.
What about the table?

A ___ I ...
What about you?

B ___ I ...
... chair?

More practice 2 | p. 116

DREAMROOMS

cushions £15.99 £9.99
lamp £29.99 £14.99
chair £30.99 £25.99
table £45.99 £25.95
bed £99.99 £79.99
poster £6.99 £2.99
wardrobe £85.95 £65.95

4 Find four different things

Partner B: Look at room B on page 110.
Partner A: Look at room A on this page. (Your partner looks at a different room B.)

Room A
a blue wardrobe
posters
a big flat-screen TV
red cushions
a black bed
a small laptop
a big table
a yellow lamp
a brown chair

Partner A: Talk to your partner about your room.
Find what's different in your partner's room (four things).

Partner A ___ My room has posters.
Partner B ___ My room has posters too.
Partner A ___ OK. My room has red cushions.
Partner B ___ My room has ...

My partner's room has:
1) green cushions
2) ...
3) ...
4) ...

1 **Before you read**

Work with a partner. Pick a picture (1–7). Answer the questions about your picture.

1 Where's Ellie? (at her mum's house / at her dad's flat / in the kitchen / in the …)
2 Is Ellie happy or unhappy?

Then tell the class: In picture 1 Ellie is at her mum's house. She's in the kitchen. She's happy.

🎧 Happy again
1.35

MONDAY
Great news! I can live with dad, Alisha and the baby, Finn.
Tomorrow is the big day! I go to dad's flat after school.
Zoe is happy. But mum isn't happy.

TUESDAY
I'm at dad's flat. I'm in my new bedroom.
I have a table and a lamp.
I can do my homework here.
No bossy Zoe. My room is pink, but it's great!

WEDNESDAY
Finn is very cute. And Alisha is really nice.
Dad and Alisha are at the cinema now.
Finn is with me.
No Conor! Now I can watch my favourite TV programmes.

THURSDAY
Dad is in town. Alisha is tired.
She's in her bedroom.
Finn is with me. He isn't very happy.

FRIDAY
Dad and Alisha are at a restaurant.
It's Alisha's birthday.
Finn is with me – again!
And he isn't very happy – again!

SATURDAY
Dad and Alisha are in town.
And Finn? Yes, he's with me – again!
Dad loves Alisha. He has no time for me.
I miss mum. And I miss Conor and Pete
and my cats … and I really miss Zoe!
Oh, a text. Is it from mum?

SUNDAY
One week at dad's flat …
I have a new idea!
Monday to Friday I'm with mum.
On Saturday and Sunday I'm with dad.
I'm really happy again.

2 Ellie's week

Read the story. Then match the phrases with the days of the week.
Monday – Good news for Ellie   Tuesday – …

| Alisha very tired | A new idea | Good news for Ellie | Alisha's birthday |

| Day one in dad's flat | Great TV programmes | Ellie misses her mum |

3  Where are they? `// ●` p. 116

Answer the questions.

1 Where's Ellie on Monday? – She's …
2 Where's Ellie on Tuesday? – She's …
3 Where are Ellie's dad and Alisha on Wednesday? – They're …
4 Where's Ellie's dad on Thursday? – He's …
5 Where are Ellie's dad and Alisha on Friday? – They're …
6 Where's Finn on Wednesday, Thursday, Friday and Saturday? – He's …

in town.
with Ellie.
at a restaurant.
in her bedroom.
in the kitchen.
at the cinema.

4  A week with dad `// ●` p. 117

dad • table • idea • live • mum

Write the sentences with the right words.

1 Ellie has good news – she can … with her dad.
2 She likes her new bedroom: it has a … and a lamp.
3 But her … and Alisha have no time for Ellie.
4 Ellie misses her …, her stepbrother and stepsister.
5 Her new …? She can live five days with her mum and two days with her dad.

More
practice 3 p. 117

My flat and my room

1 Read the story.

Write five or six sentences about your house or flat.

What can I write?

Aha! I have an idea! Here are sentences from page 34.

Homework
MY FLAT
My mum has a flat.
We live in Parkstraße.
I live with my mum.
Our kitchen is big.
We have no garden.
My bedroom is small.

My
1 ~~Ellie's~~ mum has a flat.

We live   Parkstraße.
2 ~~Ellie lives~~ in ~~Hill Road~~.

I live   my mum.
3 ~~Ellie lives~~ with ~~her dad~~.

Our
4 ~~Ellie's~~ kitchen is big.

We have no
5 ~~Ellie has a~~ garden.

My
6 ~~Ellie's~~ bedroom is small.

1 Ellie's mum has a flat.
2 Ellie lives in Hill Road.
3 Ellie lives with her dad.
4 Ellie's kitchen is big.
5 Ellie has a garden.
6 Ellie's bedroom is small.

Englische Texte zu schreiben ist leichter, wenn du kurze Sätze aus dem Buch übernimmst und sie für dich änderst.
Hier siehst du ein Beispiel. In Aufgabe 2 kannst du es selber probieren.

▶ *Skills file 2, p. 142*

2 **NOW YOU** Write about your room to a friend in England.

Page 40:
I have a table and a lamp.
My room is pink, but it's great.

Page 38:
The room is messy.
It's noisy!

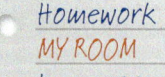

Homework
MY ROOM
In my room I have a table / a lamp / …
My room is yellow / white / pink / …
The room is / isn't messy.
And it's / it isn't noisy.
But I like my room.

Very good homework!

More practice 4   p. 117

▶ *Wordbank 5, p. 152*

1 Classroom phrases

a) Match the phrases in the box (A–I) with the pictures (1–9) in the game.

Listen please! – picture 2.

 b) Listen. When you hear the phrases, point at the pictures in the game.

1.36

| More practice 5 | p. 117 |

A Listen, please!
B Work with a partner.
C What's that in English?
D Can I go to the toilet, please?
E Your homework is exercise 3.
F Can you say that again, please?
G Write your answer.
H Please look at the picture.
I Sorry, I forgot my homework.

2 GAME The banana skin game

Play this game in groups of three or four.

WAS? 1 Würfel und 3 oder 4 Spielsteine
WIE? Landest du auf einem Nummern-Feld, nenne die *classroom phrase*. War sie korrekt, bleibe auf dem Feld. Hast du einen Fehler gemacht, gehe zwei Felder zurück. Landest du auf einem *Break*-Feld, musst du gar nichts machen. Dann ist der/die Nächste an der Reihe.

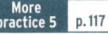

Addresses and phone numbers

1 🔘 **The alphabet song**

🎧 1.37 **a)** Listen to Cyril.

🎧 1.38 **b)** Listen again and repeat.

2 **Ellie's new address**

What's your address?

What's your phone number?

Can you say that again, please?

Can you spell that, please?

Is that right?

Is that one word?

🎧 1.39 **a)** Listen. What are the right answers?

1 Ellie talks to her friends about   Ⓐ her mum's house   Ⓑ her dad's flat   Ⓒ her new room.

2 What's her address?   Ⓐ 11 Great Field Road   Ⓑ 11 Greatfield Street   Ⓒ 10 Gratefeld Street.

3 Here is Ellie's phone number – but it's WRONG! What's the right number?

> 01 752 803 3647

> Bei Telefonnummern sagt man „Oh" für die Null.

🎧 1.40 **b)** Listen and repeat Luca's, Adam's and Berry's questions.   **More practice 6**   p. 118

3 **Berry's address and phone number**

a) Copy the notes.

🎧 1.41 **b)** Now listen to Berry. Write the missing letters and numbers.

> MER _ YW _ A _ HER   F _ _ M
> WO _ L _ E _ _
> Phone number: 0 1 _ _ 7 8 5 _ _ 8 9

4   NOW YOU

a) What's your phone number? Tell a partner. Write his / her number.

b) Ask three more partners and write their numbers. Tell them your number.

1 The kids from Harbour Road:
Homework time

a) Watch the film. Then put the photos (A–D) in the right order.

First we see photo …. After that we see …

b) Before you watch again: What's the right answer?
Then watch and check.

1 The three friends are at Sarah's / at Anna's house.

2 They do homework / look at photos.

3 They talk about shopping / football.

4 They go upstairs into Sarah's room / Tom's room.

5 Tom is Sarah's brother / dad.

6 Tom is / isn't happy because they're in his room.

2 People and places: A tour of my room

a) What are your five favourite things in your room? Write a list.
The words in the box can help you.
▶ *Wordbank 5, p. 152*

> my bed • my books • my cat • my computer •
> my cushions • my hamster • my lamp • my mobile •
> my MP3-player • my posters • my photos • my TV

Then tell a partner.

b) Now watch Joe's film.
What are his favourite things?

c) Talk to your partner.

– Joe has nice things / no nice things in his room.

– Joe is / isn't messy.

– I like / I don't like Joe's poster.

1 What's mum's problem?

1.42

Mum — Hi, Ellie.

Ellie — Hi, Mum!

Mum — This is a nice surprise. Are you OK?

Ellie — Yes, I am, thanks.

Mum — Is Finn OK?

Ellie — Yes, he is. He's great.

Mum — And Alisha? Is she OK?

Ellie — Yes, she is. She's often tired, but she's OK.

Mum — And your new room? Is it nice?

Ellie — Yes, it is. It's really nice. And what about you? Are you all OK?

Mum — Yes, we are. But ...

Ellie — Are you sure? Are you really OK, Mum?

Mum — I ... No, I'm not. I ...

Ellie — What's the problem? Is Conor too noisy?

Mum — No, he isn't.

Ellie — Are the cats a problem?

Mum — No, they aren't. Oh, it's stupid, I know. But you see, I miss you, Ellie.

Ellie — Oh Mum! Don't be silly! I'm with you tomorrow!

2 What are the right answers?

a) Read the dialogue again and put in:

it is • she is • he is • I am • we are

1 Are you OK? – Yes, ...

2 Is Finn OK? – Yes, ...

3 Is Alisha OK? – Yes, ...

4 Is your room nice? – Yes, ...

5 Are you all OK? – Yes, ...

6 Are your friends nice? – Yes, they are.

b) Put in: *he isn't • I'm not • they aren't*

1 Are you OK? – No, ...

2 Is Conor too noisy? – No, ...

3 Is Alisha OK? – No, she isn't.

4 Is your room nice? – No, it isn't.

5 Are you all OK? – No, we aren't.

6 Are the cats a problem? – No, ...

FOCUS

Wenn du im Englischen auf eine Frage nur mit *Yes* oder *No* antwortest, hält man dich für unhöflich. Verwende daher Kurzantworten wie *Yes, I am. / No, I'm not.*

Fragen mit *you:*	Antworten mit *I* oder *we:*	Fragen mit *Namen:*	Antworten mit *he, she* oder *they:*
Are you a crab, Cyril?	– *Yes, I am.*	*Is Cyril a bird?*	– *No, he isn't.*
Are you animals?	– *Yes, we are.*	*Are Cyril and Sandy friends?*	– *Yes, they are.*

▶ *Language file 4, p. 147*

3 GAME Who am I?

Play with a partner. You are a boy or a girl in the house. Your partner guesses who you are.

Are you a girl / boy?
Are you upstairs?
Are you in the kitchen / ...?
Are you in the living room?
Are you big / small?
Are you Ben / Liz / ...?

Yes, I am.

No, I'm not.

4 Ellie and her friends

Complete the answers with: *he • she • it*

1 Is Adam in Ellie's class? – Yes, ... is.
2 Is Berry Ellie's friend? – Yes, ... is.
3 Is Luca a girl? – No, ... isn't!
4 Is Ellie's house in Plymouth? – Yes, ... is.
5 Is Eggy in Germany – No, ... isn't.
6 Is Ellie happy at school? – Yes, ... is.

More practice 7 p. 118

5 ● Bossy Zoe

Zoe misses Ellie. But when Ellie is at her mum's house, Zoe is bossy again!
Write Zoe's questions and Ellie's answers.

tie

football

pullover

Is it your ...?

Yes, it is.

Are they your ...?

Yes, they are.

T-shirts

books

shoes

6 NOW YOU

a) ⊙ Write the answers for you.

1 Are you noisy? – Yes, I am. / No, I'm not.
2 Are your friends fun? – Yes, they are. / No, they aren't.
3 Is your mum bossy? – Yes, she is. / No, she isn't.
4 Is your room messy? – Yes, it is. / No, it isn't.
5 Are you and your family from Plymouth?
  – Yes, we are. / No, we aren't.

b) Work in a group.

– Pick three questions from 6a) or find new questions.
– Write the questions on a card.
– Ask students in your group the questions on your card.

1 ◯ WORDS Sandy's house

a) Match the words A–F with the places (1–6) in the picture.

A kitchen   D bathroom
B living room   E toilet
C bedroom   F garden

b) What can you see in Sandy's house?

> a table • a TV • a bed • a chair •
> a cushion • a lamp • a wardrobe

2 ◯ LANGUAGE Are you … ?

a) Answer the questions about you:
Yes, I am. • No, I'm not.
1 Are you a boy?
2 Are you 12?
3 Are you English?
4 Are you at school?
5 Are you a sister?

b) Answer the questions about Sandy's house: *Yes, it is. • No, it isn't.*
1 Is the kitchen blue?
2 Is the living room brown?
3 Is the bedroom yellow?
4 Is the toilet green?
5 Is the garden big?

c) Now answer the questions about Cyril and Sandy: *Yes, they are. • No, they aren't.*
1 Are Cyril and Sandy animals?
2 Are they in Plymouth?
3 Are they a dog and a cat?
4 Are they a crab and a bird?
5 Are Cyril and Sandy in class 7Y?

3 LANGUAGE Yes and No
Complete the answers.

1 Is Ellie happy with Zoe?

Yes, she … –   and no, she …!

2 Is Conor noisy?

Yes, he … –   and no, … …!

3 Are Cyril and Sandy friends?

Yes, … … –   and no, ……

🎧 4 LISTENING Phone codes
1.43
The phone codes for the English towns are wrong. Listen and write the right phone codes.

> Plymouth: 01758   Leeds: 0119
>
> York: 01604   London: 0110 and 0120

5 WRITING A new e-pal

a) Read Tom's email.

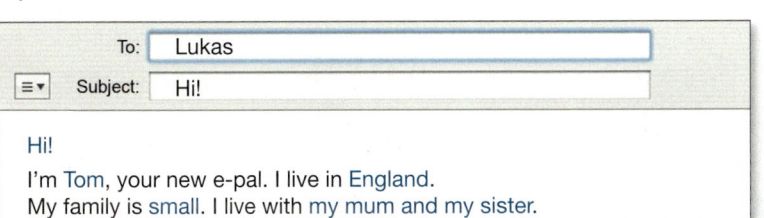

To: Lukas

Subject: Hi!

Hi!
I'm Tom, your new e-pal. I live in England.
My family is small. I live with my mum and my sister.
Our house is in Plymouth. Plymouth is nice. It's a big town in England.
My room is OK. I have a computer. I like playing games with my friends.
My school is in Plymouth. It's very big. My friends at school are cool.

Tom

b) Answer Tom's email. Write six sentences.

Hi! I'm ..., your new e-pal. I live in ...
My family is ... I live with ...

● Write eight sentences or more.

Du kannst die schwarzen Wörter in Toms Email übernehmen. Ergänze sie mit Informationen über dich.

6 SPEAKING Two sports shops

Partner B: Go to page 111.

Partner A:

Wenn du nicht verstehst, was dein Partner sagt, bitte um Wiederholung:
Can you say that again, please?

a) Your partner has a brochure about a new sports shop. Ask partner B four questions:

> What's the name of the shop, please?

> Can you spell that, please?

> What's the address?

> And what's the phone number?

Write the name of the shop, the address and the phone number.

b) Now Partner B asks you about this sports shop. Answer Partner B's questions.

Come to **SALTASH SPORTS** for all sports

34 Fore Street • Saltash PL12 6JT • ☎ 01752 848 7301

7 READING   A new hobby
a) Read the story

b) Write the right sentences.

1 Zoe is at school / in her room.
2 Conor and Zoe ask / answer questions.
3 Ellie has / has no clothes for Zoe and Conor.

4 Ellie, Zoe and Conor are / aren't at home.
5 Conor and Zoe are / aren't happy.
6 Conor is / isn't tired after tae kwon do.

8 My learner log
Write your learner log
for Unit 2.
Put it in your DOSSIER.

My learner log for Unit 2

My favourite pages are ....
My favourite text is: ....
My favourite phrases are: ....
Difficult words are: ....

My progress in English is: GREAT! 👍 / OK ✊ / NOT SO GOOD 👎

TEST AND CHECK

1 WORDS

Write the words in the right list:
kitchen, *dad*, *wardrobe*,
stepsister, *bedroom*, *chair*.

Family	House
...	...

First **test** yourself.
Then **check** your
answers on page 194.

2 WORDS   Talking about friends
Write the right word.

bossy • happy • messy • noisy • tired • unhappy

Tim is ...   Lilly is ...   Anna is ...   Jan is ...   Utku is ...   Sarah is ...

3 LANGUAGE   On the phone
Pick the right words.

1 Hi, Luca. Are you at home?
  – No, I am / I'm not.
2 Are you in town? – Yes, I am / I'm not.
3 Are your friends with you?
  – Yes, they are / they aren't.
4 Are you in a shop?
  – Yes, we are / we aren't.
5 Are Adam and Charlie with you?
  – No, they are / they aren't.
6 Is Ellie with you?
  – Yes, she is / she isn't.
  Good! I'd like to talk to her.

4 WRITING   Jake – a new friend
What are the right words?

but • have • like • live • playing • with

To:	Julia
Subject:	Hi!

Hi! I'm Jake, your new English friend.
I ... (1) in Exeter, a town near Plymouth.
I live ... (2) my mum, my dad, my sister and
my two dogs. Our house is nice, ... (3) my
room is very small. It's upstairs. I ... (4)
posters of my favourite bands.
I really ... (5) music. I often listen to music
in my room. I like ... (6) football too.
Is your family big or small? Is your house
in town?
Jake

5 SPEAKING   A dialogue
Put Sam's answers in the right order.

Emma:
– Can I see you tomorrow?
– What's your phone number?
– And what's your address?
– Can you spell that, please?
– B O R O U G H?
– Great! Thanks, Sam. Bye.

Sam:

See you.

26 Borough Road.

921 690.

Yes, I'm at home tomorrow.

B-O-R-O-U-G-H.

Yes, that's right.

Luca's birthday

1 This is my town

a) Match the phrases A–F with the pictures 1–6.

A We live in Windsor Street.
B I go to my favourite shop – a phone shop.
C I sometimes go shopping with my dad.
D We often go swimming in town.
E My brother and I ride our bikes in the park.
F On my birthday I go to the cinema.

b) Listen and check.
1.44

c) Listen again. Pick the right answers.
1.44

Family name: Boateng / Windsor
House number: 1 / 9
Name of mobile shop: Phones 4U / Mobiles 4U
Name of park: Plymouth Park / Central Park
Name of cinema: Reel Cinema / Plymouth Cinema

d) Check your notes with a partner.

2 ◯ NOW YOU

Tell your partner what you do in town.

I sometimes go	shopping.
	swimming.
	skateboarding.
	to the cinema.
	to my favourite shop.
	…

▶ *Wordbank 6, p. 153*

I often go swimming.

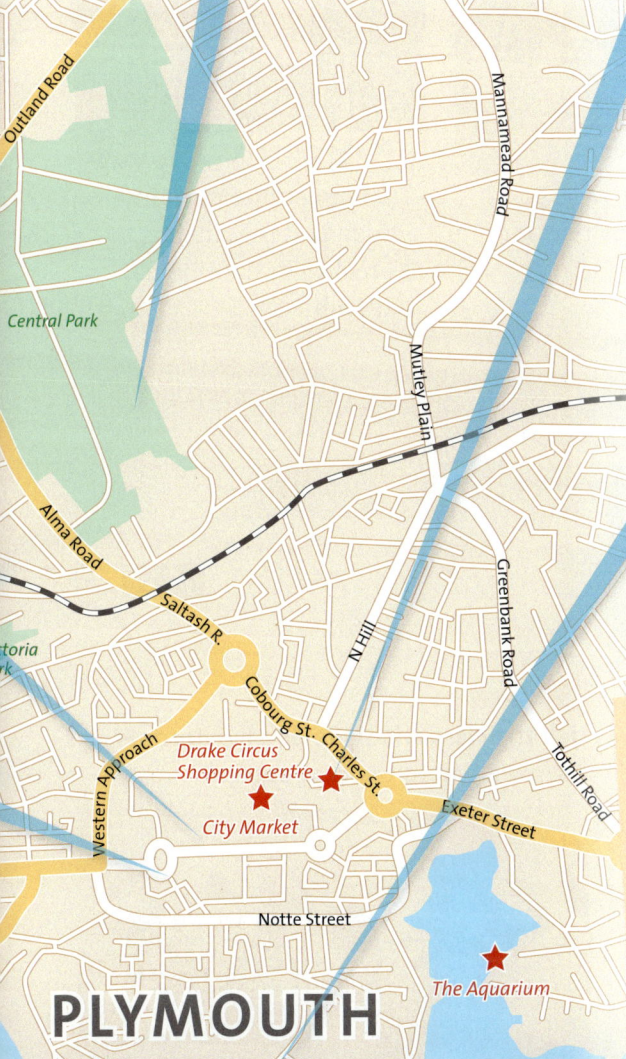

PLYMOUTH

Outland Road

Mannamead Road

Central Park

Mutley Plain

Greenbank Road

Alma Road

Saltash R.

Victoria Park

N Hill

Cobourg St. Charles St.

Western Approach

Drake Circus
Shopping Centre

City Market

Exeter Street

Tothill Road

Notte Street

The Aquarium

🎧 **3** **SONG**

1.45

This is my city

This is my town, this is my city.
Through my eyes it looks so pretty.
This is my town, this is my city now.

These are my people, this is my song.
Dirty streets, where I belong.
This is my town, this is my city now.
This is my city now.

Timothy Victor

▶ *Workbook 1–3, p. 31*

In Plymouth

1 Saturdays are great

a) 🔘 **Look at the pictures. Where is Luca?**

In picture ... Luca is at the cinema / at the market / in the park.

In the morning ...

... we go shopping with dad.
Dad buys vegetables at the
market. We often buy sweets.

In the afternoon ...

... Jack and I always go
to the park and ride our
bikes.

In the evening ...

... I sometimes meet my
friends at the cinema.
I really like the cinema.
It's fun.

b) **Read the text in a) and write Luca's sentences.**

1 In the morning we go shopping
2 At the market dad buys
3 We often buy
4 Jack and I always go
5 We ride
6 In the evening I sometimes meet

to Central Park.   my friends at the cinema.

our bikes in the park.   with dad.

vegetables.   sweets.

More practice 1   p. 118

2 🔘 **NOW YOU**

Write four sentences about your Saturdays.

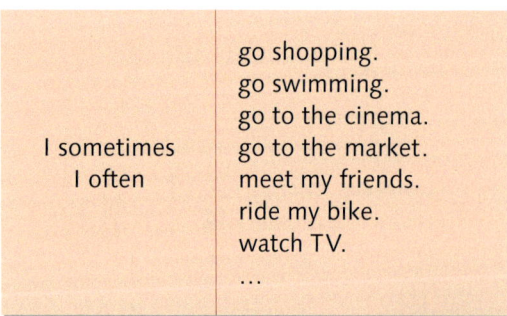

| I sometimes
I often | go shopping.
go swimming.
go to the cinema.
go to the market.
meet my friends.
ride my bike.
watch TV.
... |

More practice 2   p. 119

3 **GAME**

Tell the class what you do on Saturdays.
Throw a ball to the next student.

I go shopping.
What about you?

4 In a sports shop

a) Luca is in a sports shop with his dad.
They want to buy a birthday present for Luca.

Dad —— Look, Luca. What about the black trainers?

Luca —— Oh, no Dad! I don't like black trainers.
What about the red trainers? They're cool.

Dad —— Red? Oh no! And they're too expensive
– £99!

Luca —— What about a hoodie then? I love the
green hoodie.

Dad —— It's OK. But what about the brown hoodie?
It's nice.

Luca —— A brown hoodie? Oh Dad! Shopping with
you is terrible!

b) Which two things does Luca like?

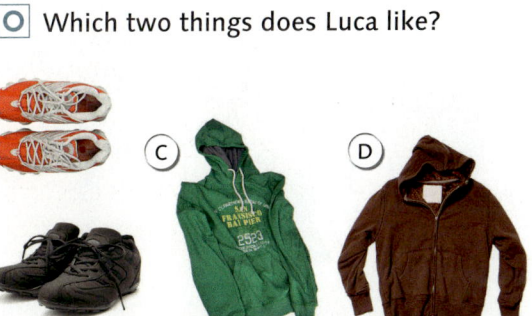

c) Finish the sentences.
1 Dad likes the ... trainers and the ... hoodie.
2 Luca likes the ... and the ...

d) Now practise the dialogue with a partner.

5 Shopping

Talk about the pictures with two partners.

> I like the shirt. What about you?

> Yes, I like the shirt too.

> Sorry, I don't like the shirt! But I love the ...

shirt

hoodie

trainers

pullover

shoes

tie

jeans

Birthdays

1 **Birthday ideas**

1.47 **a)** Listen. Which picture (A–D) is Luca's birthday, Ellie's birthday, Adam's birthday or Berry's birthday? *Picture A: ...* *Picture B: ...*

b) Match the activities with pictures A–D.
1 I sometimes go bowling with my family.
2 We always stay at home on my birthday.
3 I always have a party with my friends.
4 I sometimes go to the beach with my family.

c) Listen again. Match the names with the birthdays.

Luca
Ellie
Berry
Adam

A **9th September**
B *14th February*
C **1st August**
D **25th December**

More practice 3 | p. 119

2 **NOW YOU**

a) Write sentences – as many as you can.

On my birthday I	go swimming.
	go bowling.
	go shopping.
	go to a restaurant.
	go to the cinema.
	go to the beach.
	have a party.
	meet my friends.
	...

More practice 4 | p. 119

b) Talk to a partner about your birthday.
– On my birthday I ...
  What about you?
– I often ...
– Nice idea!

3   January, February, March, …

a) ⭕ Write the months in the right order.

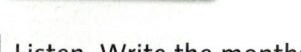

February   August   November   October

January   July   March   May   September

December   April   June

🎧 **b)** ⭕ Listen. Write the months.
1.48

🎧 **c)** Listen again. What's the right date – Ⓐ or Ⓑ ?
1.48

1	Ⓐ 15th January	Ⓑ 30th January
2	Ⓐ 1st May	Ⓑ 5th May
3	Ⓐ 2nd December	Ⓑ 22nd December
4	Ⓐ 7th October	Ⓑ 11th October
5	Ⓐ 16th July	Ⓑ 17th July
6	Ⓐ 23rd September	Ⓑ 3rd September

You write:	You say:
1st March	the first of March
2nd July	the second of July
3rd September	the third of September
4th November	the fourth of November
5th December	the fifth of December

🎧 **d)** Listen and repeat the dates.
1.49

▸ *More numbers for dates on page 190*

4   ACTIVITY   A birthday calendar

We're January.

When's your birthday, Marie?

It's on the twelfth of January.

JANUARY — Zainab: 1st January, Marie: 12th January, Jonas: 31st January

FEBRUARY — Max: 2nd February, Julian: 4th February

MARCH — Sarah: 3rd March

APRIL — Angy: 10th April, Mehdi: 28th April

Step 1
Make 12 groups in your class.
Pick a month for your group.
Draw a picture for your month.

Step 2
Find out who has a birthday in your month – and the date.
Write it on your month.

Step 3
Put all the months together.
Put the calendar on the wall of your classroom.

1 Before you read

Look at the photos. Is Luca's birthday fun? Talk to a partner.

I think Luca's birthday is / isn't fun. He's happy / unhappy in photo ...

Happy birthday, Luca!

1.50

Francis and the Drakes LIVE

Tickets: ~~£25~~ £9.99

> Can I do something with Adam, Berry and Ellie on my birthday, Mum? Something different.

> Oh, Luca loves Berry and Ellie!

> Shut up, Jack!

> What about a concert?

> Great idea, Mum. That's different!

It's Thursday. Luca's birthday is on Saturday. He wants to do something different for his birthday. But what? He has no ideas.

> Happy birthday to you. You live in a zoo ...

> Shut up, Jack!

> Happy birthday, Luca!

> Wow, this is a great surprise. Thanks!

It's Saturday morning. Luca is very happy. It's his birthday.

> We always go to the park. What about something different?

TO THE HOE ➡

> My friends are at the Hoe. We can go there.

Mum is at work. Grace and dad are at the shops. But what about Luca and Jack?

④ Great!
But ...

Jack and Luca go to the Hoe.
Jack meets his friends.

⑤ This is a bad idea.

Jack goes first. Luca goes too ...

⑥ Luca, are you OK?
No I'm not! Oh, my leg!

... but he falls.

⑦ I'm really sorry!
This is something different for your birthday, Luca!
I'm sorry too!

Luca and Jack are back from the hospital.

2 | Right or wrong?

1 Luca wants a party.
2 Luca likes mum's idea.
3 Luca and Jack go shopping with dad on Saturday.
4 Jack meets his friends at the Hoe.
5 Luca goes before Jack.
6 Luca falls.
7 Luca goes to the cinema.
8 Luca is happy in the hospital.

4 | The end of the story // ○ p.120
1.51
Listen to the end of the story.

1 Who comes to Luca's house?
2 Is Luca happy in the end?
3 Can he hear Francis and the Drakes?
4 Is the end a surprise for you?

More practice 5 | p.120

3 | Write the story.
Match the parts of the sentences.

On Thursday Luca has no ideas for

idea: a concert.

his birthday.

But his mum has a great

the Hoe.

On Saturday morning Luca is

falls.

The boys meet Jack's friends at

Luca

to the hospital.

Luca, Jack and mum go

with his leg.

Luca has a problem

very happy.

Listening to prices

1 Luca's garage sale

How can Luca get money for a new bike?
He has a garage sale.

a) Look at the picture.
What's in Luca's garage sale?
Make two lists.

▶ *Language file 5, p. 147*

a bike	two footballs
a ...	three ...
...	...

bike • calculator • cushion • computer • crab • football • hoodie • phone • pencil • pencil-case • pen • poster • T-shirt • tie • trainer

b) Look at your lists. Listen and tick (✓) in your list what you hear.
1.52

c) ◯ Listen again. //⚫ p.120
1.52
Pick the right answer Ⓐ or Ⓑ.

1 The calculator is   Ⓐ £1.   Ⓑ £10.
2 The mobile phones are   Ⓐ £7.50.   Ⓑ £9.50.
3 The crab is   Ⓐ 50 p.   Ⓑ 75 p.
4 The computer is   Ⓐ £15.   Ⓑ £20.
5 The footballs are   Ⓐ £2.   Ⓑ £4.

British money

You write: 50 p
You say: Fifty p

You write: £1.20
You say: One pound twenty

2 British money

a) Write labels for a sale.

1 One pound fifty
2 Forty-nine p
3 Seventy pounds
4 Four pounds twenty-five
5 Eighty pounds thirty
6 Seventeen pounds
7 Sixty p
8 One hundred pounds

b) ⚫ Say the prices. Practise with a partner.

 A £3.99
 B 20 p
 C £8.50
D £11.25
 E £15
F £24.90

Birthday activities

1 **Questions about birthdays**

🎧 **1.53**

a) Read or listen to the dialogue. What are Sarah's favourite birthday activities?

Daniel _ Can I ask you a question, Sarah? When's your birthday?

Sarah _ Friday 11th June.

Daniel _ And what are your favourite activities on your birthday?

Sarah _ We play games. And we sometimes watch a film.

Daniel _ Sounds fun. Thanks, Sarah.

b) Practise the dialogue with a partner.

c) 🅾 **Copy and complete this dialogue. Look at a) for help.** // ● p.120

Daniel _ Can I ... you a question, Ben? ... your birthday?

Ben ___ Thursday 21st October.

Daniel _ And what are ... favourite activities?

Ben ___ We ... games. And we sometimes ... a film.

Daniel _ Sounds ... Thanks, Ben.

More practice 6 | p.121

2 **APPOINTMENTS**

Step 1: Copy the table and everything red. Don't copy the blue words. They're examples. Write answers for you. The green box can help you.

		You	Simon	Luisa	Leyla
When's your birthday?		27th May	...	...	...
What are your favourite activities on your birthday?		watch TV go swimming	...	...	...

go to town
go to the cinema
go swimming
go bowling
watch TV
watch a film
meet my friends
ride my bike
stay at home
have a party

Step 2: Make appointments with three partners and write the names in the table.

Yes, I am.

Are you free at one o'clock?

Are you free at two o'clock?

No, I'm not. But I'm free at three o'clock.

Step 3: When your teacher says "one o'clock", go to partner 1. Ask your questions. Write the answers in the table.

Step 4: When your teacher says "two o'clock" go to partner 2. Ask your questions and write the answers in the table.

Step 5: At "3 o'clock" go to partner 3 and repeat the activity.

Plymouth posters

1   What posters?

a) Match the sentences with the posters.

1 It's on the eleventh and twelfth of August.
2 It's for fans of music and dancing.
3 You can have a party here.
4 The expensive tickets for boys and girls are £22.50.
5 It's in the afternoon and in the evening.
6 You can see this show on six days.

b) What's best for your birthday: A, B or C?

Theatre Royal Plymouth
Monday 7th – Saturday 12th February
Mon–Thu: 7 pm • Fri and Sat: 8 pm
Prices: £30, £28, £22.50, £20.50, £14
(*Children under 16* £7.50 off)

Book: 01752 267222

Fireworks Show
11th–12th August, 8 pm
The Hoe **FREE**

Supported by
drakecircus
PLYMOUTH SHOPPING

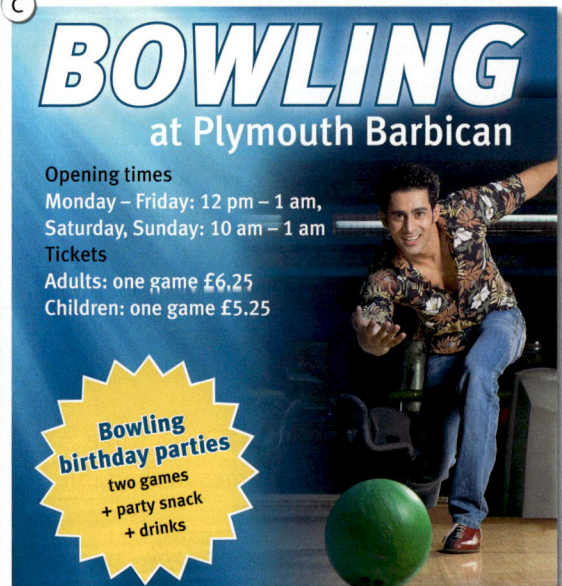

BOWLING
at Plymouth Barbican

Opening times
Monday – Friday: 12 pm – 1 am,
Saturday, Sunday: 10 am – 1 am
Tickets
Adults: one game £6.25
Children: one game £5.25

Bowling birthday parties
two games
+ party snack
+ drinks

2   How you can understand new words

What are these words in German?

1 fireworks (poster B)

2 under (poster A)
3 snack (poster C)

4 opening times (poster C)
5 adults (poster C)

So kannst du manche neue Wörter verstehen:
1) Schau auf die Bilder.

2) Gibt es ein ähnliches Wort im Deutschen?

3) Schau auf die Wörter vor und nach dem neuen Wort und rate.

▶ *Skills file 3, p. 143*

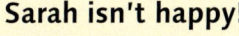

1 The kids from Harbour Road:
Sarah isn't happy!

a) Watch part 1 of the film. Why[1] isn't Sarah
with Paul and Anna at the shops?
1 Paul and Anna don't like Sarah.
2 Sarah doesn't like shopping.
3 Paul and Anna want to buy Sarah a present.

b) Now watch part 2. What's right?
Paul and Anna buy …

a hat[2]   a T-shirt   trainers   a notebook[3]

c) Watch part 2 again. What's right?
1 The price of Paul's present is £3.99 / £9.99.
2 The price of Anna's present is £7.99 / £5.99.

d) Now watch part 3. What's right at the end of the film?
Sarah is happy / unhappy.

2 People and places: Plymouth, England

a) Watch the film about Plymouth. What places can you see?

The Reel Cinema   The Hoe   The Lido   The aquarium   The shopping   The market
                                                                   centre

b) Say what *you* think about the places in Plymouth. Tell a partner.

The Reel Cinema The Hoe …	looks[4]	big. old.
		great. boring[4].
		cool. terrible.

---

[1]Why? *Warum?*   [2]hat *Hut*   [3]notebook *Notizbuch*   [4]it looks boring *es sieht langweilig aus*

1 Luca talks about his day

a) Work with a partner. Put the pictures in the right order: *C, …*

My friends meet me at school.

I come home in the afternoon.

I get up early.

Jack and I go to school by bus. Sometimes we walk.

We always have lunch at school.

I sometimes make breakfast.

b) Luca tells you about his day. Listen and check your answers in 1a).

1.54

2 Luca's dad is a firefighter

Match the sentences (1–6) with the pictures (A–F): *1B, 2…*

1 Luca's dad gets up in the afternoon.
2 He often makes dinner.
3 He has dinner with his family.
4 He goes to work after dinner.
5 He meets his friends at work.
6 He comes home in the morning.

3 The simple present

a) Look again at the texts on page 64. Make two lists:

Verb	Verb + s
I get up	Dad gets up
…	…

b) Now pick the right answers. Make the rules.

> Haha! Cyril gets up when the sea comes in!

FOCUS

Was ist richtig? Wähle Ⓐ oder Ⓑ.

Mit dem *simple present* sagst du   Ⓐ was oft passiert.
                                             Ⓑ was schon passiert ist.

Mit *I, you, we, they* verwendest du   Ⓐ das Verb mit s.
                                             Ⓑ das Verb ohne s.

Mit *he, she, it* verwendest du   Ⓐ das Verb mit s.
                                             Ⓑ das Verb ohne s.

▶ *Language file 6, p. 148*

4 Luca and his dad

a) Write the sentences for Luca. Pick the right verb.

> go • get • make • meet • have • walk

1 I … up early.
2 I often … breakfast.
3 Jack and I … to school by bus.
4 Sometimes we …
5 My friends … me at school.
6 We … lunch at school.

b) First read what Luca's dad says.

> I get up in the afternoon.
> I often make dinner.
> I meet my friends at work.
> I come home in the morning.

Then write what Luca says about his dad.

> Dad … up in the afternoon.
> He often … dinner.
> He … his friends at work.
> He … home in the morning.

5 NOW YOU

a) Write four (or more) sentences about your day.

I get up early. I go to …

b) ◉ Write about your mum, or your dad, or a friend too.

My mum gets up … She goes to work at … She …

> Du kannst Sätze aus Aufgabe 4 übernehmen und für dich ändern.

More practice 7   p. 121

🎧 6 Who is he?
1.55

Listen to the poem. Then repeat it. Who is *he*?

> He lives on the beach.
> He walks on the sand.
> He swims in the sea.
> He pinches my hand.

More practice 8   p. 121

1 WORDS In town

a) 🔘 Match the pictures A–H with the phrases 1–8.

1 I often go swimming.
2 I often meet my friends.
3 I often ride my bike.
4 I sometimes go to the cinema.

5 I sometimes go bowling.
6 I often go shopping.
7 I have lunch at school.
8 I have a party on my birthday.

b) What picture is it?

1 I can see a shirt in picture ...
2 I can see hoodies in picture ...
3 I can see sweets in picture ...
4 I can see trainers in picture ...

2 LANGUAGE Cyril's birthday

a) 🔘 Copy and complete the text.
Use the verbs in the box.

go • have • love • meet • get up • play

Cyril and Sandy ... (1) early.
Then they ... (2) to the beach.
Cyril ___ It's my birthday today. I always ... (3)
a party. I ... (4) all my friends.
Sandy ___ Great! I ... (5) your parties.
We always ... (6) games.

b) 🔘 Copy and complete the text.
Pick the right form of the verbs. // ● p.122

Sandy go / goes (1) to the market.
She buy / buys (2) nice things.
Cyril stay / stays (3) at home.
He work / works (4) in the kitchen.
He make / makes (5) a big birthday lunch.
Cyril's friends come / comes (6) in the
afternoon. They go / goes (7) swimming.
Then they play / plays (8) games.

3 LISTENING Tamara's birthday

1.56

Listen to Tamara. Pick the right answer Ⓐ or Ⓑ .

1 Tamara's birthday is in Ⓐ June. Ⓑ July.
2 It's on Ⓐ 12th. Ⓑ 20th.
3 On her birthday Tamara Ⓐ goes bowling. Ⓑ has a party.
4 She Ⓐ sometimes Ⓑ always stays at home.
5 Tamara's Ⓐ stepdad Ⓑ grandma comes for her birthday.

4 WRITING My favourite day

Write about your favourite day.

⬤ Add *sometimes*, *often* or *always* in some sentences. *I always get up at ...*

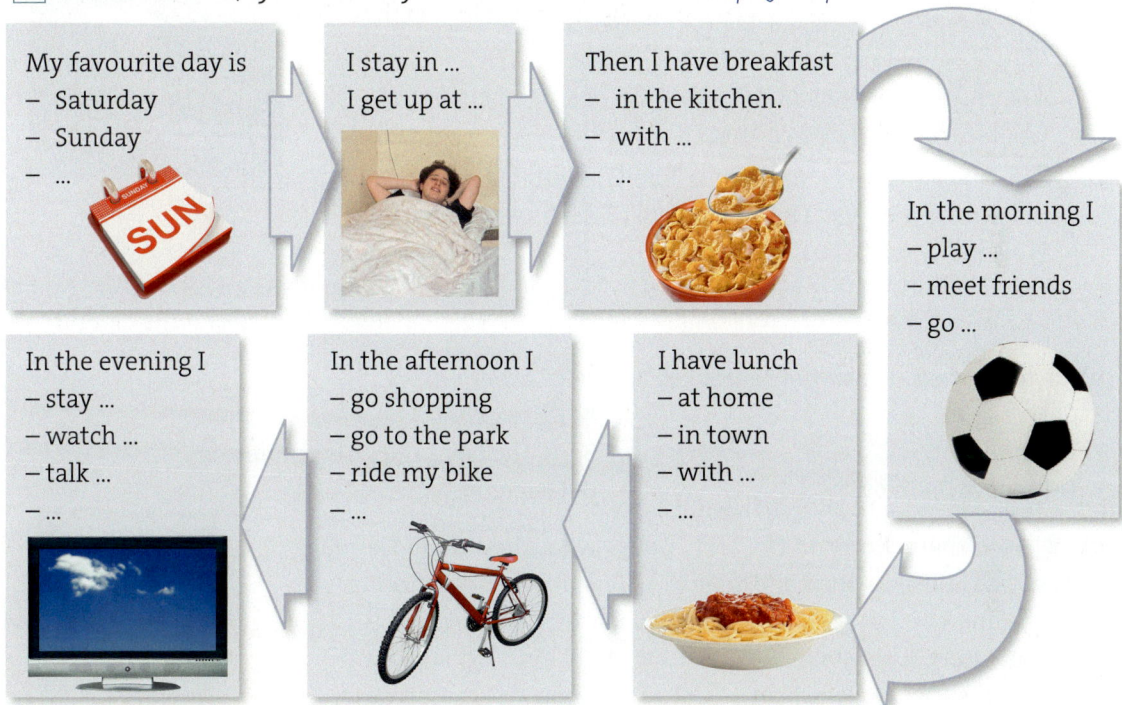

My favourite day is
– Saturday
– Sunday
– ...

I stay in ...
I get up at ...

Then I have breakfast
– in the kitchen.
– with ...
– ...

In the morning I
– play ...
– meet friends
– go ...

I have lunch
– at home
– in town
– with ...
– ...

In the afternoon I
– go shopping
– go to the park
– ride my bike
– ...

In the evening I
– stay ...
– watch ...
– talk ...
– ...

5 SPEAKING Birthdays

PARTNER B: Go to page 111.
a) PARTNER A:
Ask partner B about
his/her birthday:
– When/birthday?
– What/favourite activities?
Note the answers.

b) Now look at the pictures.
Listen to your partner and
answer his/her questions.

🎧 **6 READING Casper**

a) ⭕ Look at the text. Is it about a bus, a cat or a garden?

THE PLYMOUTH NEWS   *Saturday, 16th January 2010*

Casper

1 Casper is a cat. He's twelve. He lives in Cook Street, Plymouth with Susan Finden.

In the morning Casper leaves the house at 7.25. He walks to the bus stop. He waits there for the number 3 bus.

5 When it comes, Casper goes to town by bus. He watches the cars, the buses, the houses.

Then Casper comes home again by bus. He gets out at Cook Street and goes home.

The boys and girls on the bus like Casper. They all buy
10 tickets for the bus. The tickets cost £2.50! And Casper? He's lucky. Cats buy no tickets.

---

b) Read the text. Finish the sentences and tell Casper's story.

1 Casper is a ...   4 He watches ...
2 He's from ...   5 All the boys and girls on the bus ...
3 He goes to town by ...   6 Casper buys ...

c) 🔵 Find these words in the text. Guess what they are in German.

1 bus stop (line 4)   Ⓐ Bushaltestelle   Ⓑ Busfahrer   Ⓒ Fahrplan
2 waits (line 4)   Ⓐ schläft   Ⓑ wartet   Ⓒ trinkt
3 gets out (line 7)   Ⓐ steigt aus   Ⓑ steigt ein   Ⓒ steigt um
4 ticket (line 10)   Ⓐ Fahrplan   Ⓑ Zeitung   Ⓒ Fahrkarte

> Was hilft dir:
> • das Foto
> • ein ähnliches deutsches Wort
> • andere Wörter im Text?

---

7 My learner log
Write your learner log for Unit 3. Put it in your DOSSIER.

My learner log for Unit 3

I can	😃	😐	😟
– say what I do at the weekend:	x		
– say what I do every day:		x	
– say months and the date:	x		
– say the numbers 1–100 and prices:			x
– say what I do for my birthday:	x		

My progress in English is: GREAT! 👍 / OK 🤛 / NOT SO GOOD 👎

1 WORDS
Write the six months in the right order.

First **test** yourself. Then **check** your answers on page 195.

SPENOCTOBERENMAYTOREJULYCANDISEDECEMBEROBJUNEALNOMARCHRE

2 WORDS In a shop
What's the price of …

1 hoodies? 4 trainers?
2 sweets?   5 bikes?
3 shoes?   6 shirts?

£16 £18 35p £6.99 £99 £45

3 LANGUAGE At the weekend
a) Find the right verb.

> buy • meet • stays

1 At the weekend I often … my friends in town.
2 We sometimes … sweets there.
3 But my dad … at home.

b) Find the right form of the verb.
1 On Saturday my mum go / goes to work.
2 I often go / goes to town.
3 My two sisters go / goes swimming.

4 SPEAKING Birthdays
Copy and complete the dialogue.

> on • play • sounds • watch • what • your

Daniel _ When's … (1) birthday, Sarah?
Sarah __ Friday 11th June.
Daniel _ And … (2) are your favourite
           activities … (3) your birthday?
Sarah __ We often … (4) games. And we
           sometimes … (5) a film.
Daniel _ … (6) fun. Thanks, Sarah.

5 WRITING
Write about your Saturday and Sunday.
Write what you do
• in the morning (two sentences).
• in the afternoon (two sentences).
• in the evening (two sentences).

In the morning I In the afternoon I In the evening I	go … meet … make … walk … stay … watch … ride … buy … get up … have … play …

1 On Merryweather Farm

How many different animals can you find in the brochure? Check with a partner.

Welcome to **Merryweather Farm**

Lots of visitors come to Merryweather Farm.

Children can ride the ponies.

You can meet the animals in Pets Corner.

Everybody loves the donkeys on the farm.

You can watch the ducks.

Children love the trampolines and the zip wire.

The shop has lots of nice things.

2 Welcome to the farm

2.2

a) ⭕ Which animals are on Berry's farm?
Listen. Point at the pictures 1–12.

1 pony	2 donkey	3 cow	4 pig
5 sheep	6 duck	7 chicken	8 fish
9 hamster	10 rabbit	11 rat	12 cat

b) Listen again. Pick the right answer.
1 Berry is Ⓐ in town. Ⓑ in the shop.
2 The tickets are Ⓐ £ 15.50. Ⓑ £ 59.50.
3 The farm doesn't have Ⓐ cows. Ⓑ pigs.
4 The children don't like Ⓐ rats. Ⓑ cats.
5 The farm Ⓐ has toilets.
   Ⓑ doesn't have toilets.

More practice 1   p. 122

3 NOW YOU

a) Think: You're at Merryweather Farm.
Where do you want to go?
Pick two places.

b) Pair: Talk to a partner.
Agree on two places.
– I want to go to the zip wire / …
  What about you?
– I don't want to go to the … I want to…

c) Share: Tell the class.

We want to go to the …

And we want to go to the …

On Berry's farm

 1 **From Monday to Friday**
2.3

Berry's dog, Sam, wakes Berry at 6 o'clock in the morning.
Sam lives in the house with the family. The other animals don't live in the house. They live outside on the farm.

At 7 o'clock she looks after Harry and the other animals. She doesn't watch TV. She doesn't have time!

Before breakfast Berry feeds her pony, Harry.

After breakfast Berry goes to school. She goes by car with her dad.
Berry doesn't come home before 4 o'clock. She has a snack and then she does her homework.

Read the text. Are the sentences right or wrong?  p.122
1 In the morning Sam wakes Berry.
2 Before breakfast she feeds Sam and the other animals.
3 She goes to school by car.
4 She comes home before 4 o'clock.
5 In the evening she looks after the animals.   More practice 2 p.123

2 **NOW YOU**

Tell Berry about your day. Write five sentences. You can use these ideas:
1 My mum / my dad / my sister / my mobile / … wakes me in the morning.
2 I go to school by bus / car / bike. *Or:* I walk to school with my friends / my brother / …
3 I don't come home before one o'clock / two o'clock / …
4 In the afternoon I do my homework / do sport / meet my friends / go to town / …
5 In the evening I watch TV / read / listen to music / …

3 Activities on the farm

a) Look at the board. Then put the photos A–D in the right order.

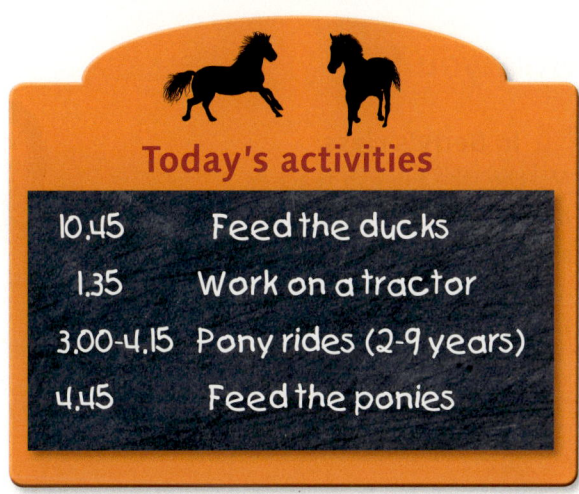

Today's activities

10.45	Feed the ducks
1.35	Work on a tractor
3.00-4.15	Pony rides (2-9 years)
4.45	Feed the ponies

b) Listen to the four dialogues with Berry and her visitors. Match the dialogues with activities A–D.
Dialogue 1 is photo ...
Dialogue 2 is ...

2.4

c) ⭘ Listen again.
What's the right time? //⏺ p.123
Dialogue 1: **A** 10.40 **B** 11.50
Dialogue 2: **A** 11.00 **B** 12.00
Dialogue 3: **A** 02.30 **B** 03.30
Dialogue 4: **A** 04.30 **B** 05.00

2.4

4 The time

a) ⭘ Listen and repeat.

2.5

| 01:00 | 10:00 | 12:05 | 05:10 | 09:15 |
| 08:25 | 12:30 | 11:35 | 02:45 | 06:50 |

You write:	You say:
2.00	two o'clock
2.05	two oh five
2.10	two ten
2.15	two fifteen
2.30	two thirty
2.45	two forty-five

b) Work with a partner. Say one of the times in a). Your partner points at it.

c) Listen to three dialogues. Write the times.

2.6

5 What's the time, please?

a) Draw a digital clock and write a time on it.

b) Talk to a partner.
A What's the time, please?
B It's ...
A Thanks.
B You're welcome.

c) Walk around: Find a new partner. Talk to as many partners as you can.

More practice 3 p.123

How you feel

🎧 **1** **In Berry's class**
2.7
Ms Lee, the English teacher, has two questions for the students in her class.
a) **Partner A:** Copy table A.
Partner B: Copy table B.

b) Who says your sentences? Adam, Luca, Berry or Ellie? Listen and write the names.

Ⓐ *I feel great when* …	
I do sport.	Luca, …
I'm with my animals.	
I'm with my friends.	
I listen to music.	
I don't have homework.	

Ⓑ *I feel fed up when* …	
my sister is bossy.	Ellie
my mobile doesn't work.	
my friends don't text me.	
people don't talk to me.	
I have lots of homework.	

c) Swap tables with your partner. Listen again and check your partner's answers.

2 **NOW YOU**
When do **you** feel great? When do **you** feel fed up? Write as many sentences as you can. You can put the text in your DOSSIER.

More practice 4 p.124

I feel great when	I play football/… I'm in my room/… I have no maths/… I'm with my family/… I watch TV/a DVD/… I listen to music/…
I feel fed up when	my friends don't text me/… I have lots of homework/… my sister is noisy/… my bus is late. my bike doesn't work. I do sport.

3 **What about your partners?**
Double circle: Make two circles and talk to different partners.
A I feel great when …
 And you?
B I feel great when …
 But I feel fed up when …
 And you?
A I feel fed up when …

4 Berry's homework

2.8

a) ◯ Read Berry's text.
Put the photos in the right order.

How I feel by Berry Donovan

I feel great when I'm with the animals at home. I really love animals.

I sometimes feel a bit fed up because I'm the only student at school in a wheelchair. I'm always different.

But I feel great when I'm with my friends. With my friends I'm not "the girl in the wheelchair". I'm a normal teenager!

I feel great when I do sport. My favourite sport is wheelchair basketball.

I feel really fed up when people don't talk to me because I'm in a wheelchair.
They ask: "How is Berry?"
They don't ask ME: "How are YOU?"

b) Copy and complete Berry's notes.

😄 I feel great	🙁 I feel fed up
when I'm with …	because I'm …
when …	when …

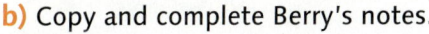

c) ⬤ Look again at exercise 2.
Pick **one** time when you feel really great.
Then pick **one** time when you feel really fed up. Write more about it.
You can put your text in your DOSSIER.

I feel great when I do sport.
My favourite sport is …
I often play with …

I feel fed up when my parents are bossy or my … is …
They often don't know how I feel.
They don't listen.
And they often say: "You can't …"

1 Before you read

Look at the pictures. Who is it – Adam, Berry, Ellie or Luca?

1 Ellie, ... and ... are on the bus.
2 ... doesn't have his sweets.
3 ... has a problem with animals.
4 ..., ..., ... and ... go to Pets Corner.
5 ... doesn't like the chipmunk.
6 ... is unhappy at night.

🎧 Let's go to the country
2.9

1 Scene 1

Berry writes to her friends.
This is her email.

> Hi!
>
> 5 Can you come to the farm
> for a sleepover? What about
> next Saturday? There's a bus
> at 3 o'clock.
>
> Berry

10 Scene 2

It's 3 o'clock on Saturday.
Luca, Ellie and Adam are excited.
"OK. Let's go!" Ellie says.
"Yeah, let's go to the country!" Adam says.
15 "Yippee!" Luca says.

Scene 3

It's 3.45.
The three friends are in Woolwell.
But Luca is unhappy.
"Oh no!" he says. "I don't have my sweets." 20
"It's OK, Luca," his friends say.
"We have lots of nice things."

Scene 4

It's 4.30.
The four friends are on the farm and go to 25
Pets Corner.
"This is Lulu, our chipmunk," Berry says.
"Oh, she's so cute!" Ellie says.
"Look!" Adam says.
"Oh no! My shoulder is wet!" Luca says. 30
Everybody laughs.

Scene 5

It's 5.30. "Let's eat," Ellie says.

"I don't like your things," Luca says.

35 "I want to buy sweets. Can I go to Woolwell?"

"Go through that field," Berry says.

Scene 6

It's 6.15. Adam gets a text from Luca:

40 They go to the field.

"Help! It's a bull!" Luca says.

"It isn't a bull. It's a cow," Berry says. "Cows aren't dangerous!"

Everybody laughs.

45 But Luca doesn't laugh.

Scene 7

It's 11 o'clock at night.

"Oh, no! What's that noise?" Luca asks.

"Oh, Luca! It's only a chicken," Berry says.

"Good night, everybody!"   50

"Good night," Ellie and Adam say.

Scene 8

On Sunday the friends play on the zip wire and the trampolines.

They ride Harry, Berry's pony.   55

They feed the animals.

In the afternoon Ellie, Adam and Luca go back to Plymouth by bus.

"Thanks Berry. It's great here," Ellie says.

"Yeah, I love the country," Adam says.   60

"It's nice, but I'm a city boy," Luca says.

"And I'm a country girl," Berry says.

2   What are the right scenes?

a) Match the titles with the scenes 1–8 in the story.

A cute animal

Time to go home

Let's go to the country

Come to a sleepover

Noises at night

No sweets!

Is it a cow or a bull?

Time to eat

b) Check with a partner.

3   At the farm

Copy and complete the sentences.

1 The three friends go to Woolwell by …

2 Luca doesn't have his …

3 Ellie thinks that Lulu is …

4 Luca goes to a field and meets a …

5 At night Luca hears a …

6 Luca is a … boy and Berry is a … girl.

4   THEATRE TIME

Work in groups or teams.
Pick a scene from the story.
Read and act the scene.

Signs

1 **In Plymouth**

Look at the signs. Then match the sentences 1–5 with the signs A–E.

1 You can get the bus here. → *Sign* ...
2 You can see this sign at a cafe.
3 This sign is on Berry's farm.
4 This sign is in a park in Plymouth.
5 People in wheelchairs, please go left.

▶ *Skills file 3, p. 143*

> Du kannst die Schilder verstehen, auch wenn du nicht jedes Wort kennst.

2 ◉ **MEDIATION**

Partner A: Stell dir vor, du bist in Plymouth.
Beantworte die Fragen von Partner B – auf Deutsch.

Partner B: Du kannst die Schilder nicht verstehen. Stelle Partner A folgende Fragen auf Deutsch. Tauscht nach zwei Fragen die Rollen.

Schild A: Warum ist der Hund hinter Gittern? Ist er im Gefängnis?
Schild B: Ich habe Hunger. Können wir hier frühstücken?
Schild C: Es geht um *animals*, also Tiere. Was dürfen wir nicht tun?
Schild D: Wer sollte hier links gehen?
Schild E: Wie können wir herausfinden, wann der nächste Bus kommt?

Invitations

1 An invitation to a sleepover
Read the invitation.
1 Where is Mike's sleepover?
2 When is it?
3 What can Moona bring?

6.00 pm = 18.00 Uhr
11.00 am = 11.00 Uhr

More practice 5 p.124

Invitation to:
A sleepover at Mike's house

Dear Moona,

Please come to my sleepover.
It's on Friday, 23rd May.
It's at my house: 12 Ambrose Street
It's from 6 pm to 11 am.
I want to play games and watch a film.
Please bring some sweets and chocolate.
I hope you can come.
Mike

2 Answers to an invitation
Read the two answers.
Can Moona and Steve
come to Mike's sleepover?

Dear Mike,
Thank you for the invitation.
I'd love to come!
Best wishes
Moona

Dear Mike,
Thank you for the invitation.
I'm sorry, but I can't come. Have a nice time!
Steve

3 NOW YOU
a) Write an invitation to a friend for a party at your house.

Write your friend's name.

Write the times here.
Example:
From 6 pm to 9 pm

What can you do together?
– go swimming
– watch a film
– listen to music
– ride bikes
– …

INVITATION TO
a party at … 's house

Dear …,

Please come to my party.
It's on …
It's at my house: …

It's from … to …
I want to … and …
Please bring … and …
I hope you can come.

Write your name here.

Write the day and the date of your party here. Example:
Saturday, 25th May

Write your address here.

What can people bring?
– swimming things
– trainers, a pullover
– DVDs, CDs
– funny photos
– …

b) Swap invitations with your partner. Then write an answer to your partner's invitation.
Look at Moona's and Steve's answers! You can put your texts in your DOSSIER.

▶ Wordbank 7, p.153

Guess and check

1   A poem
2.10

Read and listen to the poem.
Then answer the questions.

1 What's the title of the poem? Can you say it?
2 Who do you think speaks in the poem:
   a mum / a dad / a child?
3 What does he / she want?
4 Do you like the poem? Is it funny?

2   Can you guess some words?

a) Read the poem again and find the English
words for these animals. Check with a partner.

Greife nicht sofort zum Wörterbuch.
• Manche Tierwörter kennst du schon, z.B. *rabbit*.
• Andere sind auf Deutsch ganz ähnlich, z.B. *goldfish*.

b) Write these words on pieces of paper.

stoat   budgie   guinea pig   parrot

kitten   horse   puppy   peahen

Put the pieces of paper in alphabetical order.
Then check the words in the Dictionary (pages 174–181).

c) ⬤ Read the poem again. What other words are new?
Can you guess them? Check them in the Dictionary.
Tell your partner what they mean in German.

Muuuuuuummmmmmm

Can we have a kitten
Can we have a dog
Can we call her Frisky
Can we call him Bob?
I can take him out each day
I can brush his fur
I will buy the dog meat
And milk to make her purr
Mum!!

Oh … no … well –

Can we have a donkey
Or can we have a horse
A monkey or a parrot
Hamster or a snake?
Can we have a guinea pig
A peahen
Or a stoat
Llama or a budgie
A rabbit or a goat?

No, WE DON I WANT stick insects
And goldfish aren't much fun …
Oh can we have a puppy …
Mum, mum, muuuuuuummmmmmm.

Peter Dixon

Du kannst Wörter schneller im
Wörterbuch finden, wenn du sie
in alphabetischer Reihenfolge
suchst.

▶ *Skills file 4, p. 144*

1 **The kids from Harbour Road:**

A class project

a) Watch the film.

Then find the right sentences.

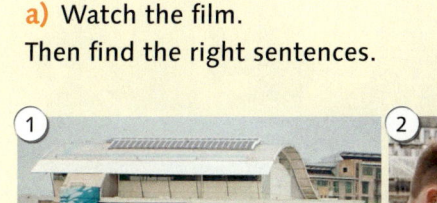

Sarah   Paul   Anna

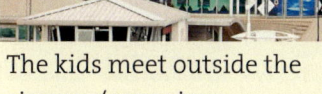

1
The kids meet outside the cinema / aquarium.

2
Paul has a new camera / mobile.

3
First they look at the people / fish.

4
Then they ask lots of people / questions.

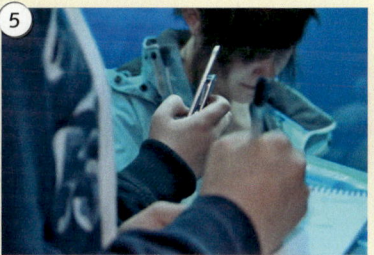

5
Sarah and Anna write notes, but Paul uses his computer / mobile.

6
Paul has a big problem with his pen / mobile.

b) Watch the film again. Who says it – Anna, Paul or Sarah? Can you remember?

1 Let's do our project on sharks[1].
2 I love my new mobile.
3 I don't have a ticket.

4 Your phone is terrible!
5 This is our project – but you don't listen!
6 But what can I do now?

2 **People and places:** **A normal day at school**

a) Watch the film. Then complete the sentences and say how Emily feels in scenes A–D.

Emily feels ... when she can't do things alone[2].

Emily feels ... when people are normal with her.

Emily feels ... when people don't listen to her.

Emily feels ... when Laura invites[3] her.

b) Watch the film again. Is it a good or bad day for Emily?

[1]shark *Haifisch*   [2]alone *allein*   [3]invite *einladen*

🎧 1 Pets
2.11

Berry has lots of pets. What about you?
Do you have a pet? What's your favourite pet?

1 *Adam* — We don't have a pet.
Luca — What about you, Ellie?
Ellie — I have two cats at mum's house.
But Dad and Alisha don't have
5 a pet. They don't have time.
Berry — And what about you, Luca?
Luca — No, we don't have a pet. I want
a dog, but dad doesn't like dogs.
Adam — What about other pets?
10 *Luca* — Well, I love cats too, but mum
doesn't like cats. But I want a pet!
Ellie — I have an idea. What about
a chipmunk?
Luca — A chipmunk?
15 *Berry* — I don't know. A chipmunk is a wild
animal. It isn't really a good pet for
a house.
Luca — And I remember Lulu and my wet
shoulder. I don't want a chipmunk,
20 thank you!

2 The simple present – negative sentences

a) Put in *doesn't* or *don't*.

1 We ... have a pet. (line 1)
2 Dad and Alisha ... have a pet. (lines 4/5)
3 They ... have time. (line 5)
4 Dad ... like dogs. (line 8)
4 Mum ... like cats. (lines 10/11)
5 I ... want a chipmunk. (line 19)

I don't like dogs!

b) Make rules for negative sentences with *doesn't* or *don't*.

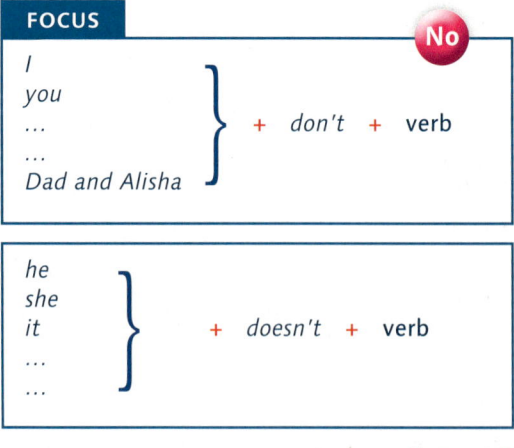

FOCUS No

I		
you		
...	+ *don't* + **verb**	
...		
Dad and Alisha		

he		
she		
it	+ *doesn't* + **verb**	
...		
...		

► *Language file 7, p. 148*

3 NOW YOU

Write sentences about you.

1 I have / don't have a pet.
2 My mum likes / doesn't like animals.
3 We have / don't have a big garden.
4 I like / don't like dogs.
5 My best friend has / doesn't have a pet.
6 He / She wants / doesn't want a hamster.

4 ○ That's wrong! //● p.125

Copy and complete the orange sentences.

1 Berry lives in the city. – Wrong! She doesn't live in …
2 Berry's parents have a pet shop. – Wrong! They don't …
3 Berry rides a donkey. – Wrong! She doesn't …
4 Berry has a cat. – That's wrong! She doesn't …
5 Berry's mum and dad have cows.– Wrong! They don't…
6 Berry goes to school in Woolwell. – Wrong! She doesn't …
7 Luca and Adam have dogs. – That's wrong! They don't…
8 Ellie has two ponies. – That's wrong! She doesn't …

5 My pets

Copy and complete the sentences. Put in *don't* or *doesn't*.

1 I live in a small flat. We … have a garden.
2 My mum likes small pets. She … want a big pet.
3 I … have a "normal" pet, like a dog. I have lots of fish.
4 I often watch my favourite fish, Sam. He … like the other fish.
5 Mum … feed the fish. I look after my pets.
6 My pets … come from England. They come from Africa. <u>More practice 6</u> p.125

6 NOW YOU

Write about your pet or a friend's pet. Write as many sentences as you can.
Pick A or B. You can put the text in your DOSSIER.   ▶ *Wordbank 8, p. 154*

Ⓐ
My favourite pet
I want a …
I don't want a …
Cats / … are nice.
But I don't like …

Ⓑ ● People and pets
I have / I don't have …
My grandma / friend has a …
But it doesn't live in the house / kitchen / …
It lives in the garden / outside …
My … feeds / looks after it.

1 WORDS On Merryweather Farm

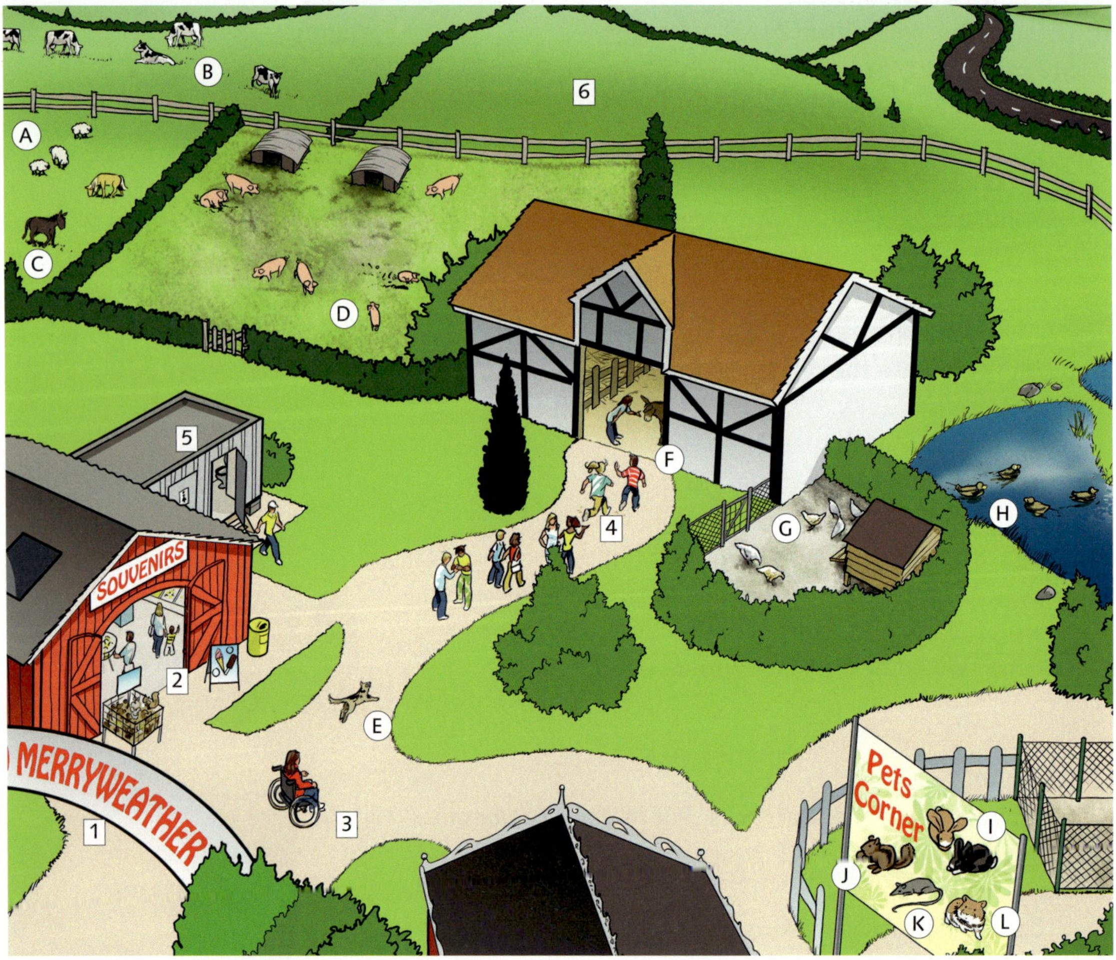

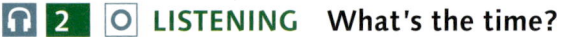

a) Match 1–6 in the picture with the words in the green box.

b) Name the animals A-L in the picture.

field • toilet • shop • sign • visitors • wheelchair

2 LISTENING What's the time?

2.12

p.125

Listen to eight dialogues. Match pictures A–H with the dialogues. *Dialogue 1: picture ...*

A

B

C

D

E

F

G

H

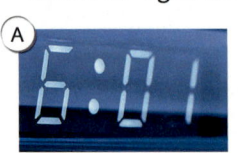

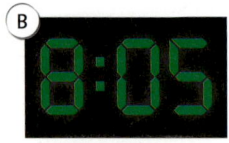

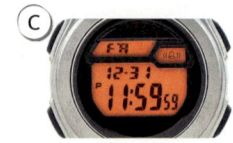

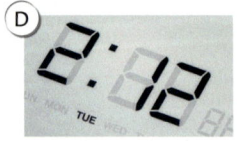

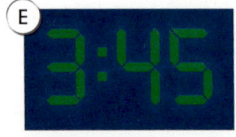

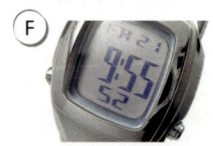

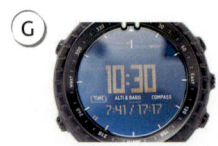

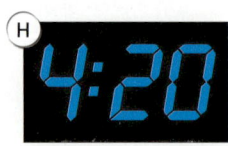

3 READING   On Berry's farm

a) Berry writes about a day on the farm. Read her text.

> In the morning mum, dad and I get up at 6 o'clock. Sam always wakes me, but he doesn't wake mum or dad! I feed my pony before breakfast. After breakfast I go to school by car with my dad. Dad then sometimes goes shopping in Plymouth (we don't have big shops here in the country!). Mum doesn't come with us because the first visitors come to the farm at 9 o'clock.
>
> Mum and dad have lunch at 1 o'clock. After lunch dad stays in the shop and mum works with the ponies. A friend, Mr Jones, looks after the children on the trampolines because it can be dangerous when the children are stupid!
> When I come home from school, dad has a snack with me. Then I do my homework. Sam is always under my table! We have dinner in the evening, so it's late when dad and I look after the animals, and I'm often tired when I go to bed. Work on the farm is great on a good day. It's not so good when it's wet!

b) You're a reporter for the school magazine.

- ◯ Make notes about six activities.
- ● Make notes about a day on the farm.

When?	Who?	What?
in the morning	Mrs Donovan, Mr Donovan, Berry Donovan	get up

c) Write the right words.

> at • before • by • in • on • with

1 I feed my pony ... breakfast.
2 I go to school ... car.
3 We don't have big shops ... the country.
4 The first visitors come ... 9 o'clock.
5 After school dad has a snack ... me.
6 We have lots of work ... the farm.

4 ● WRITING   A day with my family

Write about a day in your family. Use ideas in Berry's text in exercise 3 and in the red box. Write as many sentences as you can.
eight sentences: **good**   nine and more sentences: **very good!**

> Write about how you feel too:
> *I feel great when ...*
> *I feel fed up when ...*

When?	Who?	What?
In the morning/afternoon/evening Before school/lunch/dinner/... After breakfast/lunch/... At 10 o'clock/at 11.15/...	I	have breakfast/feed my cat have lunch/have a snack/... do sport/meet friends/play a game/ ... don't go to bed before ...
	my mum my brother ...	goes to work/stays at home doesn't come before ... watches TV/plays ...

In the morning I get up at ... I have breakfast ... Then I go to school. I don't walk, I get the bus. ...

5 LANGUAGE   Crabs and birds

Write Cyril's sentences. Pick the right answer: red or blue.

1 I have a friend, Sandy – but she doesn't live / don't live on the beach.

2 Sandy and her sisters like visitors. I doesn't like / don't like visitors.

3 They feed Sandy, but they doesn't feed / don't feed me.

4 Sandy has three sisters, but she doesn't have / don't have a brother.

5 I have a brother and a sister. They doesn't like / don't like birds.

6 Birds are noisy. We crabs doesn't make / don't make lots of noise.

7 They wake us very early in the morning. I say to them:
  "You doesn't have / don't have friends here on the beach!"

6 SPEAKING   Partner game

a) Partner A writes a time in the morning – but doesn't show it.
Partner B guesses the time.
Partner A says "Earlier" or "later".
How often does Partner B guess?

b) Swap roles.
How often does Partner A guess?

It's 11 o'clock.

No, earlier!

It's 10.15.

No, later!

7   My learner log

Copy and complete your learner log. You can put it in your DOSSIER.

My learner log for Unit 4

Now I can ...
– say the names of lots of animals: ...
– talk about activities in my day: ...
– say the time: ...
– say when I feel great or fed up: ...
– write an invitation: 😀 😐 🙁
– find new words in a dictionary: 😀 😐 🙁

– My favourite text is on page ...
– My favourite words are ...
– My favourite phrases are ...
– My favourite people are ...
– Difficult words are ...

My progress in English is: GREAT! 👍 / Ok 👊 / NOT VERY GOOD 👎

1 WORDS Activities

Write the sentences. Pick the right verbs.

> feeds • has • comes • goes • wakes • works

First **test** yourself. Then **check** your answers on page 196.

1 Dad ... mum in the morning.

2 First he ... all the animals.

3 He often ... shopping.

4 Then he ... on the farm.

5 He has a snack when Berry ... home.

6 He ... dinner with Berry.

2 LANGUAGE What's the time?

Match the sentences with the pictures.

1 It's four fifteen.
2 It's ten ten.
3 It's four forty.
4 It's four twenty-five.
5 It's ten thirty.
6 It's ten fifty-five.

A 4:40
B 10:10
C 10:30
D 4:15
E 4:25
F 10:55

3 LANGUAGE Family and animals

Write the sentences.

1 I doesn't like / don't like hamsters.
2 My sister doesn't like / don't like bulls.
3 My parents doesn't like / don't like rats.
4 My grandma doesn't like / don't like pets.
5 My dad doesn't like / don't like zoos.
6 We all doesn't like / don't like snakes.

4 READING

Where can you see these signs?

1 in a zoo
2 on a farm
3 in a park
4 near a cafe
5 in a cinema
6 on a zip wire

A The next film begins at 6.30

B Please don't walk on the grass.

C ! Be careful: These monkeys can be dangerous!

D No children under 8.

E Please don't feed the donkeys

F Food and snacks

5 WRITING

Write an invitation to a sleepover. Write:

• the name of your friend
• when (day, date, time) and where
• what you want to do
• what your friend can bring

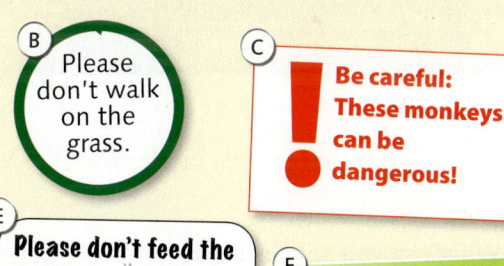

Invitation to a sleepover
Dear ...,
Please come ... ...
...
I hope you can come!
...

1 Plymouth

a) Do you know the people in photos A–D? Who are they? Can you guess?
I think the boy in photo B is ...

b) What can you see on pages 88–89? Pick the right words from the boxes.

There's a ...

> boy • cafe • child • ferry • pony •
> kitchen • road • woman • man

There are some / lots of ...

> birds • boats • buses • cars • chairs •
> houses • people • shops • tables •
> trees • women

c) Now collect all the class's ideas for words on pages 88–89. Make two lists. Collect as many words as you can.

There's a ...	There are some / lots of
...	...

▶ Language file 9, p. 149

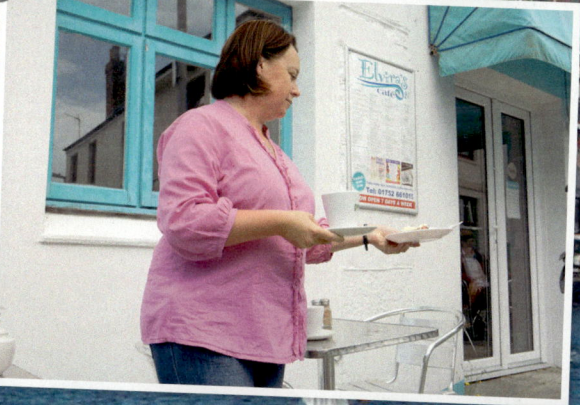

C

D

🎧 **2** **Adam's family**
2.13
a) Listen to Adam and Ellie. Look at photos A–D.
What's the right order of the photos?

b) Listen again. Answer the questions.
1 Where does Adam go after school?
  Ⓐ To the harbour.   Ⓑ To the cafe.   Ⓒ Home.
2 Where does Adam's dad work in summer?
  Ⓐ In the cafe.   Ⓑ On the ferry.   Ⓒ In France.
3 What does Adam do after school?
  Ⓐ He helps in the cafe.   Ⓑ He plays football.
  Ⓒ He goes to the cinema.
4 Where is Adam's brother Zack in the afternoons?
  Ⓐ With his mum.   Ⓑ At school.   Ⓒ With his babysitter.

▶ *Workbook 1–2, p. 53*

Cafe work and school work

1 After school

2.14

a) What work does Adam do in the cafe? Read and find out.

Luca talks with Adam after school.

Luca ___ Can you come to town, Adam?

Adam ___ Sorry, I can't. I help mum in the cafe after school.

Luca ___ Oh? That's new! What do you do there?
Do you cook?

Adam ___ No, never. I wash up and …

Luca ___ And where do you do your homework?

Adam ___ In the cafe. But I don't always have time.

Luca ___ Does your dad work in the cafe too?

Adam ___ No, he doesn't. He works on the ferry in summer.

Luca ___ Oh … Do you miss your dad?

Adam ___ Yes, of course. I only see him at the weekend.

Luca ___ That's hard.

Adam ___ Oh, it's 3.45! Sorry, Luca, I must go.

Luca ___ OK. Bye, Adam. See you tomorrow!

b) Find a sentence in the dialogue for each picture.

A
after school:
help mum in
cafe

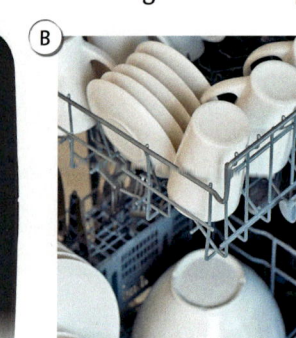
B

C

D

**c) In the evening Luca and his mum talk about Adam. Luca's mum asks lots of questions.
Pick the right answer for Luca.**

1 Does Adam often help his mum in the cafe after school?
  A Yes, he does.   B No, never.

2 Does he wash up?
  A Yes, sometimes.   B No, never.

3 Does he eat in the cafe?
  A Yes, always.   B I don't know.

4 Does Adam's dad work in the cafe too?
  A Yes, of course.   B No, he doesn't.

5 Does Adam meet his dad at the weekend?
  A Yes, he does.   B Yes, and on weekdays too.

6 Does Adam have time for his homework?
  A Yes, always.   B No, not always.

2 A letter from school

a) Read the letter. Is it good news or bad news for Adam?

b) 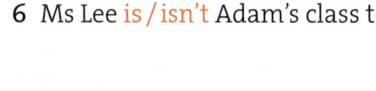 Pick the right words. **//** ● p.126

1 Adam is / isn't often tired at school.
2 He listens / doesn't listen in class.
3 He does / doesn't do his homework.
4 Adam is / isn't happy at school.
5 Ms Lee wants / doesn't want to talk with Adam's mum.
6 Ms Lee is / isn't Adam's class teacher.

Eggbuckland Community College
A DCSF Designated Technology College • Principal : Katrina Borowski

Dear Mr and Mrs Osmanovic

Adam is often tired at school, and he doesn't listen in class.
He doesn't always do his homework.
And he isn't very happy at school.

Please phone me and we can talk about it.

Best wishes

R Lee

Class 7 Teacher

🎧 3 Go home, Adam!
2.15

a) Listen to Adam and his mum. Pick the right words.

1 They're in the cafe / at home.
2 Adam's mum needs / doesn't need help.
3 At the end Adam goes home / eats in the cafe.

b) Listen again. Are the sentences right or wrong?

1 Adam's mum says her work in the cafe is OK.
2 She has a letter from Ms Lee.
3 Adam likes maths.
4 He has science homework today.
5 There's a computer in the cafe.

More practice 1 | p.126

4 Do you often …?

a) Look at the box. Pick a question.
b) Double circle: Make two circles and talk to different partners.

Partner A __ Do you often …?
Partner B __ Yes, I do. / Yes, sometimes. / No, never. Do you …?
Partner A __ Yes, I do. / Yes, sometimes. / No, I don't.

Do you often	do your homework?
	help in the kitchen?
	wash up?
	listen to music
	text your friends?
	watch TV?
	play games?
	read?
	…?

It's boring at home!

🎧 **1**   **Trouble for Adam**

2.16   **a)** ⭕ Look at the pictures. Where's Adam? Who is with Adam?

A

Go home, Adam. You must do your homework.

It's Tuesday after school.
Adam is in his mum's cafe.

B

I don't want to go home! No mum, no dad and Zack is with his new babysitter. Let's meet at the harbour.

Adam phones his friends.

C

Now Adam and his friends are at the harbour. They want to dive there. It's fun. But it's dangerous too.

D

At about five o'clock Zack and Alisha are at the harbour too. They see Adam.

E

Don't dive here, Adam! It's dangerous. Go home!

It's boring at home!

You need a hobby, Adam.

F

Hi, Josie. Can you send me a brochure for PMZ, please?

Alisha has a good idea. Her friend Josie works at the PMZ music club.

b) Match the questions with the answers.

1 Why does Adam phone his friends?
2 Where do Adam and his friends dive?
3 When are Zack and Alisha at the harbour?
4 Who do Zack and Alisha see?
5 Where does Alisha's friend Josie work?
6 What does Alisha ask Josie?

A At about five o'clock.
B Because it's boring at home.
C They see Adam.
D "Can you send me a brochure, please?"
E At the harbour.
F At PMZ music club.

c) 🔵 Pick a photo for 1, 2 and 3.
Who says it?

1 Look, Alisha. It's Adam.

2 Hi, Dan. Let's go to the harbour!

3 PMZ sounds good. I like music!

2 Welcome to PMZ

a) O Look at the brochure. Find out: What does PMZ mean? What days is PMZ open?

MAKE MUSIC FOR FREE

AT PLYMOUTH MUSIC ZONE

www.plymouthmusiczone.org.uk

MON	**THE PMZ GUITAR CLUB** 4 pm–6.15 pm ⦙ Everybody welcome! Learn to play the guitar.
TUE	**THE BIG BASH** 5 pm–6 pm ⦙ 8–18 yrs Play the drums in a group.
WED	**JAM BAND** 4 pm–5 pm ⦙ 8–18 yrs Bring your instrument. Play in a band.
THUR	**BEATS PER MINUTE (BPM)** 4.30 pm–5.30 pm ⦙ 11–25 yrs Instrument workshop for young disabled musicians. Make some new music.
FRI	**STREETBEATZ** 4 pm–6.15 pm ⦙ 12–19 yrs For all young rappers. Make your music in the PMZ studio.
SAT	**THE ROOF RAISERS** 10 am–12.30 pm ⦙ 11–18 yrs For young singers. Sing with a real band.

b) O Listen to Adam. Pick A, B, C or D.
2.17
1 What does Adam like?

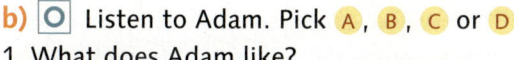

A
rapping

B
the drums

C
the guitar

D
the piano

2 What group does Adam want to join?
A *The PMZ Guitar Club*   B *Streetbeatz*
C *The Big Bash*   C *Jam Band*

c) O Copy the table. Then listen again and finish the notes. // ● p.126
2.17

1 PMZ address	R _ gl _ n Road
2 Bus number	3 _
3 Times (Mon–Fri)	From 4 pm to …
4 Times (Sat)	From 10 am to …
5 Price	Free!

3 NOW YOU

a) **Ask your partner.**
Do you like music? – Yes, I do. / Yes, sometimes. / No, I don't.
Who's your favourite band / singer? – It's …
Do you play an instrument? – Yes, I do. / No, I don't.
    What instrument? – I play the drums / the guitar / …
Do you sing / rap? – Yes, sometimes. / No, never.

b) **Walk around:** Find new partners and ask your questions. Talk to as many partners as you can.

▶ *Wordbank 9, p. 154*

More practice 2 p.127

🎧 **1** **Before you read**
2.18
Listen to the songs. Do you like them?

> I like / I don't like
> song number …

🎧 ## Music makes a difference
2.19

It was Friday afternoon. Adam was on the
bus to PMZ. Some kids were on the bus too.
"Hey babyface, how old are you?" a girl
asked.
5 "Five?"
The other boys and girls laughed.
Adam said nothing.

Ten minutes later Adam was at PMZ with
his rap teacher, Josie.
10 He was angry.
"Why are you angry, Adam?" Josie asked.
"Some kids on the bus were mean," Adam
said.
"That's terrible," Josie said.
15 "But you can use that in your rap."

In the lesson, Josie talked about rap.
"In rap music, you must sing about your life.
– for example, about problems in your life.
What problems for example?"
"Problems at school … trouble with parents   20
… trouble with other kids …," the students
said.
"OK. We have a rap battle here at PMZ next
week. You can write a rap," Josie said.

Come to a
RAP BATTLE
at PMZ on Friday evening
Everybody welcome –
friends and family

On Monday morning Adam was at school.   25
"There's a rap battle at PMZ next Friday,"
Adam said. "Do you want to come? You can
hear my new rap."
"I'd love to come," Ellie said.
"And I want to come too," Berry said.   30
"Me too!" Luca said.

On Friday after school everybody was at PMZ. And Adam was very happy because his dad was there.

35 "Welcome to our rap battle," Josie said. Adam was nervous. His friends were excited.

"Go, Adam, go!"

Adam's rap was great. He was second in the
40 rap battle.

"Well done, Adam," his mum said.

"I'm very proud of you, Adam," his dad said.

"Thanks," Adam said. "Music really makes a difference."

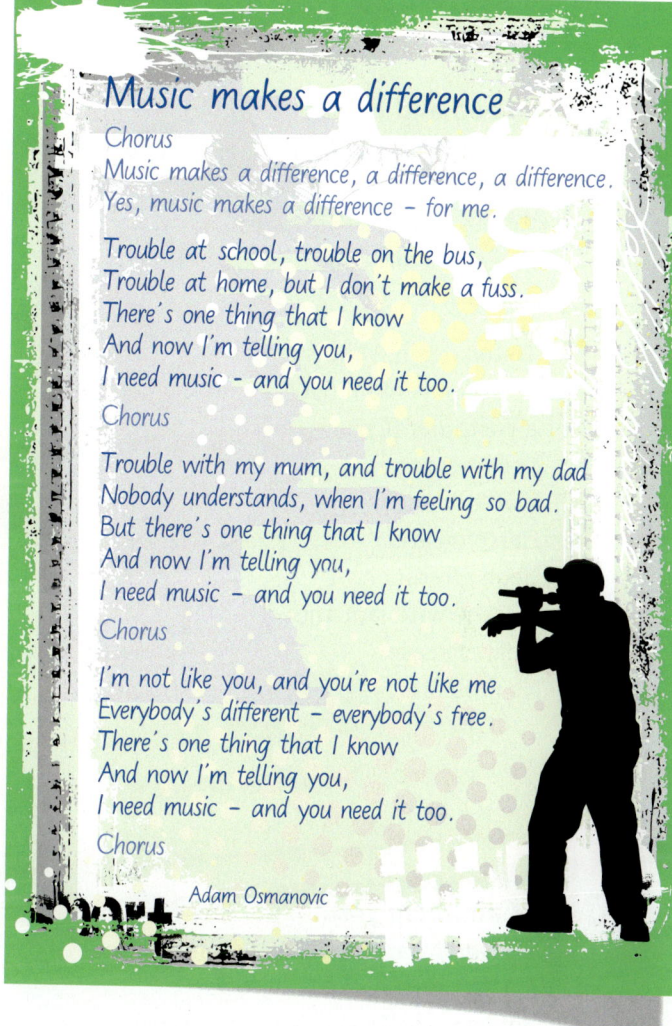

Music makes a difference

Chorus
Music makes a difference, a difference, a difference.
Yes, music makes a difference – for me.

Trouble at school, trouble on the bus,
Trouble at home, but I don't make a fuss.
There's one thing that I know
And now I'm telling you,
I need music – and you need it too.
Chorus

Trouble with my mum, and trouble with my dad
Nobody understands, when I'm feeling so bad.
But there's one thing that I know
And now I'm telling you,
I need music – and you need it too.
Chorus

I'm not like you, and you're not like me
Everybody's different – everybody's free.
There's one thing that I know
And now I'm telling you,
I need music – and you need it too.
Chorus

Adam Osmanovic

2 ◉ Check in the story!

a) Who said this in the story?

1 "Hey, babyface!" (line 3)
2 "Some kids on the bus were mean." (l. 12)
3 "You must sing about your life" (l. 17)
4 "I'd love to come." (l. 29)
5 "Go, Adam, go!" (l. 38)
6 "Music really makes a difference." (ll. 43–44)

b) Who in the story was …

1 mean?
2 angry?
3 nervous?
4 excited?
5 proud of Adam?

Check with a partner.

3 ◉ What's right? ⫽ ● p. 127

Pick the right answer.

1 The girl on the bus was nice / mean.
2 Josie was Adam's rap teacher / mum.
3 The rap battle was on Thursday / Friday.
4 Adam's dad was there / wasn't there.
5 Adam was first / second in the rap battle.
6 Music is / isn't important for Adam.

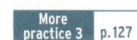

More practice 3 p. 127

4 RAP   Music makes a difference

2.20
2.21
a) Listen to Adam's rap. Do you like it?

b) Pick one verse of Adam's rap. Learn it. Rap for the class. Who's the best rapper?

In a cafe

FOOD

a chicken sandwich

fish and chips

a cheese sandwich

a soup

scone, jam and cream

a salad

1   Food and drinks

a) Listen. You hear four customers. What does each customer want (A–J)?

Customer 1: … and …
Customer 2: …

b) Listen again. Who says this – Adam's mum (M) or a customer (C)?
1 Can I help you?
2 Water or juice?
3 Here you are.
4 Good afternoon.
5 A scone with jam and cream, please.
6 No problem.   **More practice 4** p.127

2   Can I help you?

DRINKS

tea

coffee

juice

water

a) Listen. What does the customer want?
Adam ——— Hello, can I help you?
Customer — Hi. Yes, a chicken sandwich, please.
Adam ——— A chicken sandwich. Anything else?
Customer — Yes, a bottle of water, please.
Adam ——— Here you are. Anything else?
Customer — No, that's all, thanks.
Adam ——— That's £5.45, please.
Customer — £5.45. Here you are.   **More practice 5** p.128

b) Practise the dialogue with a partner.

3   NOW YOU

Make a dialogue in a cafe.

You	Your partner
Hello, can I help you?	– Hi. Yes, …, please.
Anything else?	– Yes, …, please.
Here you are. Anything else?	– No, that's all, thanks.
That's £…, please.	– Thank you.

MENU

Soup of the day	£2.50
Chicken sandwich	£3.95
Cheese sandwich	£4.50
Fish and chips	£6.50
Salad	£3.00
Scone, jam and cream	£3.95
Orange juice	£1.90
Bottle of water	£1.50

▶ *Workbook 10–12, p. 57*

Text messages

1 Hi!

a) Look at the four text messages. Are they from Adam, Adam's mum, Luca or Josie?   I think text message A is from …

In einer SMS lässt man oft die Artikel *(the / a)* weg. Diese musst du beim Lesen wieder einfügen:

in cafe => in the cafe
at market => at the market

A Hi, Adam. Rap was gr8. PMZ is cool. C U at school on Monday.

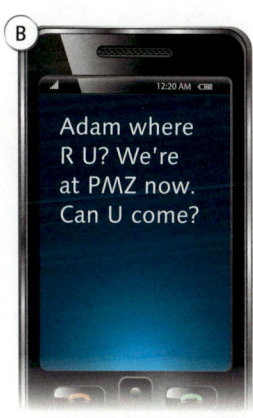

B 12:20 AM

Adam where R U? We're at PMZ now. Can U come?

C Mum I'm at home. Have science home-work. Can't come 2 cafe.

PHONE   PROGRAMS

D I'm not in cafe now. I'm at market. C U soon. XX

b) Match the red text messages symbols with the words in the green box.

1 science + maths
2 can U come?
3 C U soon
4 Can U come 2 cafe?

5 film was gr8
6 R U at home?
7 C U L8r
8 XX

and • are you • great • kisses •
later • see you • to • you

More practice 6 p.128

2 Amanda and the party

a) Mediation You and your partner get a text from an English friend, Amanda. She lives in your town. Work with your partner. How do you say it in German?

12:20 AM

Hi U 2. Where R U? I'm at party + it's gr8! Can U come 2? C U L8r.
X Amanda

b) Answer Amanda's text. You can put your text in your DOSSIER. Here are some ideas:

I'm at home / …
I feel gr8 / happy / terrible / …
Can come 2 party. Where is it?
Sorry. Can't come 2 party.

Talking about pictures

1 **Who is it – Cyril or Sandy?**

on the bike   under the chair   in front of the bag   behind the bag   next to the dog

Work with a partner. Ask questions: Who is …
a) in front of the bag   b) behind the bag   c) under the chair   d) on the bike   e) next to the dog?

2 **Oh, no! It's Mr Johnson!**

2.24 **a)** Listen. What's the right order of the scenes A, B and C?

b) Pick one of the pictures A–C in exercise 2. Talk about it with a partner.

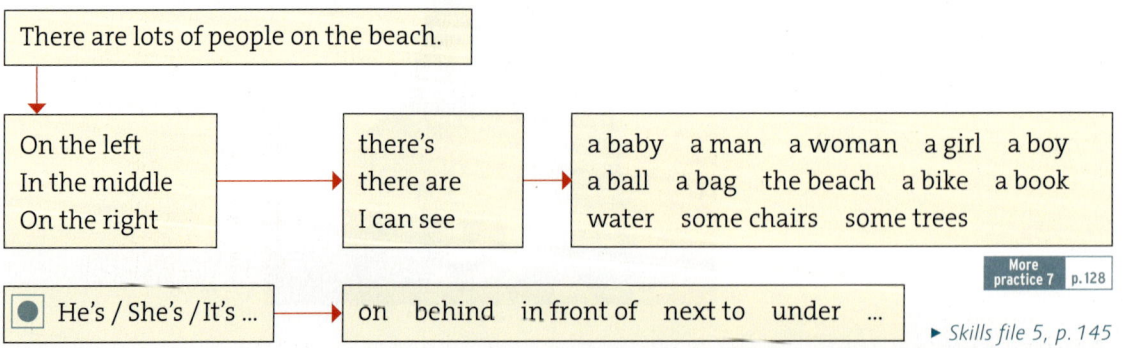

There are lots of people on the beach.

On the left	there's	a baby a man a woman a girl a boy
In the middle	there are	a ball a bag the beach a bike a book
On the right	I can see	water some chairs some trees

More practice 7 p.128

He's / She's / It's …   →   on   behind   in front of   next to   under   …

► Skills file 5, p. 145

                    ► Workbook 16–18, pp.59–60

Sarah   Paul   Anna

1 The kids from Harbour Road:

What's your talent?

a) Tell a partner about your talents: I can …

b) What about Anna, Paul and Sarah? Can you guess?

I think Anna can …   I think Sarah can …   And I think Paul can …

c) Now watch part 1 of the film and check.

d) Look at the photo. Put the sentences in the right order. Then watch part 2 and check.

A That's four pounds for you, and four pounds
for you, please.
B I'm hungry! Can I have a muffin, and
a hot chocolate[1], please?
C Thank you!
D Chocolate or blueberry[2]?
E I'll have[3] a chocolate muffin, please.
F And yourself[4]?
G A hot chocolate and a blueberry muffin, please.
H Thanks.

e) Act the scene for the class.

2 People and places: A visit to PMZ

a) Watch the film. Who are these people?

Photo 1 is …
Photo 2 is …   **Debbie**   **Jimmy**
Photo 3 is …

Simon

b) Watch again. Who …

1 works at PMZ?
2 shows the people around[5] PMZ?
3 is in the recording studio?
4 plays the drums?
5 sings *Music makes a difference*?

---

[1] hot chocolate *heiße Schokolade*   [2] blueberry *Heidelbeere, Blaubeere*   [3] I'll have … *Ich nehme …*
[4] And yourself? *Und du?*   [5] show around *herumführen*

1 An interview

2.25

a) ◯ A girl from the school magazine talks to Adam. She has lots of questions.
Read the interview. What music does Adam's family like?

Adam likes ...   Mrs Osmanovic likes ...   Mr Osmanovic doesn't like ...

Girl ____ Congratulations on your second prize for the rap battle, Adam.
Adam _ Thanks.
Girl ____ You like rap music. Do you like other music too?
Adam _ Well, I like hip hop. But my favourite music is rap.
5 *Girl* ____ Where do you practise?
Adam _ At home, in my room.
Girl ____ Do your parents listen to you?
Adam _ No, they don't!
Girl ____ Does your mum like music too?
10 *Adam* _ Yes, she does.
Girl ____ Does she like rap?
Adam _ Rap? No, she doesn't. She likes rock music.
Girl ____ And what about your dad? Does your dad like rock?
Adam _ No, he doesn't. He doesn't like music.
15 *Girl* ____ But I'm sure your parents like your rap?
Adam _ Yes, they do. Well, that's what they say ...
Girl ____ Thank you, Adam. And good luck with your rapping!

b) ◯ Write the questions with *do* or *does*.
Check in the dialogue.

1 ... you like other music too? (line 3)
2 ... your parents listen to you? (l. 7)
3 ... your mum like music? (l. 9)
4 ... your dad like rock? (l. 13)

c) ⬤ Write the right questions.

1 Where do / does you practise?
2 Do / Does your mum go to PMZ?
3 Do / Does Josie help you?
4 Do / Does you sometimes go to concerts?
5 Do / Does your friends like rap too?
6 Do / Does they come to your rap battles?

2 The simple present – questions with *do* and *does*

Make the rules. Copy and complete the tables with *he, you, they, she*.

Why do I like visitors? Because they feed me!

FOCUS			?
Do	*I* *...* *we* *...* *your parents*	+	verb

FOCUS			?
Does	*...* *...* *it* *your mum* *your dad*	+	verb

▶ *Language File 8, p. 149*

3 An interview with Cyril
Write the reporter's questions. Pick *do* or *does*.

1 Do / Does you like Plymouth?
2 Do / Does you have a best friend?
3 Do / Does you and Sandy live here?
4 Do / Does Sandy like Plymouth too?
5 Do / Does Sandy have a best friend?
6 Do / Does you like Mr Johnson?
7 Do / Does you live in a flat?
8 Do / Does you and Sandy go to school?
9 Do / Does Sandy like visitors?
10 Do / Does Sandy eat crabs?

– Yes, it's great.
– Yes, I do. Her name is Sandy.
– Sure, here in Kingsand.
– Sandy? She loves Plymouth!
– Yes, of course. It's me!
– No, he's terrible.
– No, I don't. I live in a big house.
– No, we aren't children!
– Yes, because they feed her.
– No, of course not!

More practice 8 p. 129

4 Berry and you
a) Write the dialogue with Berry in your exercise book. Write as much as you can.

BERRY	YOU
Hi. I'm Berry. What's your name?	– Hi, Berry. I'm …
Do you live in England?	– No, I live in …
Do you live in the country?	– Yes, I do. / No I don't. I live in a city / town / village.
Do you like English?	– Yes, it's great. / No, it's difficult.
Do you have a pet?	– Yes, I have a … / No, but I'd like a …
Do you like rock music?	– Yes, I do. My favourite singer is … / No, I don't. I like …
Do you like sport?	– Sometimes. I play … / No, not really. But I like …

b) ● Write two more questions and answers.

5 Your interview
a) Think of good questions for an interview. Write as many questions as you can. Here are some ideas for interview questions.

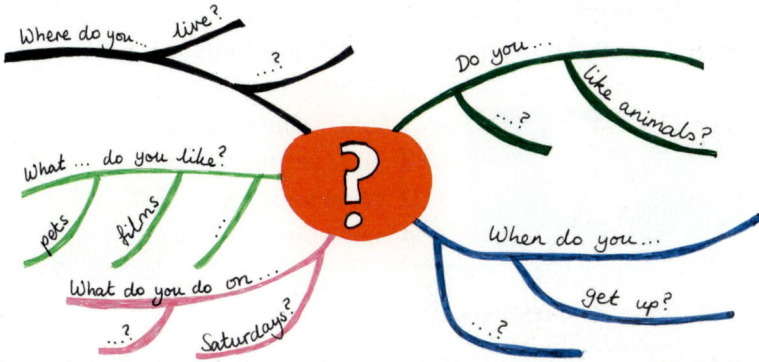

Where do you ... live?
...?
Do you ...
...? like animals?
What ... do you like?
pets films ...
What do you do on ...
...? Saturdays?
When do you ...
get up?
...?

b) Walk around. Find a partner and ask your questions. Your partner answers your questions.

PRACTICE

1 WORDS Food and drinks

a) ⓞ Find the odd word out.

1 sweets, tea, chicken, cafe
2 breakfast, soup, lunch, dinner
3 cream, jam, scone, chips
4 coffee, cheese, tea, juice
5 scones, bananas, salad, vegetables

b) Complete the sentences with answers from a).

1 You can buy food and drinks in a ...
2 I often have vegetable ... for lunch.
3 My favourite food is fish and ...
4 I'd like a ... sandwich, please.
5 We often have tea and ... in a cafe at the weekend.

2 WORDS In a cafe

Look at the pictures. Then copy and complete the sentences.

①  ②  ③  ④  ⑤

1 We ⬜⬜⬜⬜ food. (p. 90)   2 We ⬜⬜⬜⬜ up. (p. 90)   3 We often ⬜⬜⬜⬜. (p. 94)

4 We ⬜⬜⬜ in the kitchen. (p. 90)   5 We ⬜⬜⬜⬜ brochures about our cafe. (p. 92)

3 LANGUAGE Questions and answers

a) What do you know about crabs?

Crab quiz

1 Do crabs live in towns?
2 Do crabs live on the beach?
3 Do crabs eat fish?
4 Do normal crabs sing?

5 Does Cyril live in a house?
6 Does Cyril talk?
7 Does Cyril go to school?
8 Does Cyril like people?

Write your answers:

Yes, they do / No, they don't.   Yes, he does. / No, he doesn't.

b) Now make a birds quiz. Write the questions.

Bird quiz

1 birds / sing or make a noise?
2 birds / drink water?
3 some birds / eat crabs?
4 some birds / live near the sea?

5 Sandy / live in a house?
6 Sandy / eat crabs?
7 Sandy / talk?
8 Sandy / like visitors?

c) Answer the questions about birds.

d) ⚫ Make a quiz about another animal. Put it on the board. Who knows the answers?

Donkeys   Do they live in Germany / in zoos / on farms / ...?   Do ... eat other animals?
... they like people?   Do ... make lots of noise?
... they make good pets?   Do ... sing / ...?

4 LISTENING   About Adam

2.26

Ms Lee talks to Adam's mum a month later.

a) Listen. Pick the right answer.
1 Ms Lee is happy / unhappy with Adam.
2 PMZ is good / bad for Adam's school work.

b) Now listen again. What are the right answers?
1 Adam listens / is tired in his lessons.
2 He does / doesn't do his homework.
3 Adam's dad is at home / on the ferry.
4 Adam goes to PMZ on Saturday / Friday.
5 Ms Lee wants to meet / knows Josie.

5 WRITING   You and music

Write to an English friend about you
and music.
You can put the text in your DOSSIER.

No ideas?
– Look again at page 93.
– Look at the ideas in the email.

Hi …,

I love pop / rap / rock … music.
My favourite band / singer is …
My favourite English song is …
I play / don't play an instrument.
I play the piano / the guitar / the drums / …
I can sing / rap / …
What about you? Do you like music?

Best wishes

…

---

6 MEDIATION   I'm hungry!

Du bist mit einem Freund
in Plymouth. Beantworte
seine Fragen auf Deutsch.

1 Ich habe Hunger.
   Was gibt es hier zu essen?
2 Ich habe auch Durst.
   Was kann ich hier trinken?
3 Gibt es auch etwas Süßes?
4 Gibt es auch Eis?
   Wieviele Sorten?
5 Wir haben £10 für uns beide.
   Was schlägst du vor?

Harbour Cafe

Tea / coffee   £2.55
Cold drinks   £1.50
Juices   £1.99
Sandwiches   £3.50
Scone and butter   £1.75
Chocolate cake   £2.25
Fruit salad   £2.50
Ice cream — 16 flavours:
                    big   £2.00
                    small   £1.50

PRACTICE

7 READING On a Saturday morning …
Read the story. Match the phrases (A–G) with the scenes (1–7).

Can you help me outside, Adam?
…

1 The cafe was very busy.

Hello, Adam. How are you?
…

2 Ms Lee was in the cafe.

…
Tea and a scone, please.

3 She was hungry.

Thank you, Adam.
…

4 Adam was very fast.

Is everything OK at school?
…

5 Oh no! Trouble?

Listen, Ms Lee. That's my rap.
…

6 It was Adam's rap!

The tea was very good. Thanks, Adam.
…

7 Ms Lee was happy.

A **Can I help you?**

B **OK, Mum**

C **That's a great rap!**

D **You're welcome. Bye.**

E **Hello, Ms Lee. I'm fine, thanks.**

F **Here you are. One tea and a scone.**

G **Oh, yes. No problems. I'm very happy with Adam.**

8 My learner log
Copy and complete the learner log. You can put it in your DOSSIER.

My learner log for Unit 5

Now I can …
- ask what people do 😄 😐 🙁
- talk in a cafe 😄 😐 🙁
- read a text message 😄 😐 🙁
- talk about a picture 😄 😐 🙁

- The best page is page …
- The story is OK / boring / good.
- My favourite food is …
- Difficult new words are …

My progress in English is: GREAT! 👍 / OK 👊 / NOT VERY GOOD 👎

▶ Text file 5, p. 139 ▶ Workbook 1–3, p. 64

TEST AND CHECK

1 WORDS

Complete the network with words from the box.

First **test** yourself. Then **check** your answers on page 197.

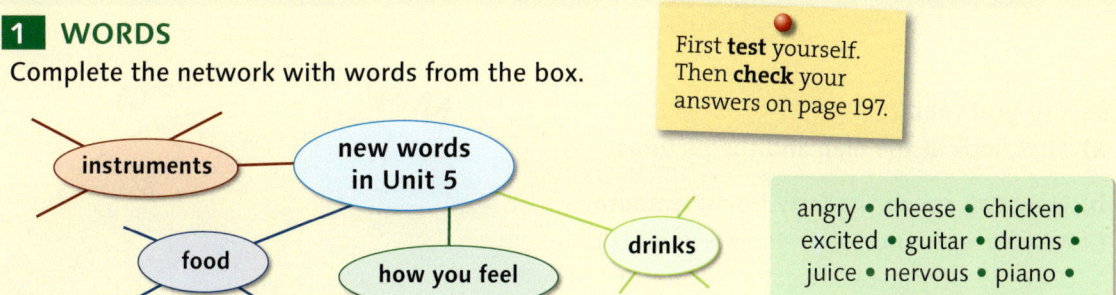

instruments — new words in Unit 5 — drinks

food — how you feel

angry • cheese • chicken • excited • guitar • drums • juice • nervous • piano • scone • tea • water

2 WORDS   What's in the picture?

Look at the picture. Then write sentences with *there is / there are.*

How many sentences can you write?

There's a cafe.
There are two / three ...

3 LANGUAGE   An English friend

Write the questions to your friend.

1 Do / Does you watch sport on TV?
2 Do / Does your house have a garden?
3 Do / Does you live near a school?
4 Do / Does your parents like rap?
5 Do / Does you have lots of homework?
6 Do / Does your town have a good cinema?

4 MEDIATION   Help your friend.

Write the text in German.

R U at school? We have no school + no homework today, it's gr8. C U L8er. Chris

5 WRITING and SPEAKING   In the Harbour Cafe

a) ● Write a dialogue in your exercise book. Here are some ideas.

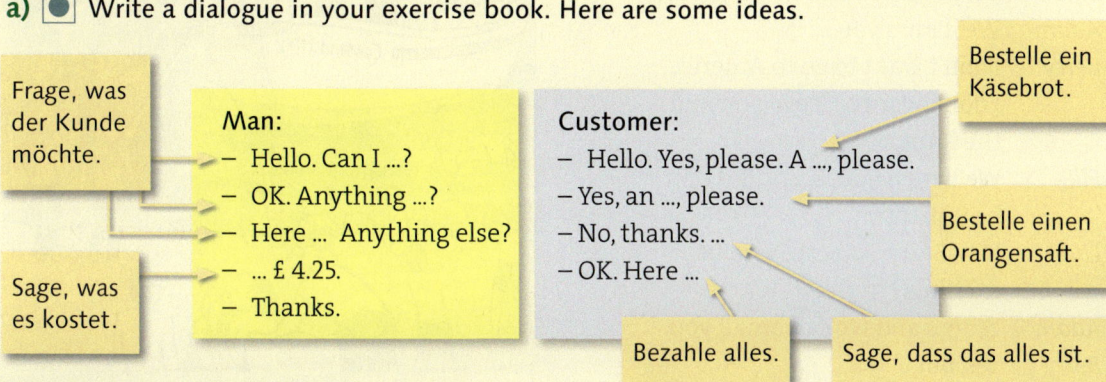

Frage, was der Kunde möchte.

Man:
– Hello. Can I ...?
– OK. Anything ...?
– Here ... Anything else?
– ... £ 4.25.
– Thanks.

Sage, was es kostet.

Customer:
– Hello. Yes, please. A ..., please.
– Yes, an ..., please.
– No, thanks. ...
– OK. Here ...

Bestelle ein Käsebrot.

Bestelle einen Orangensaft.

Bezahle alles.

Sage, dass das alles ist.

b) Practise your dialogue with a partner.

Summer is here!

Before you read

a) First, look at the map and the pictures.

🎧 **b)** Now you are on the ferry from Plymouth.
2.27
Close your eyes and listen. Have a good trip!

1 Does the ferry go to Cawsand or Kingsand?
2 Is it a good trip?

🎧 ## Great news, great trip
2.28
In June, Berry's parents organize a trip for
Berry and her friends. They take[1] a ferry
from Plymouth to two smuggler villages –
Cawsand and Kingsand. Berry's dad

5 wants to meet her friends in Cawsand with
a big picnic.

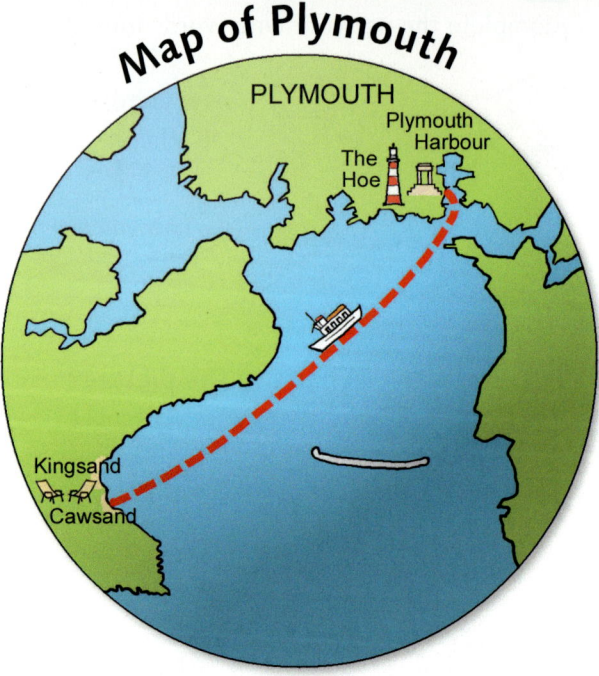

Scene 1 *On the ferry*

The ferry trip is great – but Berry isn't
happy.

10 *Ellie* —— You don't look happy, Berry.
Is everything OK?

Berry — Well, no. It isn't.

Luca —— What's the problem?

Berry — I'm going to America with mum
15 and dad in August.

Adam —— Holidays in America? That's great!

Berry —— Not for holidays! Mum and dad
have new jobs in America.

Luca —— What? New jobs? You mean[2] ...
20 a new life in America?

Ellie —— Oh no! Don't leave, Berry!

Adam —— We'll miss you ...

Berry —— I don't want to go to America.
I don't want to leave you and
25 the farm.

Ellie —— We'll miss you, Berry. But don't
be unhappy.

Luca —— Hey, Berry. America will be
exciting[3]!

30 *Adam* —— Yeah ... and we can email you.

Berry —— Yes, but ...

Luca —— Hey, we can visit[4] you!

Ellie —— Berry, you'll be OK. America will be
great!

35 *Berry* —— Yeah! I feel better now.
Thanks guys.

Luca —— Look, here we are in Cawsand.

Berry —— But where's dad? I can't see him.

---

[1]take *nehmen* [2]mean *meinen* [3]exciting *aufregend* [4]visit *besuchen*

Scene 2 *A message in a bottle[1]*

2.29

Berry	Where's dad? He's late.
Luca	And he has our picnic!
Adam	Look, there's a map of Cawsand. And there's a bottle.
Ellie	Let's go and look!
45 *Adam*	And what's in the bottle? A message?
Luca	It's a message for you, Berry.

> To Berry and her friends!
> **W**e have our dad,
> And he can't swim!
> 50 You have 30 minutes
> – can you find him?
> Go to the square[2] and then stop.
> Find the next bottle outside the shop.
> From a Kingsand smuggler

55 *Berry*	We must find dad!
Adam	Let's look at the map. There's a shop on the square!
Ellie	That's it. Let's go.
Luca	Look – that's the old woman from the ferry.
60	

Scene 3 *Only 25 minutes!*

Luca	Here's the shop.
Berry	Look, there's a bottle on the chair!
Ellie	And here's the message:

> 65 **S**mugglers always want to eat.
> Find a cafe where smugglers meet.

Luca	We must find a cafe. We only have
70	25 minutes!
Adam	Look, there's the old woman.
Ellie	Come on!

Scene 4 *Only 20 minutes!*

75 *Adam*	Look, a cafe!
Ellie	The *Smuggler's Cafe*. That's it!
Adam	Look, another bottle.

> **W**hat's the time?
> You don't know?
> 80 Find a big clock.
> Go, go, go!

Luca	We must find a big clock.
Ellie	I can't see a clock. Can you see the old woman?
85 *Adam*	No, she isn't here. What can we do?
Luca	We only have twenty minutes …

[1] message in a bottle *Flaschenpost*   [2] square *Platz*

Scene 5 *Only 10 minutes!*

2.30

Ellie ___ Look, there's the clock!

Berry ___ Oh, yes! A really big clock!

90 *Ellie* ___ There's the bottle!

Adam ___ Good! We only have ten minutes.

Luca ___ Here's the message.

> **C**ows give us milk
> And cows give us cream.
> 95 Look for the cows
> If[1] you want an ice cream.

Ellie ___ Cows?

Adam ___ Here in Cawsand?

Berry ___ Look. I can see cows.

100 *Ellie* ___ Me too.

Luca ___ And a bottle. Quick[2].

Scene 6 *Only one minute!*

Berry ___ Read the message, Ellie.

Ellie ___ OK.

> 105 **Y**our dad's on the beach
> And he can't swim.
> Only one minute
> Can you find him?

Adam ___ Let's look on the beach.

110 *Ellie* ___ I can see the old woman.

Luca ___ But where's Berry's dad?

Adam ___ Quick! We only have one minute!

Berry ___ There he is – in the sand! Hey Dad!

Dad ___ Help!

115 *Luca* ___ Really exciting!

Mum ___ Hello, everybody.

Berry ___ Mum! You are the Kingsand smuggler!

Ellie ___ That was a great game!

120 *Adam* ___ Yeah, it was really good.

Mum ___ Are you OK now? Are you hungry?

Luca ___ Yes!

Dad ___ Your picnic is

125 over there[3]. With Sam.

Berry ___ Oh no! Sam! Stop!

---

[1] if *wenn, falls* [2] quick *schnell* [3] over there *da drüben*

1 The kids from Harbour Road:
Summer holidays

Sarah Paul Anna

a) Pick five important things for camping.

1 ice cream   2 a tent   3 sandwiches   4 sausages   5 a can of beans   6 a bike   7 matches   8 a can opener

b) Watch the film. Which things do the kids take[1]?

c) Put the photos in the right order.

A

B

C

D

d) Talk to a partner about the kids from Harbour Road.

I like Paul because …

Yes, Paul is nice. But my favourite kid is … because …

I think … is cool.

2 People and places: A ferry trip to Cawsand

a) You go by ferry to Cawsand.
What do you think you can see? Make a list.

bags • a beach • bikes • birds • boats • buses • cars • a cinema • crabs • dogs • a ferry • fish • food • a harbour • kids • people • picnics • a school • water • shops • tents •…

b) Watch the film. What things on your list do you see?

---

[1] take *mitnehmen*

8 SPEAKING   What lessons on Monday?   ▶ *Unit 1, p. 32*

a) Partner B: Copy the Tuesday timetable into your exercise book. Answer partner A's questions about Monday. Then ask partner A and complete the Tuesday timetable.

Lesson	Monday
1	maths
2	history
3	ICT
4	technology
5	geography

Lesson	Tuesday
1	....
2	....
3	....
4	....
5	....

What's lesson one on Monday?

It's maths. What's lesson one on Tuesday?

It's ...

Check your answers with your partner's timetable.

4   Four different things   ▶ *Unit 2, p. 39*

a) Partner B: Look at room B on this page. (Your partner looks at a different room A.)

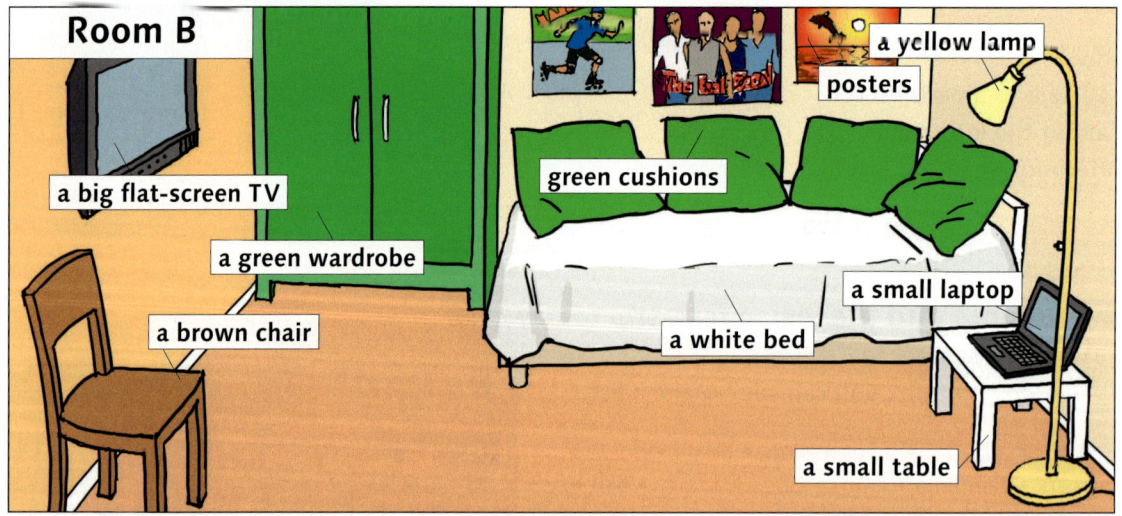

Room B

a big flat-screen TV

a green wardrobe

a brown chair

green cushions

a white bed

posters

a yellow lamp

a small laptop

a small table

b) Partner B: Talk to your partner about your room.
Find what's different in your partner's room (four things).
Partner A _ My room has posters.
Partner B _ My room has posters too.
Partner A _ OK. My room has red cushions.
Partner B _ My room has ...

My partner's room has:
1) red cushions,
2) ...
3) ...
4) ...

6 SPEAKING Two sports shops ▸ *Unit 2, p.49*

a) Partner B: Answer partner A's questions about this shop:

JD SPORTS

52 George Street
Plymouth PL1 RR

☎ Tel. 01752 806 4895

b) Ask partner A four questions about a sports shop in Plymouth.
Write the name, address and phone number of the shop.

> What's the name of the shop, please?

> Can you spell that, please?

> What's the address?

> And what's the phone number?

Unit 3 ▸ STOP AND PRACTISE

5 SPEAKING Birthdays ▸ *Unit 3, p.67*

PARTNER B: Stay on this page.

a) Look at the picture.
Listen to your partner and answer his/her questions.

b) Now ask partner A about his/her birthday:
– When / birthday?
– What / favourite activities?
Note the answers.

Your birthday: 24th October

or

Hi! What's your name!

More practice 1 **Hi! What's your name?** ▸ *p. 8*

Read the dialogue with a partner.

*Sarah*___Hi. I'm Sarah. What's your name?

*Daniel*___Hi, I'm Daniel.

*Sarah*___I'm eleven. What about you?

*Daniel*___I'm ten.

*Sarah*___I'm from Plymouth, in England. What about you?

*Daniel*___I'm from Lüneburg, in Germany.

Lest den Dialog so oft, bis ihr ihn auswendig könnt. Dann spielt ihn in der Klasse vor.

More practice 2 **Write about you.** ▸ *p. 10*

I'm (name)
I'm ...
I'm from ... in ...

• Suche im Schülerbuch die Wörter, die du brauchst, und schreibe sie ab.
• Prüfe, ob du sie richtig geschrieben hast.

Unit 1

More practice 1 **Photos from Eggy** ▸ *Unit 1, p. 19*

He • She • It • They

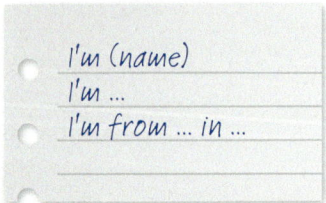

① ...'s a car.

② ...'s a boy.

③ ...'s a bike.

④ ...'re girls.

⑤ ...'s a teacher.

⑥ ...'s a timetable.

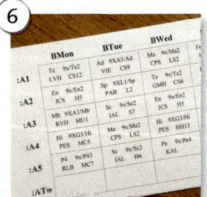

⑦ ...'s a school.

⑧ ...'re sweets.

⑨ ...'re birds.

⑩ ...'s a football.

More practice 2 Days and lessons ▸ *Unit 1, p. 21*
Write five days and four lessons.

More practice 3 The timetable ▸ *Unit 1, p. 21*
a) Write right and wrong sentences about the timetable on page 21 – as many as you can.

Lesson one on Friday is ...
Lesson ... on Thursday is science.
Lesson three on ... is ...
Lesson ... on ... is ...

...

b) Read your sentences to your partner. He/She says *right* or *wrong*.

More practice 4 The story ▸ *Unit 1, p. 23*
Put the sentences in the right order.

Part 1

1 Luca says, "Where's your tie, Ellie?"
2 But Ellie has no tie.
3 It's Tuesday morning at Eggy.
4 Berry says, "Where's your tie, Ellie?"
5 Miss Borowski says, "The uniform is important!"

It's Tuesday morning at Eggy.
...

Part 2

1 Now Ellie has a tie.
2 Class 7Y is in the art lesson.
3 Then class 7Y is in the canteen.
4 It's a great tie. But it isn't the school tie.
5 Luca has an idea.

Class 7Y is in the art lesson.
...

Unit 1

More practice 5 **Make a school tie** ▸ *Unit 1, p. 23*

> I like orange and blue. What about you?

> Er, ... blue is OK. What about white and blue?

1 Pick your colours.

2 Make the tie.

3 Pick the best tie.

> I like the red and green tie!

> I like the black and white tie!

2 NOW YOU ▸ *Unit 1, p. 26*

Write the dialogue with a partner. Then practise it with your partner.

A Hi, ... ! How ... you?
B Hi, ... I'm ... What about you?
A I'm ... Can I borrow a ..., please?
B Sure, here ...
A Thanks. ...'s the next lesson?
B It's ... I like ... It's my ... lesson.

6 What's right? ▸ Unit 1, p. 29
Write the six sentences.

	is	a boy."
Eggy	isn't	students at Eggy.
Cyril and Sandy	are	a girl."
Berry: "I'	aren't	a school in Plymouth.
	'm	in Germany.
	'm not	animals.

  7 At Eggy ▸ Unit 1, p. 29
Complete the sentences.

1 Eggy is my new school. …'s big.
2 Ellie is a new girl at Eggy. …'s great!
3 Mr Brown is at Eggy. … isn't our art teacher. …'s our ICT teacher.
4 Mrs Ford is a teacher too. … isn't the principal. …'s our maths teacher.
5 Ms Lee, Mrs Ford and Mr Brown are my new teachers. … aren't bad.

More practice 6 Cyril isn't a bird ▸ Unit 1, p. 29
Match the sentences.

1 Plymouth isn't in Germany.
2 Eggy isn't in London.
3 Cyril isn't a bird.
4 Sandy isn't a crab.
5 Mr Brown isn't a maths teacher.
6 The four friends aren't from Germany.
7 Ellie and Berry aren't teachers at Eggy.
8 Luca and Adam aren't girls.
9 Ms Lee and Mr Brown aren't students.

A He's a crab.
B They're teachers.
C It's in Plymouth.
D They're boys.
E They're from England.
F It's in England.
G She's a bird.
H They're students at Eggy.
I He's an ICT teacher.

Unit 2

More practice 1 My dream house ▸ Unit 2, p. 35

My dream house is	new / old / big / small / … in England / in Germany / in …
My dream house has	four big bedrooms / three bathrooms / two kitchens / …
My dream bedroom is	big / new / blue and white / …
My dream house has	a pony / monkeys / … in the garden.

1 //● At Ellie's house ▸ Unit 2, p. 36

c) Make sentences.

Ellie lives with Conor lives with Berry lives with Ellie's dad lives with Ellie's mum lives with	his her	mum and dad. new partner. new partner and Ellie, Zoe and Conor. mum and her brother Conor. two sisters, Zoe and Ellie.

2 //● Ellie isn't happy ▸ Unit 2, p. 38

b) Read the dialogues again. Then pick the right words: *he • it • she • they*

1 Is Zoe happy? – No, ... isn't.
2 Are Ellie's shoes in the room? – Yes, ... are.
3 Are Ellie and her mum in the kitchen?
   – Yes, ... are.

4 Is the kitchen noisy? – Yes, ... is.
5 Is Ellie OK? – No, ... isn't.
6 Is the kitchen a good place for
   homework? – No, ... isn't.

More practice 2 ○ Things in a room ▸ Unit 2, p. 39

Write the names of the things in the room.

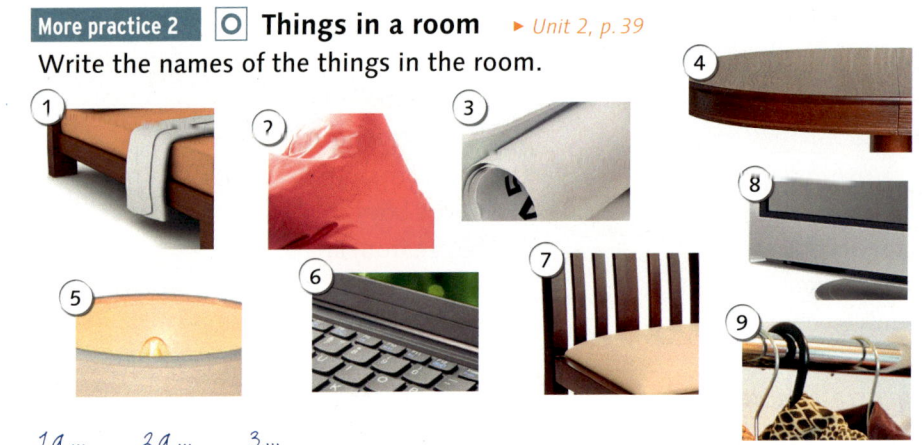

a bed
a chair
a computer
a cushion
a lamp
a poster
a table
a TV
a wardrobe

1a ...   2a ...   3 ...

3 //● Where are they? ▸ Unit 2, p. 41

Answer the questions.

1 Where's Ellie on Monday?
2 Where's Ellie on Tuesday?
3 Where are Ellie's dad and Alisha on Wednesday?
4 Where's Ellie's dad on Thursday?
5 Where are Ellie's dad and Alisha on Friday?
6 Where's Finn on Wednesday, Thursday, Friday
   and Saturday?

He's She's They're	in town. with Ellie. at a restaurant. in her bedroom. in the kitchen. at the cinema.

4 //● **A week with dad** ▸ *Unit 2, p. 41*

Write the sentences with the right words.

1 Ellie has ... news – she can ... with her dad.
2 She likes her ... bedroom: it has a ... and a lamp.
3 But her ... and Alisha have no ... for Ellie.
4 Ellie ... her ..., her stepbrother and stepsister.
5 Her new ...? She can live ... days with her mum and two days with her dad.

> dad • table • five • good
> • idea • live • misses •
> mum • new • time

More practice 3 **Words** ▸ *Unit 2, p. 41*

a) Write the phrases from the story in two lists: ☺ ☹

b) Check your lists with a partner.

> Great news! • Dad has no time for me. •
> No bossy Zoe. • Finn is cute! •
> Alisha is nice. • He isn't very happy. •
> Tomorrow is the big day. • I miss mum. •
> I have a new idea! • I'm really happy.

More practice 4 **My brother's room** ▸ *Unit 2, p. 42*

Now write about a different room, for example
• your brother's room
• or your sister's room
• or a friend's room
• or ...

I like my brother's room / I don't like my friend's room.
In his/her room he/she has a big desk and a ...
The desk is white and the ...
My brother/sister/friend has great posters and ...
In his/her room my brother / sister / friend can listen ... / play ...

More practice 5 **Classroom phrases** ▸ *Unit 2, p. 43*

Write it in English, please. Look at the phrases in the box.

1 Wie fragst du, was „Fenster" auf Englisch heißt?
2 Wie fragst du, ob du zur Toilette gehen kannst?
3 Wie bittest du jemanden, etwas zu wiederholen?
4 Wie fragst du, ob du dir einen Radiergummi leihen kannst?
5 Wie fragst du, was ihr in der nächsten Stunde habt?
6 Wie sagst du, dass dir etwas leidtut?
7 Wie bedankst du dich?

> Can I ... toilet, please?
> Can you ... again, please?
> What's „Fenster" in ...?
> Can I ... your rubber, please?
> Sorry!
> Thanks!
> What's the ... lesson?

▶ *Unit 2, p. 44*

> Unit 2

More practice 6   **The alphabet**

Work with a partner.

Partner A: Pick a word in box A. Spell it.
Partner B listens and writes the word.
Then listen and write Partner B's word.

Partner B: Listen and write Partner A's
word. Then pick a word in box B.
Spell it for Partner A.

More practice 7   **Ellie and her family**   ▶ *Unit 2, p. 47*

Match the questions and answers.

1 Is Finn cute?
2 Is Berry Ellie's friend?
3 Is Ellie's house very big?
4 Are Ellie's cats in her mum's house?
5 Is Alisha Ellie's sister?
6 Is Conor Ellie's dad?

A – Yes, they are.
B – No, she isn't.
C – No, he isn't.
D – Yes, he is.
E – Yes, she is.
F – No, it isn't.

> Unit 3

More practice 1   **Mehmet's Saturday**   ▶ *Unit 3, p. 54*

Write Mehmet's sentences.

1 In the morning I ... comics.
2 I ... shopping with mum and dad.
3 We often ... fish.
4 In the afternoon I often ... my friends.
5 We ... football in the park.
6 In the evening I ... TV.

> buy • go • meet • play • read • watch

More practice 2 **My Sundays** ▶ *Unit 3, p. 54*

Write six or more sentences about your Sundays.

		go … meet … watch … play … ride … …	with my friends. in town. in the park. with my mum and dad. in my room. …
I	sometimes often		

More practice 3 **Birthdays in Plymouth** ▶ *Unit 3, p. 56*

Write the dialogue in your exercise book.

> go bowling • go swimming •
> go to the beach • go dancing •
> stay at home

Luca ___ I sometimes  on my birthday.

What about you, Adam?

Adam __ I always

Berry ___ That's cool. What about you, Ellie?

Ellie ___ Me? I  with my parents and we sometimes  .

Luca ___ And you, Berry?

Berry ___ My birthday is 25th December. I  .

More practice 4 **In my holidays** ▶ *Unit 3, p. 56*

Write sentences – as many as you can.

> Du weißt nicht mehr, was
> die Wörter bedeuten? Dann
> sieh dir die Seiten 52–66
> noch einmal an oder schlage
> die Wörter im *Dictionary*
> nach (Seite 174–181).

			to Turkey/to … a party. at home. bowling. my friends. my bike. to the sea. shopping. swimming. to the park. to town. to the cinema. TV. …
In my holidays I	always often sometimes	go have meet stay ride watch …	

Unit 3

🎧 //O **4** **The end of the story** ▶ *Unit 3, p. 59*

a) Read and listen to the end of the story.

Luca is at home.

Luca ___ Who's at the door?

Mum ___ Adam ... Ellie ... Berry ... Hi! This is a surprise! Come in ... Luca is in the living room.

Ellie ___ Happy Birthday, Luca!

All ___ Happy Birthday to you, Happy Birthday to you,
Happy Birthday dear Luca, Happy Birthday to you ...

Luca ___ Hi everybody! Thanks ... This is a great surprise!

Berry ___ Oh Luca, are you OK?

Luca ___ I'm OK. But I can't walk. I have a sore leg.

Berry ___ So no concert for you! Aw!

Adam ___ But we have this cake for you! And some chocolate ...

Ellie ___ And a CD ... *Francis and the Drakes*!

Luca ___ Wow, thanks!

Adam ___ Let's have a party.

Luca ___ Great idea. This is a good birthday!

b) Now answer the questions.

1 Who comes to Luca's house?   3 Can he hear *Francis and the Drakes*?
2 Is Luca happy in the end?   4 Is the end a surprise for you?

More practice 5 **Act the scene** ▶ *Unit 3, p. 59*

Read the end of the story. Practise the dialogue in small groups. Then act the scene for the class.

//● **1** **Luca's garage sale** ▶ *Unit 3, p. 60*

c) Listen again and finish the sentences.

1 The calculator is ...   4 The computer is ...
2 The mobile phones are ...   5 The footballs are ...
3 The crab is ...

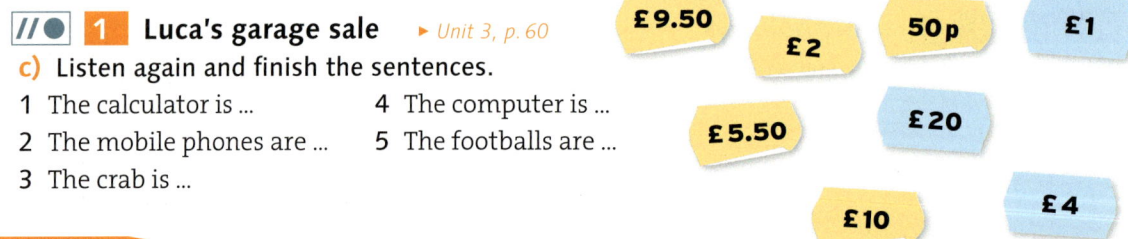

£9.50   £2   50p   £1   £5.50   £20   £10   £4

//● **1** **Questions about birthdays** ▶ *Unit 3, p. 61*

c) Put the sentences in the right order and write the dialogue.

Daniel ___ a question? / Can I / you / ask
birthday? / your / When's

Ben ___ 21st / Thursday / October.

Daniel ___ And what are / favourite / your / on your birthday? / activities

Ben ___ We / games. / play
And / watch / sometimes / a film. / we

Daniel ___ Sounds fun. Thanks, Ben.

More practice 6   **When's your birthday?**   ▶ *Unit 3, p. 61*

Play the birthday game. Throw the ball. Ask the question.

When's your birthday?

It's on the sixth of May.

More practice 7   **Ellie's weekends**   ▶ *Unit 3, p. 65*

Write the text for Ellie. Pick the right form of the verb.

Ellie ___ At the weekend I go / goes (1) to my dad's flat. He always get up / gets up (2) first. He make / makes (3) breakfast for me and the baby. My stepmum stay / stays (4) in bed. We sometimes go / goes (5) shopping at the market. After lunch I meet / meets (6) my friends in town. In the evening dad watch / watches (7) TV with Alisha. I sometimes watch / watches (8) too. I sometimes play / plays (9) with Finn. On Sunday evening I go / goes (10) to my mum's house.

I play
You play
He plays
She plays
It plays
We play
They play

More practice 8   **Cyril and Sandy's day**   ▶ *Unit 3, p. 65*

Write about Cyril's and Sandy's day. Find the right verb forms.

get • go • have • meet

In the morning I ... up early.

Sandy ... up in the afternoon.

I ... breakfast on the beach.

I often ... my friends.

We ... swimming.

Sandy ... to town.

Unit 3 ▶ STOP AND PRACTISE

//● **2** LANGUAGE **Cyril's birthday** ▶ *Unit 3, p. 66*

b) Copy and complete the text.
Find the right forms of the verbs.

Sandy ... (1) to the market.
She ... (2) nice things.
Cyril ... (3) at home.
He ... (4) in the kitchen.
He ... (5) a big birthday lunch.
Cyril's friends ... (6) in the afternoon.
They ... (7) swimming.
Then they ... (8) games. It's a great day!

> buy
> come
> go (2x)
> make
> play
> stay
> work

Unit 4

More practice 1 **Animal words** ▶ *Unit 4, p. 71*
Copy the diagram and complete it.
Write as many animals as you can.

Pets   Farm animals

hamsters   cats   cows

Or write three lists, like this:

Pets	Zoo animals	Farm animals
...	...	...

//● **1** **From Monday to Friday** ▶ *Unit 4, p. 72*
The sentences are wrong. Write correct sentences.

1 In the morning Berry wakes Sam.
2 Before breakfast she feeds Sam and the other animals.
3 She goes to school by bus.
4 She comes home before 3 o'clock.
5 In the evening she looks after her grandma.

More practice 2 **Berry's day** ▸ *Unit 4, p. 72*

Copy the sentences and complete them with the right verbs from the box.

> does • feeds • comes home • goes • looks after • wakes

Sam ... Berry in the morning.

Berry ... Harry before breakfast.

She ... to school by car.

She ... after 4 o'clock.

She ... her homework.

She ... the animals on the farm.

3 **Actitivites on the farm** ▸ *Unit 4, p. 73*

c) Listen again. What's the time in the dialogues?

Dialogue 1: Ⓐ 10.40 Ⓑ 10.50 Dialogue 2: Ⓐ 12.45 Ⓑ 12.00
Dialogue 3: Ⓐ 02.30 Ⓑ 02.45 Dialogue 4: Ⓐ 04.30 Ⓑ 04.15

More practice 3 **Say the times** ▸ *Unit 4, p. 73*

a) Match the times A–F with sentences 1–6.

1 It's seven twenty.
2 It's three o'clock.
3 It's nine thirty.
4 It's ten forty-five.
5 It's eleven fifty-five.
6 It's four fifteen.

b) Work with a partner. Pick a time and ask: "What's the time in A?"
He/She answers: "It's ..."
After three questions swap roles.

c) Draw six more clocks with different times. Write the times in words.

Unit 4

More practice 4   **When students in 7Y feel great or fed up**   ▸ *Unit 4, p. 74*

a) Copy and complete the sentences with verbs from the box.

> are • go • have • is • 'm • play • text • watch

I feel great when I ... to a concert.

Steve
1

I feel great when I ... table tennis.

Amy
2

I feel fed up when my parents ... bossy.

Katherine
3

I feel great when I... with my family.

Dan
4

I feel fed up when the bus ... late.

Emily
5

I feel great when I ... a DVD.

Olivia
6

I feel fed up when my best friend doesn't ... me.

Nasser
7

I feel fed up when I ... lots of work at school.

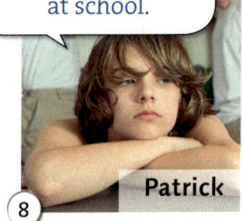

Patrick
8

b) 🔵 Now write the eight sentences again – but find new ideas for the words in blue.
Write as many sentences as you can!
Example: *I feel great when I go to the cinema / to town / to a party / ...*

More practice 5   **Mike's invitation**   ▸ *Unit 4, p. 79*

You're Mike. Complete his invitation.

> ... Steve,
>
> Can you ... to my sleepover ... Friday?
> It's at my ... from 6 pm to ... am.
> I want to listen to music.
> Please ... your favourite music.
> I ... you can come!
>
> Mike

 4 That's wrong! ▸ *Unit 4, p. 83*

Correct the sentences. Use *doesn't / don't*.

1 Berry lives in the city. – Wrong! She doesn't live in ...
2 Berry's parents have a pet shop. – Wrong! They don't ...
3 Berry rides a donkey. – Wrong! She ...
4 Berry has a cat. – That's wrong! She ...
5 Berry's mum and dad have cows. – Wrong! They ...
7 Berry goes to school in Woolwell. – Wrong! She ...
8 Luca and Adam have dogs. – That's wrong! They ...
9 Ellie has two ponies. – That's wrong! She ...

More practice 6  **City girl and country boy** ▸ *Unit 4, p. 83*

Read Hanna's sentences. Then copy and complete Josh's sentences.

Hanna, a city girl

1 I live in town.
2 My dad works in a hospital.
3 My mum works in a college.
4 I go to school by bus.
5 We live in a flat.
6 I often walk in our park.

Josh, a country boy

1 I don't live in town. I live in the country.
2 My dad _ _ in a hospital. He works on the farm.
3 My mum _ _ in _ _. She works on the farm too.
4 I _ _ _ _ _ _. I _ _ _by car.
5 I _ _ _ _ _. I _ _ _ house.
6 I _ _ _ _ _ _. I _ through fields.

Unit 4 **STOP AND PRACTISE**

2 LISTENING What's the time? ▸ *Unit 4, p. 84*

Listen to eight dialogues. Write the time.

1 It's 6. ...   3 It's ...   ...
2 It's 9. ...   4 ...

//● **2** **A letter from school** ▶ *Unit 5, p. 91*

b) Make the sentences.

1 Adam is often ...	A happy at school.
2 He doesn't listen ...	B his homework.
3 He doesn't do ...	C in class.
4 Adam isn't ...	D talk with Adam's mum.
5 Ms Lee wants to ...	E Adam's class teacher.
6 Ms Lee is ...	F tired at school.

More practice 1 ● **Adam's mum phones Ms Lee** ▶ *Unit 5, p. 91*

a) Put the sentences in the right order and write the dialogue.

Ms Lee ___ Hello, Ms Lee here.
Adam's mum ___ Good morning. I'm ...

– Hello, Ms Lee here.

– Fine, at 10.30. Goodbye, Ms Lee.

– Goodbye, Mrs Osmanovic. See you on Wednesday.

– Yes, I'd like to talk about Adam with you. Can you come to school this week?

– Yes, it is. At 10.30?

– It's about your letter ...

– Good morning. I'm Mrs Osmanovic.

– Yes. Is Wednesday morning OK?

– Ah, good morning, Mrs Osmanovic.

b) Act your dialogue with your partner.

//● **3** **Welcome to PMZ** ▶ *Unit 5, p. 93*

c) Copy this table in your exercise book.
Then listen again and finish the notes.

1 PMZ address	... Road
2 Bus number	...
3 Times (Mon–Fri)	From ...to ...
4 Times (Sat)	From ... to ...
5 Price	...

More practice 2 **Tell the class** ▸ *Unit 5, p. 93*

Tell the class about one partner.
These ideas and sentences can help you.

> ... likes music.
> He / She has a favourite band – ...
> ...'s favourite singer is ...
> ... plays / doesn't play an instrument.
> ...

//● 3 What's right? ▸ *Unit 5, p. 95*

True or false? Correct the wrong sentences.

1 The girl on the bus was mean.
2 Josie was Adam's rap teacher
3 The rap battle was on Thursday.

4 Adam's dad was there.
5 Adam was first in the rap battle.
6 Music is important for Adam.

More practice 3 ● **An email to Adam** ▸ *Unit 5, p. 95*

You were at the rap battle and you liked Adam's song.
Write an email to Adam (6-8 sentences). Here are some ideas.

> Dear Adam
> I was at the rap battle on Friday.

I think	you were ...
	the rap battle was ...
	Josie was ...
	your rap is ...
	PMZ is ...
	your parents are ...

good different friendly nervous
important great boring nice proud
stupid interesting happy terrible

> Best wishes
> ...

More practice 4 **Food and drinks words** ▸ *Unit 5, p. 96*

a) Write the words in the green box in four lists. The same words can be in different lists!

hot (heiß)	cold (kalt)	sweet (süß)	not sweet
soup	...	...	soup
...	...	...	...

coffee • cheese sandwich •
chicken sandwich • cream • fish
and chips • jam • juice • salad •
soup • tea • water

b) Look at pictures A–J on page 96 for one minute. Then close your book. Now say the things in the photos – as many as you can! Can you write them?

Unit 5

More practice 5 What's that in English? ▶ Unit 5, p. 96

1 Sonst noch etwas?
2 Kann ich Ihnen helfen?
3 Das macht (Preis), bitte.
4 Das ist alles.
5 Eine Flasche Wasser, bitte.
6 Bitte schön.

More practice 6 Four messages ▶ Unit 5, p. 97

Write the four messages in full sentences.

Hi, Adam.
The rap was great.
And PMZ is cool.
See …

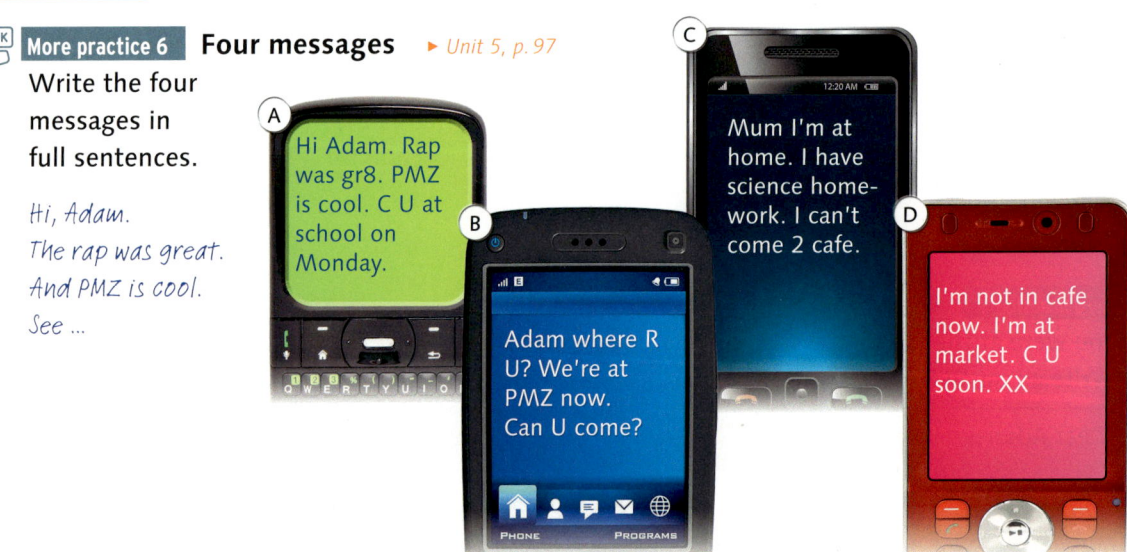

A Hi Adam. Rap was gr8. PMZ is cool. C U at school on Monday.

B Adam where R U? We're at PMZ now. Can U come?

C Mum I'm at home. I have science homework. I can't come 2 cafe.

D I'm not in cafe now. I'm at market. C U soon. XX

More practice 7 Talking about a picture ▶ Unit 5, p. 98

a) Pick one of the pictures. Talk about it to a partner. What picture (A–D) is it?

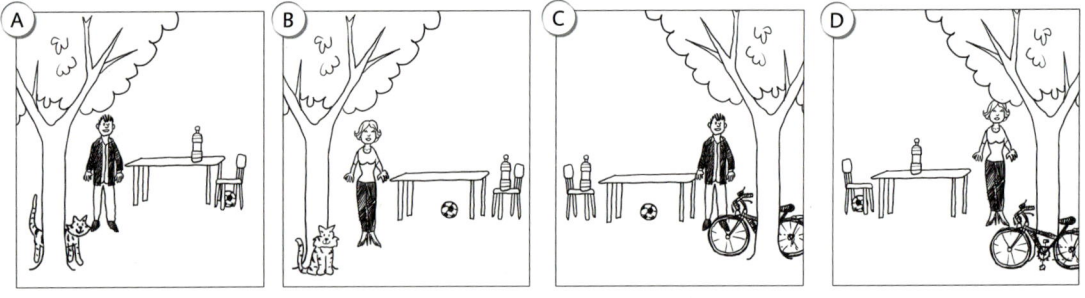

A   B   C   D

b) ● Draw a picture. Talk about it to your partner. He/She listens and draws the picture. Is your partner's picture the same as your picture?

► Unit 5, p. 101

More practice 8   **Questions to a new friend in England**

a) Copy and complete the questions with *do* or *does*.

1 Where ... you live?
2 ... your house have a garden?
3 ... you do your homework in the kitchen or in your room?
4 ... students in your school go to school by bike?
5 When ... the first lesson start at your school?
6 What ... you do after school?

b) Swap questions with your partner. Check your partner's questions.
Then answer your partner's questions.

Lösung:

Unit 1

1   **The unit quiz**   ► Unit 1, p. 28

Check your anwers:

1 PE
2 Ellie and Berry
3 Adam
4 Luca and Jack
5 Ms Lee
6 Grace / Luca's sister
7 Berry
8 (your name)

TF 1 You stupid boy!

It's Sunday morning at Kingsand. Cyril is on the beach. No people. No boys and girls. Cyril is happy!

Sandy isn't happy. No people. No boys and girls. No lunch for Sandy!

Look! It's Mr Johnson, Mrs Johnson and Toby Johnson! They're very happy – a great day on the beach!

Look! Sandy is on the beach now. She's with Cyril. Cyril isn't happy now.

Can Toby Johnson see Cyril? Can he see Benny and Babe?

But now Toby can see Cyril!

Go, Cyril, go!

Toby has Cyril!

⑩ Now I have a pet crab[1]. Hee, hee, hee!

Cyril isn't very happy. But Toby is happy!

⑪ Two crabs! Great!

Benny and Babe are Cyril's friends. They're next!

⑫ It's Super Sandy! Yeeeehaaaaa!

⑬ You stupid bird!

Toby isn't very happy now!

⑭ Help!

Where's Toby?

⑮ Thanks, Sandy.

Cyril is OK now!

⑯ Are you OK, Toby? Toby?!?!

Mrs Johnson can't[2] see Toby.

⑰ I don't like crabs.

Toby is wet[3]. He's cold[4]. He isn't happy.

⑱ You stupid boy!

The nice day on the beach is over[5]!

---

[1] a pet crab *ein Krebs als Haustier*   [2] can't *nicht können*   3 wet *nass*   [4] He's cold. *Ihm ist kalt.*   5 over *vorbei*

🎧 TF 2 The best Christmas present[1]
2.31

1 Before you read
What do you know about Christmas in Britain[2]? Can you think of two things?

It's 24th December and lots of[3] people are in Plymouth. They all buy things for Christmas.

Ellie and her mum are in Plymouth too. Ellie buys a present for Finn – a small red crab.

5 Now Ellie and her mum are at home. Pete and Conor are there too. But Zoe isn't at home. She's with her boyfriend[4], Alan.

In the evening Conor and Ellie put[5] the decorations on the Christmas tree.
10 "It's great!" Pete says.
"It's really nice!" mum says.

"Ding-dong". Some people are at the door[6]. They sing a carol[7]:

> *"We wish you a Merry Christmas,*
15 > *We wish you a Merry Christmas,*
> *We wish you a Merry Christmas*
> *And a Happy New Year."*

"Ding-dong". Now Zoe is at the door too. But she isn't happy.
"Hi, Zoe," mum says. "What's the problem?" 20
"Alan and me," Zoe says. "He's ... oh, I don't know!" And she goes to her room.

---

[1] Christmas present *Weihnachtsgeschenk*   [2] Britain *Britannien*   [3] lots of *viele*   [4] boyfriend *(fester) Freund*
[5] put *aufhängen*   [6] door *Tür*   [7] carol *Weihnachtslied*

🎧 It's 6 o'clock on Christmas morning, 25th December.
2.32 Ellie is in bed.
25   "Zoe! Zoe!" she says.
     "What?" Zoe says.

"It's Christmas morning! And look!
Our Christmas stockings[1] are
here!" Ellie says.

30   Ellie looks into her stocking.
     "Oh, look, Zoe. A computer game, great!
     And a new T-shirt ... and
     a book ... and chocolate ...
     Thank you, Father Christmas,"
35   Ellie says and she laughs[2].
     Then Zoe looks into her stocking.
     She finds lots of presents for her too!

After breakfast, the family goes to the
living-room. It's present time – again.
"Here's a present for you, Conor. It's from   40
Pete," mum says.
"Thanks Dad," Conor says. "Oh, speakers –
great!"
"And here's a present from me for you, Zoe,"
mum says.   45
But Zoe isn't happy.
She has no present from Alan.

Christmas dinner is turkey[3], potatoes[4],
vegetables[5], and then Christmas pudding.
And they all have Christmas crackers.   50
"Conor, pull[6] a cracker with me," Ellie says.
BANG! In the cracker is a small present
(a pen) and a green paper hat[7].

"Zoe, pull a cracker
with me," Pete says.   55
"No thanks," Zoe says.

Christmas cracker

Christmas dinner

Christmas pudding

---

[1] stocking *(langer) Strumpf*   [2] laugh *lachen*   [3] turkey *Truthahn*   [4] potatoes *Kartoffeln*   [5] vegetables *Gemüse*
[6] pull *ziehen*   [7] paper hat *Papierhut*

🎧 After lunch Ellie goes to her dad's flat.
2.33 "Happy Christmas, Dad," Ellie says.
"Happy Christmas, Ellie."

60 It's Finn's first Christmas. He's very happy.
And his present from Ellie is great.
At 3 o'clock the Queen is on TV.
"At Christmas, family and friends are very
important …," the Queen says.

65 Later, it's time for Christmas cake[2].

"Christmas is great!" says Ellie.
"I'm so happy … and I hope Zoe is happy
now too."
Then Ellie gets a
70 text from Zoe:

The Queen[1] is on TV

Hi Ellie. Alan was
here[3] this evening
– that's my best
Christmas present!
Zoe

2 Christmas things
What are the Christmas things (1–5)
in the photo?

> a Christmas cracker • a Christmas tree •
> Christmas cards • a paper hat • a turkey

3 Christmas in Britain
a) What do you know about Christmas in Britain?
1 In Britain people open presents **A** in the evening of 24th December. **B** on 25th December.
2 Children open presents from Father Christmas **A** in the morning. **B** in the evening.
3 Presents from **A** family and friends **B** Father Christmas are under[4] the Christmas tree.
4 There's **A** a small present and a paper hat **B** a cake and a pudding in a Christmas cracker.
5 People have **A** fish **B** turkey for lunch.

b) 🔘 Write more things about Christmas in Britain. You can write sentences about these
things: cards – carols – the Queen – cake …

---

[1] queen *Königin* [2] cake *Kuchen* [3] Alan was here *Alan war hier* [4] under *unter*

TF 3 What's bicycle[1] motocross?

Bicycle motocross (BMX) is a popular sport. It's an Olympic sport too.

Your BMX bike:

low[2] saddle
special handlebar
small wheel
chain
brake
stunt peg[3]
frame
fork
helmet
tyre
gloves
pedal
pads

You can ride on a track[4].

You can ride in a special park.

And you can sometimes ride in town.

THE PLYMOUTH NEWS

A world champion

This is Shanaze Reade. She's from England. Her dad is from Jamaica. Her mum is from Ireland.
Shanaze rides on BMX tracks. She's the world champion. She got[5] her first BMX bike when she was[6] 10. It was £1!

Shanaze Reade

Find a picture of your bike or your dream bike. Make labels for the bike.

[1] bicycle *Fahrrad*   [2] low *niedrig*   [3] peg *Füßstütze*   [4] track *Piste*   [5] she got *sie bekam*   [6] she was *sie war*

🎧 **TF 4 The circus**
2.34

It's 9 o'clock on Friday morning. The students
are happy. They like Fridays.
But one boy isn't happy. He has no friends in
the class.

5 "Good morning," Ms Lee says. We have a
new student today. This is Ben. Ben is from
Russell's Circus".
"Wow – a circus!" Luca says.
"Do you live in Plymouth?" Ellie asks.

10 "Well, we're in Central Park now," Ben says.
"But we go to different towns and I go to
different schools."
"Cool," Berry says.

1 How is Ben at 9 o'clock?
    What do you think – how is he
    at 1 o'clock?

At 1 o'clock, Ellie, Adam, Luca and Berry are
15 in the canteen with Ben.
 "Do you live in a tent[1]?" Ellie asks.
"No, in a caravan," Ben says.
"Cool – it's like camping[2]!" Luca says.
"And what do you have in your circus?" Adam
20 asks.
"Clowns, acrobats, jugglers[3]...," Ben says.
"You can visit our circus, if you like[4]."
"Really? That's great!" says Luca.
"When can we come?" Berry asks.
25 "Tomorrow is Saturday. Come tomorrow
morning," Ben says.
"OK. See you tomorrow morning."

2 What can Ellie, Berry, Adam and Luca
    do on Saturday ?

---

[1] tent *Zelt*   [2] it's like camping *es ist wie Camping*   [3] juggler *Jongleur/in*   [4] if you like *wenn ihr wollt*

It's Saturday morning and Ellie, Luca, Adam
and Berry are in Central Park, at Russell's
30　Circus.
"Hi. Welcome to my home," Ben says.
Ben brings the four kids to his caravan.
"This is cool," Ellie says. "And so big!"
"This isn't like camping!" Luca says.

35　The friends meet Ben's mum. She works
in the ticket office[1].
And they meet Ben's dad. He's a clown.

It's time for a tour of the circus. There are lots
of people in the big tent.
40　"This is Maria. And this is Darek. They're from
Poland. And they're acrobats," Ben says.
"Do you like your work?" Berry asks.
"Yes, we love it," Maria says.

The juggler, Raymond,
is from France.　　　　　　　　　　　　　　45
"Do you want to try[2]?"
he asks Ellie.
"OK," she says. But she's
terrible. The other kids
laugh.　　　　　　　　　　　　　　　　　　50

Then they see Ben's dad.
He's on the shoulders of two other clowns –
but then they all fall. The friends laugh.

They have lunch in Ben's caravan.
"Do you want to see the show today?" Ben's　　55
mum asks. "It's at 3 o'clock."
"Wow. Yes please. That's great!" the kids say.
"Good," Ben's dad says. "You can help us."

3 Is Ben's caravan like camping?
4 What circus people do the kids meet?

---

[1] ticket office *Kasse*　　[2] try *ausprobieren*

2.36 It's 2.30 on Saturday afternoon. Lots of people are at Russell's Circus. Berry is in the ticket office with Ben's mum. Then she sees her mum and dad.

"Hi, Mum. Do you want a brochure?" she asks.

65 Luca is in the big tent. He helps people to their places[1].

"Hi, Luca," Berry's mum and dad say.

"Hello, Mr and Mrs Donovan," he says. "Here are your places."

The circus starts at 3 o'clock. First there's
70 music. Then the ringmaster[2] says, "Welcome to Russell's Circus! And here are my two helpers – Ben and Ellie!"

The first act is the clowns. It's Ben's dad and the two other clowns. Today there's a fourth
75 clown – it's Adam!

5 Who has the best job at the circus - Adam, Berry, Ellie or Luca? What do you think?

Two weeks later the four friends are at Russell's Circus again. But the big tent isn't there. The circus is over[3]. It's time to go to the next town.

"Bye, Ben. Thanks for a great day at
the circus!" Berry says. 80

"You're welcome. See you next year!" Ben says.

Theatre time

Work in groups. Pick a scene from the story. Read and act the scene. Or draw a comic of this text.

---

[1] to their places *zu ihren Plätzen*   [2] ringmaster *Zirkusdirektor/in*   [3] over *vorbei*

TF 5 Cream tea

What is cream tea?

In England cream tea is a special afternoon snack.
Cream tea is: • a cup of tea,
  • a scone,
  • jam,
  • cream.

Why is cream tea special?

Because it isn't with normal cream.
It's with 'clotted cream'.
• Normal cream is 35 % fat.
• Clotted cream is 55–65 % fat.

How do you make scones?

1 Put flour[1] (225 g), sugar[2] (50 g), baking powder[3]
   (3 teaspoons[4]) and salt[5] (a half teaspoon) in a bowl.
2 Rub butter (50 g) into the flour with your fingers.
3 Add milk (75 ml) and one egg.
4 Mix everything.
5 Make 12 scones with a glass.
6 Put the scones in the oven (230 °C) for 8 – 10 minutes.
7 Cut a scone, when it's warm.
8 Put cream and jam on it – and eat it!

1 Can you put pictures A–H
   in the right order?

2 Can you make scones at home? (No clotted
   cream? Use mascarpone or crème fraîche.)

A   B   C   D

E   F   G   H

[1] flour *Mehl*   [2] sugar *Zucker*   [3] baking powder *Backpulver*   [4] teaspoon *Teelöffel*   [5] salt *Salz*

SF 1 Vokabeln lernen

▶ Unit 1, p. 25

> – Lerne nur 5 bis 10 Vokabeln auf einmal.
>
> – Lerne und wiederhole regelmäßig. Versuche, jeden Tag 10 Minuten zu lernen.
>
> – Lerne mit jemandem zusammen. Es macht mehr Spaß, und ihr könnt euch gegenseitig abfragen.
>
> – Beim Wiederholen solltest du die Vokabeln laut aussprechen **und schreiben**.

What's *Lieblingstier* in English?

Favourite animal

1 Vokabeln lernen mit dem *Vocabulary*

Das *Vocabulary* in deinem Englischbuch (S. 155–173) hilft dir beim Vokabellernen. Auf S. 155 kannst du sehen, wie es aufgebaut ist.

– Lies das englische Wort laut.

– Lies dann die deutsche Übersetzung und den Beispielsatz.

– Wenn du testen möchtest, ob du die Wörter weißt, gehe eine Seite Zeile für Zeile durch:

– Decke zuerst die beiden **rechten** Spalten ab und sage die deutsche Übersetzung.

– Gehe dann die Seite erneut durch, decke die **linke** Spalte ab und sage die englischen Wörter.

school	Schule	
at school	in der Schule	! Englisch: they're **at school** Deutsch: sie sind **in der Schule**
boy	Junge	
girl	Mädchen	
teacher	Lehrer/in	
car	Auto	

> Schreibe schwierige Vokabeln auf Zettel. Klebe die Zettel zu Hause an Gegenstände, die du oft siehst: deinen Schrank, deine Zimmertür, deine Nachttischlampe, etc.

2 Vokabelheft

Schreibe neue Wörter in ein Vokabelheft oder -ringbuch. Trage in die linke Spalte das englische Wort ein und daneben die deutsche Übersetzung. Du kannst auch ein Bild malen.

3 Sammeln und ordnen

Du merkst dir neue Vokabeln besser,
wenn du sie in Gruppen ordnest.
Du siehst hier ein Beispiel - ein *network*.

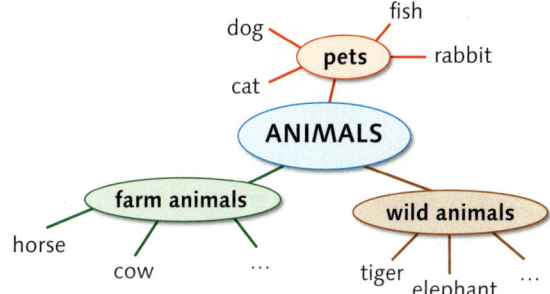

4 Vokabeln lernen mit Karteikarten

1. Du kannst neue Vokabeln auch auf Karteikarten schreiben.
Dazu brauchst du:
– viele kleine Kärtchen (oder gleich große Zettel)
– einen passenden Kasten (oder einfach zwei Gummibänder)
– eine **OK**- und eine **?**-Karte.

2. Auf die Vorderseite der Kärtchen schreibst du die englischen
Wörter – vielleicht malst du noch ein Bild oder klebst ein
Foto dazu? Auf die Rückseite schreibst du das deutsche Wort.
Am Anfang stehen alle Kärtchen im **?**-Fach.

3. Nun sortiere alle Karten so, dass das deutsche Wort vorne
steht. Bearbeite jede Karte.
Du weißt das englische Wort?
▸ Die Karte wandert in das **OK**-Fach (oder auf den **OK**-Stapel).

Du weißt es nicht?
▸ Die Karte kommt zurück in das **?**-Fach (oder auf den **?**-Stapel).

Beim nächsten Mal beginnst du mit diesen Karten.

Wiederhole auch regelmäßig die Vokabeln aus dem **OK**-Fach. Wenn
du sie nach zwei bis drei Wochen noch weißt, sortiere sie aus.

5 Vokabellernen am Computer

Mit dem e-Workbook oder mit der elektronischen Vokabelkartei
kannst du am Computer üben.

SF 2 Eigene Texte schreiben

▶ Unit 2, p. 42

1 Ideen sammeln

– Sammle zuerst wichtige Ideen und Wörter, z.B. in einem Gedankennetz oder einer Liste.

– Suche in deinem Buch nach weiteren Ideen oder tausche dich mit einem Partner / einer Partnerin aus.

> **My flat/house**
>
> *Where is it?:* in ... Street.
> *It's:* new, old, big, small, noisy, quiet ...
> *It has:* ... rooms, a garden, ...
> *I live with:* my mum, dad, brother,...
> *Rooms:* kitchen, bathroom, ...

2 Textentwurf schreiben

– Jetzt mache einen Textentwurf auf einem Zettel oder am Computer.

– Texte oder Sätze aus dem Buch sind oft eine gute Vorlage. Ersetze die Wörter, die nicht stimmen, und ergänze eigene Ideen.

– Schreibe kurze, einfache Sätze auf.

– Überlege dir eine sinnvolle Reihenfolge. Womit fängst du an? Welches ist der beste Schlusssatz?

> TUESDAY
> I'm at dad's flat. I'm in my new bedroom.
> I have a table and a lamp.
> I can do my homework here.
> No bossy Zoe. My room is pink,
> but it's great!

3 Textentwurf überarbeiten

– Hast du alles richtig geschrieben? Wenn du nicht sicher bist, suche das Wort im Dictionary (S. 174–181).

– Fange nicht jeden Satz gleich an:
  My room is pink. My room is small. ⇨ *My room is pink. It's small.*

– Aus zwei mach eins: Wenn du zwei sehr kurze Sätze hast, verbinde sie mit *and* und mach einen daraus:
  I have a lamp. I have a bed. ⇨ *I have a lamp and a bed.*

– Suche dir einen Partner oder eine Partnerin und tauscht eure Texte aus. Versteht ihr die Texte des anderen? Findet ihr noch Fehler?

4 Text schreiben

Schreibe am Ende den korrigierten Text noch einmal ab. Dann hast du ihn sauber im Heft.

SF 3 Unbekannte Wörter verstehen

▶ *Unit 3, p. 62*

Du kannst englische Texte verstehen – auch wenn du nicht alle
Wörter kennst.

1 Schau auf die Bilder

Bilder sind eine große Hilfe und erklären Vieles.
Was bedeuten z.B. *forefinger* und *wrist* im folgenden Text?

> How to check your pulse:
>
> Put your forefinger and your
> middle finger on your wrist.
> Count your pulse for 60 seconds.

2 Denke an ähnliche Wörter im Deutschen

Viele englische Wörter werden ähnlich wie im Deutschen
geschrieben oder klingen ähnlich wie deutsche Wörter,
z.B. in dem kleinen Text oben:
– *pulse* hat Ähnlichkeit mit dem deutschen Wort "Puls"
– *middle finger* ist natürlich im Deutschen der "Mittelfinger"

Was bedeuten die folgenden Wörter auf Deutsch?

> cost • fresh • half • price • hang • loud speaker •
> nervous • ocean • penguin • plan • study • tomato sauce

Hmm, *nervous*
sieht so aus wie
das deutsche Wort
„nervös", oder?

Ja, das ist es!

3 Schau auf den ganzen Satz

Häufig kannst du ein unbekanntes Wort aus dem
Satzzusammenhang erschließen. Dabei helfen dir die Wörter,
die vor oder nach dem unbekannten Wort stehen.
Was könnten *building* und *stay* bedeuten?

> 1 Our school is new. It's a very nice building
>   with lots of classrooms.
> 2 Mum: You can't see your friends this afternoon.
>   Stay at home and do your homework!

Also, es
geht um
die Schule
und …

Ich hab's!

forefinger *Zeigefinger* wrist *Handgelenk* cost *kosten* fresh *frisch*
half *halb* price *Preis* hang *hängen* loud speaker *Lautsprecher*
ocean *Ozean* penguin *Pinguin* plan *Plan* study *studieren, lernen*
tomato sauce *Tomatensauce* building *Gebäude* Stay at home *Bleib zu Hause*

SF 4 Im Wörterbuch nachschlagen

▶ *Unit 4, p. 80*

1 Wörter alphabetisch ordnen

> **Uncle Ernie's farm**
>
> Uncle Ernie has got a farm near Bristol.
> On his farm there are lots of animals.
> He has 20 pigs and 85 cows.
> But his favourite animal is his donkey.

Wenn du in einem englischen Text ein Wort noch nicht kennst oder vergessen hast (z.B. *donkey*), dann hilft dir das *English-German Dictionary* (S. 174–181) weiter. Dort kannst du Wörter nachschlagen.

Alles ist alphabetisch aufgelistet:

– *D* kommt vor *F*

– *dad* kommt vor *dog*

– *draw* kommt vor *dream*

– Wo findest du also *donkey* im *Dictionary*? Zwischen *dive* und *dock* oder zwischen *do* und *door*?

Ordne nun diese *farm animals* alphabetisch. Denke daran:
h kommt vor *p*, *do* vor *du*, *dog* vor *don*.

> horse • cat • bull • donkey • sheep •
> chicken • duck • pig • dog • rabbit

2 Zusammengesetzte Ausdrücke erkennen

Manche Wörter sind fett hervorgehoben. Das sind zusammengesetzte Wörter (z.B. *family tree*) oder Redewendungen (z.B. *I feel fed up*).

3 Ganzen Eintrag lesen

Die Ziffern 1, 2 usw. (z.B. *finish*) zeigen, dass ein Wort mehrere Bedeutungen haben kann. Lies daher immer den ganzen Eintrag und entscheide dann, welche Bedeutung in deinem Fall die richtige ist.

Welche Mehrfachbedeutungen kannst du für folgende Wörter finden?

> text • phone • too • right

> **family** ['fæməli] Familie 2 (36)
> **family tree** (Familien-)Stamm-
> baum 2 (37)
> **farm** [fɑːm] Bauernhof 4 (70)
> °**fast** [fɑːst] schnell
> **favourite** ['feɪvərɪt] Lieblings- (13)
> **favourite thing** Lieblingssache
> (13)
> **February** ['februəri] Februar 3 (56)
> **fed up** [fed ˈʌp]: **feel fed up** ge-
> nervt sein, sauer sein; die Nase
> voll haben 4 (74)
> **feed** [fiːd] füttern 4 (72)
> **feel** [fiːl] sich fühlen; fühlen 4 (74)
> **ferry** ['feri] Fähre 5 (88)
> **field** [fiːld] Feld; Weide 4 (77)
> **fifty** ['fɪfti] fünfzig 3 (60)
> **film** [fɪlm] Film 3 (61)
> °**find** [faɪnd]: finden **find out**
> herausfinden
> **fine** [faɪn] gut, schön 1 (17) **I'm**
> **fine.** Es geht mir gut. 1 (17)
> °**finish** ['fɪnɪʃ]:
> **1.** beenden, enden
> **2.** Ende, Ziel

bull - cat - chicken - dog - donkey - duck - horse - pig - rabbit - sheep

donkey kommt zwischen do und door.

SF 5 Über Bilder und Fotos sprechen

▶ Unit 5, p. 98

Es ist leichter, über ein Bild oder ein Foto zu sprechen, wenn du folgende Schritte beachtest:

1 Beginne allgemein

Sage zunächst in ein oder zwei Sätzen, was du allgemein auf dem Bild siehst: Welcher Ort, welcher Gegenstand oder welche Personen sind zu sehen?

In the picture I can see a messy room.

2 Teile das Bild in drei Teile

Sage, was sich links, in der Mitte und rechts auf dem Bild befindet.

> **On the left** I can see a red bed, three cushions, …

> **In the middle** there are trainers, a green rucksack, a …

> **On the right** there's a table, a chair, a …

3 Beschreibe die drei Teile genauer

Fange mit dem linken Teil des Bildes an und sage genau, was sich wo befindet:

On the left I can see a red bed.
Next to the bed there's a wardrobe. The doors of the wardrobe are open.
In front of the bed there's a blue rucksack. In front of the rucksack I can see a football.

Dann mach genau so mit dem mittleren Teil des Bildes weiter:

In the middle there are lots of trainers and socks.
Next to a blue trainer there's a green rucksack.
Behind the rucksack there's a blue chair.

Schließlich kommt der rechte Teil des Bildes an die Reihe:

On the right I can see a table.
On the table there are lots of books, exercise books and a lamp.
Next to the table there's a green chair.
Behind the table there's a black bed. On the bed I can see a …
Under the bed there's a book and a white sock.
Behind the bed I can see a window. Next to the window …

LF 1 Personalpronomen ▸ *Unit 1, p. 28–29*

I	you	he	she	it

we	you	they

Die deutschen Pronomen *du*, *ihr* und *Sie* heißen im Englischen alle *you*.

LF 2 'm – 's – 're ▸ *Unit 1, p. 28*

Kurzformen	Langformen
I'm eleven.	I am eleven.
He's in my class.	He is in my class.
She's our teacher.	She is our teacher.
We're here.	We are here.
They're old.	They are old.

Es gibt Kurz- und Langformen. Bei den Kurzformen ist ein Buchstabe weggefallen. Dafür steht ein Auslassungszeichen (').

a) Bejahte Sätze

Kurzformen	
I'm	
You're	
He's	
She's	from Plymouth.
We're	
They're	

Die Kurzformen benutzt du nach Pronomen (*I, we, he, she, it, they*).

Langformen	
Adam is	
Ms Lee is	
The bike is	from Plymouth.
Adam and Ellie are	

Die Langformen benutzt du meistens hinter Eigennamen (*Ellie, Ms Lee*) oder Nomen (*bike*).

LF 3 b) Verneinte Sätze ▶ Unit 1, p. 29

Kurzformen	Langformen
I'm not old.	I am not old.
We aren't old.	We are not old.
Adam isn't old.	Adam is not old.
Ms Lee isn't old.	Ms Lee is not old.
The bike isn't old.	The bike is not old.
They aren't old.	They are not old.

Bei der Verneinung benutzt du fast immer die Kurzformen.

Benny and Babe aren't birds – they're crabs!

LF 4 c) Fragen und Kurzantworten ▶ Unit 2, p. 46

Are you eleven? – Yes, I am. / No, I'm not.
Bist du elf? – Ja. / Nein.
Is your room nice? – Yes, it is. / No, it isn't.
Ist dein Zimmer schön? – Ja. / Nein.

Antworte auf eine Frage im Englischen nicht einfach mit *yes* oder *no*. Das klingt oft unhöflich. Verwende besser Kurzantworten.

Fragen	Kurzantworten
Are you here, Ali?	Yes, I am.
	No, I'm not.
Are you all OK?	Yes, we are.
	No, we aren't.

Bei Fragen mit *you* antwortest du mit *I* oder *we*.

Is Timo at home?	Yes, he is.
	No, he isn't.
Is mum tired?	Yes, she is.
	No, she isn't.
Is your room nice?	Yes, it is.
	No, it isn't
Are the cats here?	Yes, they are.
	No, they aren't.

Bei Fragen mit Eigennamen oder Nomen antwortest du mit *he*, *she*, *it* oder *they*.

Is your house nice?

Yes, it is!

LF 5 Plural von Nomen ▶ Unit 3, p. 60

a bird	two birds
a bike	three bikes
a pencil	four pencils
a football	five footballs

Du bildest den Plural (die Mehrzahl) von Nomen, indem du *s* an das Wort anhängst.

Simple present ▶ *Unit 3, p. 65*

LF 6 a) Bejahte Sätze

I go to school by bike.
Ich fahre mit dem Rad zur Schule.

My friends meet me at school.
Meine Freunde treffen mich in der Schule.

My mum works in a shop.
Meine Mama arbeitet in einem Laden.

She starts early.
Sie fängt früh an.

Mit dem *simple present* (einfache Gegenwart) sagst du, was oft oder jeden Tag passiert.

I get up early.

bejahte Sätze	Yes	
I often You often We often They often		play football.
He She It		starts early.

Mit *I*, *you*, *we*, *they* verwendest du das Verb ohne *s*.

He, she, it, ein s muss mit!

Mit *he*, *she*, *it* musst du immer ein *s* ans Verb anhängen.

LF 7 b) Verneinte Sätze ▶ *Unit 4, p. 82*

I don't have a pet.
Ich habe kein Haustier.

We don't live in town.
Wir wohnen nicht in der Stadt.

My dad doesn't like dogs.
Mein Papa mag keine Hunde.

Mit *don't* oder *doesn't* sagst du, was normalerweise nicht geschieht.

verneinte Sätze	No	
I You We They		don't watch TV.
He She It		doesn't play.

Mit *I*, *you*, *we*, *they* verwendest du *don't*.

I don't know the answer.

Mit *he*, *she*, *it* verwendest du *doesn't*.

LF 8 c) Fragen ▸ *Unit 5, p. 100*

Do you like rap music?
Magst du Rap?

Does your dad like rock music?
Mag dein Papa Rockmusik?

Do your parents listen to you?
Hören dir deine Eltern zu?

Mit *Do* oder *Does* kannst du Fragen stellen.

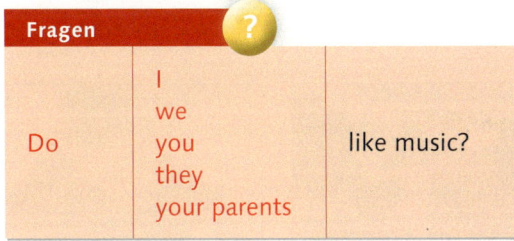

Fragen ?		
Do	I we you they your parents	like music?

Does	he your dad she your mum it	like music?

Mit *I, you, we, they* verwendest du *Do …?*

Do you live in Plymouth?

Yes, I do!

Mit *he, she, it* verwendest du *Does …?*

Where do you live?
Wo lebst du / Wo leben Sie?

What do you like?
Was magst du / Was mögen Sie?

Why do we have so much homework?
Wieso haben wir so viele Hausaufgaben?

Manche Fragen beginnen mit Fragewörtern.

LF 9 There's … / There are … ▸ *Unit 5, p. 88*

There's a ferry in the photo.
Es gibt eine Fähre auf dem Foto.

There are two girls in front of the shop.
Es stehen zwei Mädchen vor dem Laden.

There's	a boat. a bike.
There are	two boats. three bikes.

Mit *there's (= there is)* oder *there are* sagst du,
dass etwas vorhanden ist.
Im Deutschen heißt es:
– Es gibt …
– Da sind …
– Es stehen …

Wordbank 1: Sports and hobbies

▶ p. 11

I like	dancing. playing football. playing computer games. reading. skateboarding. riding. swimming. watching TV.

boxing

climbing

canoeing

cycling

doing athletics

drawing

playing ice hockey

ice skating

in-line skating

listening to music

making models

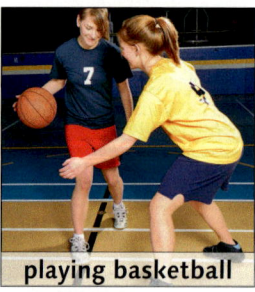
playing basketball

playing table tennis

snowboarding

skiing

surfing the internet

taking photos

trampolining

Wordbank 2: My favourite thing

▶ p. 13

    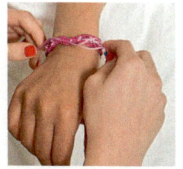 

| bag | cap | card collection | DVD player | friendship bracelet | game console |

| MP3 player | necklace | key ring | poster | skateboard | TV |

Wordbank 3: Timetable

▶ Unit 1, p. 32

I have art, drama, English, French, geography, history, ICT, maths, music, PE, science, technology, …

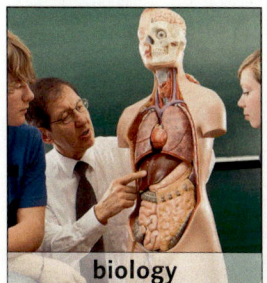   

| biology | chemistry | ethics | German |

   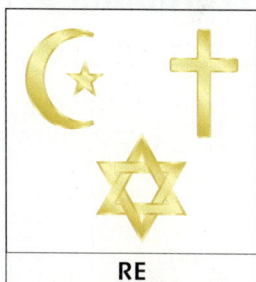

| homework club | home economics | physics | RE |

| social studies | special needs training | textile technology | tutor period |

---

homework club *Hausaufgabenbetreuung*   home economics *Hauswirtschaftslehre*   RE = religious education *Religions-lehre*   social studies *Gesellschaftslehre*   special needs training *Förderunterricht*   textile technology *Textiles Gestalten*   tutor period *Klassenlehrerstunde*

Wordbank 4: My family

▶ Unit 2, p. 37

My uncle Peter. He's my dad's brother. He's Silke's husband.

My aunt Silke. She's married to Peter. She's Peter's wife.

My uncle Holger. He's single. He and Theresa's mum are divorced.

My aunt Anja. She's my mum's sister.

My mum

Me

My dad

My grandma and her grandson Tim.

My sister Lisa

Charly

My cousin Tim. He's Peter's and Anja's son.

My grandpa and his granddaughter Anna.

My cousin Theresa. She's Holger's daughter.

aunt *Tante* uncle *Onkel* grandson *Enkel* granddaughter *Enkelin* cousin *Cousin, Cousine* husband *Ehemann*
wife *Ehefrau* single *alleinstehend* married to *verheiratet mit* divorced *geschieden*

Wordbank 5: My room

▶ Unit 2, p. 42

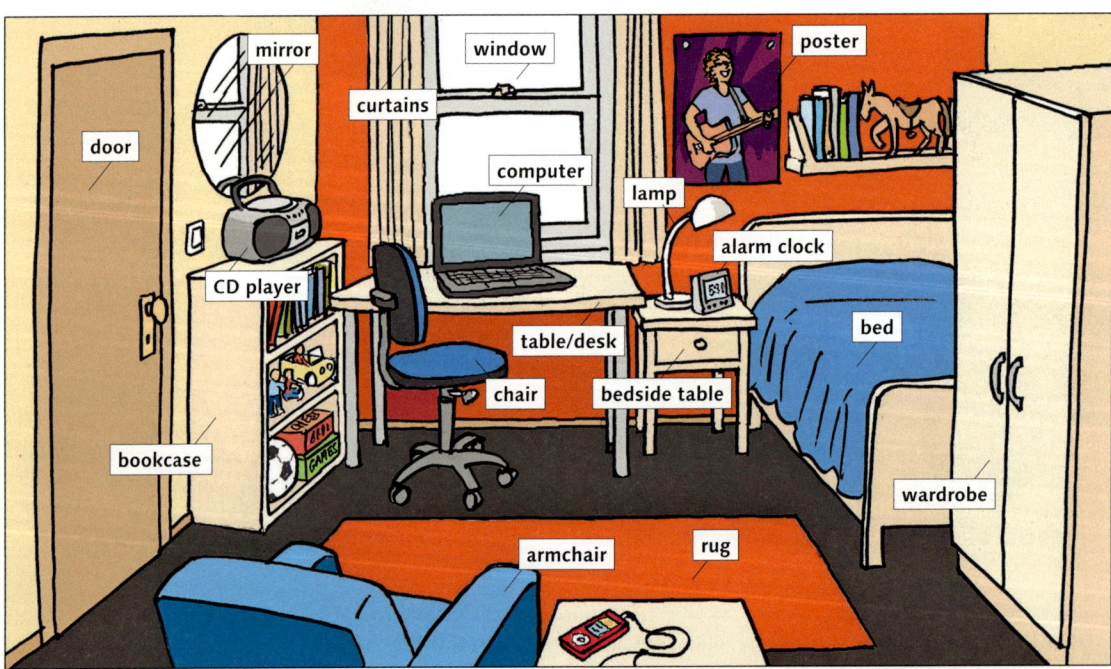

mirror

window

poster

curtains

door

computer

lamp

CD player

alarm clock

bed

table/desk

chair

bedside table

bookcase

wardrobe

armchair

rug

Wordbank 6: My town

▶ Unit 3, p. 52

a fast food restaurant

the swimming pool

the park

a video shop

the zoo

I sometimes go to …

the football stadium

a sports club

the shopping centre

the youth centre

the skate park

Wordbank 7: Things for a party

▶ Unit 4, p. 79

I want to …
go swimming, watch a film,
listen to music, ride bikes,
play games, have fun, dance.

Please bring:
swimming things, trainers, a pullover,
DVDs, CDs, funny photos, games.

make popcorn

have a water fight

balloons

biscuits

have a barbecue

camp in the garden

a sleeping bag

pyjamas

play musical chairs

have a fancy dress party

fancy dress

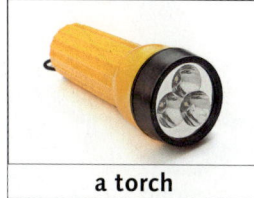
a torch

play musical chairs *"Die Reise nach Jerusalem"/Stuhltanz spielen* fancy dress *Verkleidung*
water fight *Wasserschlacht*

Wordbank 8: Talking about pets

▶ Unit 4, p. 83

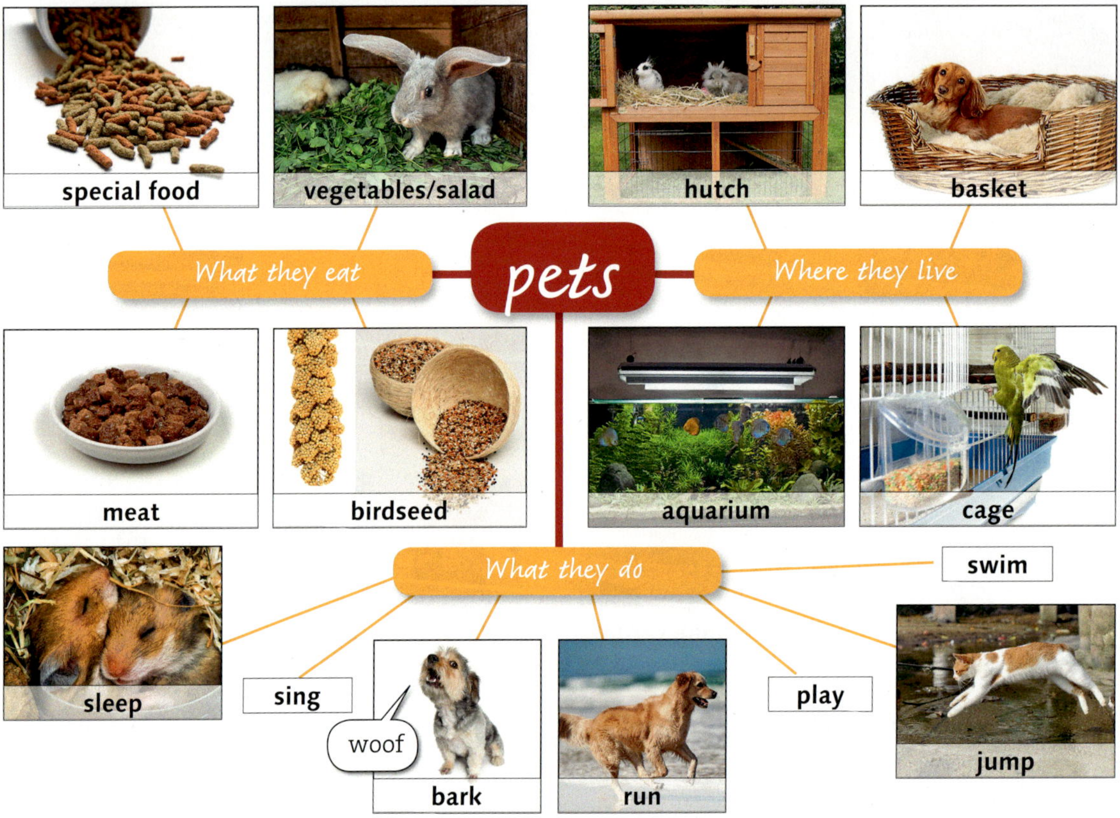

What they eat
- special food
- vegetables/salad
- meat
- birdseed

pets

Where they live
- hutch
- basket
- aquarium
- cage

What they do
- sleep
- sing
- bark — woof
- run
- swim
- play
- jump

birdseed *Körnerfutter, Vogelfutter*   hutch *Hütte, kleiner Stall*   meat *Fleisch*   special food *Spezialfutter*
vegetables *Gemüse*

Wordbank 9: Instruments

▶ Unit 5, p. 93

I play the drums, the guitar, the piano, the ...   **I don't play an instrument. I like the ...**

cello *Cello*

clarinet *Klarinette*

saxophone *Saxophon*

recorder *Blockflöte*

violin *Geige*

flute *(Quer-)flöte*

trumpet *Trompete*

keyboard *Keyboard*

Das **Vocabulary** (S. 155–173) enthält alle neuen Wörter und Wendungen des Buches, die du **lernen** musst.
Sie stehen in der Reihenfolge, in der sie im Buch zum ersten Mal vorkommen.

Hier siehst du, wie das **Vocabulary** aufgebaut ist:

> Diese Zahl gibt die **Seite** an, auf der die Wörter zum ersten Mal vorkommen.
> p. 13 = Seite 13

> Dies ist das „Gegenteil"-Zeichen.
> **new ◄► old** bedeutet:
> „**new** ist das Gegenteil von **old**".

> **Blau** gedruckte Wörter kennst du wahrscheinlich schon aus dem Englischunterricht in der Grundschule.

> Das **rote Ausrufezeichen** bedeutet: Vorsicht, hier macht man leicht Fehler!

p. 13	my	mein/e
	favourite thing	Lieblingssache
	thing	Ding, Sache
	bike	Fahrrad 
	it's (= it is)	es ist *(bei Sachen und Tieren auch:* er ist, sie ist)
	great	großartig, toll
	small	klein
	old	alt
	but	aber
	camera	Fotoapparat; Kamera
	mobile (phone)	Handy
	new	neu
	big	groß
	group work	Gruppenarbeit
p. 14	the last day	der letzte Tag
	holidays	Ferien
	the last day of the holidays	der letzte Tag der Ferien →
	story	Geschichte
	Hello.	Hallo.
	It's me.	Ich bin's. →
	no	

! Deutsch: **Handy**
Englisch: **mobile phone** oder **mobile**

new ◄► old

big ◄► small

> **of**
> • the colour **of** my bike
>   (die Farbe meines Rades)
> • the last day **of** the holidays
>   (der letzte Tag der Ferien)
>
> „ich": **me** statt **I**
> • Hello, Ellie. It's **me**, Luca.
>   (Hallo, Ellie. Ich bin's, Luca.)
> • I'm twelve. – **Me** too.
>   (Ic...

> Der **blaue Pfeil** heißt:
> Zu diesem Eintrag gibt es in der rechten Spalte einen blauen Kasten.

> Die **blauen Kästen** solltest du dir immer besonders gut ansehen. Dort stehen wichtige Hinweise zu den neuen Wörtern.

Tipps zum Wörterlernen findest du im **Skills file** auf den Seiten 140 bis 145.

Im **Vocabulary** werden folgende **Abkürzungen und Symbole** verwendet:

p. = page (Seite)
pl = *plural* (Mehrzahl)

Wenn du **nachschlagen** möchtest, was ein englisches Wort bedeutet oder wie man es ausspricht, dann solltest du das **Dictionary English – German** auf den Seiten 174–181 verwenden.

Und wenn du vergessen hast, wie etwas auf Englisch heißt, dann kann dir das **Dictionary German – English** auf den Seiten 182–188 eine erste Hilfe sein.

Hi! What's your name?

p.8	**Hi!**	Hallo!
	What's your name?	Wie heißt du? (*wörtlich:* Was ist dein Name?)
	What's …? (= What is …?)	Was ist …?
	your	dein/e; eurer/eure
	name	Name

	I'm (= I am)	ich bin
	the crab	der Krebs
	the	der, die, das
	four	vier →
	What about you?	Und du?/Was ist mit dir?
	you	du; dich; dir; ihr; euch
	from Plymouth	aus Plymouth
	in England	in England ❗ Ländernamen werden immer großgeschrieben.
	Germany	Deutschland
	partner	Partner/in — one partner – two partner**s**
	class	(Schul-)Klasse — one class – two class**es**
p.9	**game**	Spiel
	I can see …	Ich kann … sehen.
	can	können
	see	sehen
	and	und
	a **beach**	ein Strand
	song	Lied
p.10	**colour**	Farbe
	Welcome to Plymouth.	Willkommen in Plymouth!
	green	grün →
	red	rot
	yellow	gelb
	brown	braun
	black	schwarz
	blue	blau
	white	weiß
	pink	rosa
	orange	orange
	Ellie **says**	Ellie sagt

1 one	6 six	11 eleven	
2 two	7 seven	12 twelve	
3 three	8 eight	13 thirteen	
4 four	9 nine	14 fourteen	
5 five	10 ten		

red	rot	orange	orange
yellow	gelb	pink	pink, rosa
blue	blau	white	weiß
green	grün	black	schwarz
brown	braun		

say	sagen	
like	mögen	I **like** red.
sweets	Bonbons, Süßigkeiten	
I don't like …	ich mag … nicht	
p.11 **sport**	Sport; Sportart	
hobby	Hobby	**!** Englisch: one hobby – two hobb**ies** Deutsch: ein Hobby – zwei Hobby**s**
playing football	Fußballspielen	
football	Fußball	
watching TV	Fernsehen	
TV	Fernseher	
too	auch	**!** steht immer am Ende des Satzes: I'm from Berlin **too**. = Ich bin **auch** aus Berlin.
swimming	Schwimmen	
dancing	Tanzen	
skateboarding	Skateboardfahren	
reading	Lesen	
riding	Reiten	
playing games	Spiele spielen	
What are …?	Was sind …?/Welche(s) sind …?	
p.12 **animal**	Tier	
have	haben	
pony	Pony	
cat	Katze	
bear	Bär	
rat	Ratte	
monkey	Affe	
bird	Vogel	
an elephant	ein Elefant	→ **a – an** **a** dog – **an** elephant
snake	Schlange	
dog	Hund	
crocodile	Krokodil	
fish	Fisch(e)	**!** one fish – two **fish**
rabbit	Kaninchen	
hamster	Hamster	
tiger	Tiger	
different	unterschiedlich, verschieden, anders	
partner work	Partnerarbeit	

p. 13	**my**	mein/e
	favourite thing	Lieblingssache
	thing	Ding, Sache
	bike	Fahrrad
	it's (= it is)	es ist *(bei Sachen und Tieren auch:* er ist, sie ist)
	great	großartig, toll
	small	klein
	old	alt
	but	aber
	camera	Fotoapparat; Kamera
	mobile (phone)	Handy
	new	neu
	big	groß
	group work	Gruppenarbeit
p. 14	**the last day**	der letzte Tag
	holidays	Ferien
	the last day **of** the holidays	der letzte Tag der Ferien
	story	Geschichte
	Hello.	Hallo.
	It's me.	Ich bin's.
	no	nein
	yes	ja
	go away	weggehen
	go	gehen; fahren
	away	weg, fort
	stupid	dumm, blöd
	This is … [ˈðɪs ɪz]	Dies ist …/ Das ist …
	help	Hilfe
	help	helfen
	Goodbye.	Auf Wiedersehen.
p. 15	**yippee**	hurra

! **Deutsch: Handy**
Englisch: **mobile phone** oder **mobile**

new ◄► old

big ◄► small

of
- the colour **of** my bike
  (die Farbe meines Rades)
- the last day **of** the holidays
  (der letzte Tag der Ferien)

„ich": **me** statt **I**
- Hello, Ellie. It's **me**, Luca.
  (Hallo, Ellie. Ich bin's, Luca.)
- I'm twelve. – **Me** too.
  (Ich bin zwölf. – Ich auch.)

yes ◄► no

This is Cyril the crab.

Oh go away, you stupid bird.

Unit 1: Welcome to our school

p.16	**our**	unser/e	
	school	Schule	
	at school	in der Schule	❗ Englisch: they're **at school** Deutsch: sie sind **in der Schule**
	boy	Junge	
	girl	Mädchen	
	teacher	Lehrer/in	
	car	Auto	
p.17	**first (= 1st)**	erste, erster, erstes	the **first** day ◄► the **last** day
	How are you?	Wie geht's?/Wie geht es dir/euch?	
	how	wie	**How** old are you? – I'm 13.
	I'm OK.	Es geht mir gut.	
	I'm fine.	Es geht mir gut.	I'm **fine** = I'm **OK**
	fine	gut, schön	
	thanks	danke	
	Bye.	Tschüs.	**Hello.** ◄► **Bye./Goodbye.**
	Have a good day.	Ich wünsche dir einen schönen Tag./Schönen Tag noch.	
	good	gut	
	See you.	Bis dann./Tschüs.	
p.18	**Good morning.**	Guten Morgen.	
	Ms Lee	Frau Lee	
	English	Englisch; englisch	**what?** was? **who?** wer? **how?** wie?
	Who are you?	Wer bist du?/Wer seid ihr? →	
	brother	Bruder	
	sister	Schwester	
	we're (= we are)	wir sind	
	best	beste(r, s); am besten	
	friend	Freund/in	
	they're (= they are)	sie sind	
	no	kein, keine	We have **no** car.
	he's (= he is)	er ist	
	she's (= she is)	sie ist	
p.19	**Mr** Smith	Herr Smith	
	Mrs Smith	Frau Smith	❗ **Ms** = *allgemeine Anrede für Frauen* **Mrs** = *Anrede für verheiratete Frauen*
	or	oder	
p.20	a **tour of** the school	ein Rundgang durch die Schule	

maths	Mathematik	
geography	Geografie, Erdkunde	
here	hier; hierher	
science	Naturwissenschaft	
ICT (information and communication technology)	Informations- und Kommunikationstechnologie	
art	Kunst	
PE (physical education)	(Schul-)Sport	
where?	wo? / wohin?	Nicht verwechseln: ➡ **who?** wer? **where?** wo?
he/she/it isn't (= is not)	er/sie/es ist nicht	
not	nicht; kein/e	➡ I'm **not** ten. And I'm **not** a boy. Ich bin **nicht** zehn. Und ich bin **kein** Junge.
lesson	(Unterrichts-)Stunde	
now	nun, jetzt	
p.21 **timetable**	Stundenplan	
time	Zeit; Uhrzeit	
Monday	Montag	❗ Die Wochentage werden immer großgeschrieben.
Tuesday	Dienstag	
Wednesday	Mittwoch	
Thursday	Donnerstag	
Friday	Freitag	
music	Musik	
technology	Technik, Technologie	
history	Geschichte	
French	Französisch; französisch	
break	Pause	
lunch	Mittagessen	
drama	Schauspiel, darstellende Kunst	
on Monday	am Montag	What's lesson one **on Monday**?
right	richtig	
wrong	falsch	**wrong** ◀▶ **right**
p.22 **before** you read	bevor du liest	
read	lesen	
tie	Krawatte	
Ellie **has** …	Ellie hat …	
Miss Borowski	Frau Borowski	❗ **Miss** = Anrede für unverheiratete Frauen
principal	Schulleiter/in	
please	bitte	

remember	daran denken, nicht vergessen; sich erinnern an	**Remember**, this is important! (Denk dran!) Can you **remember** my name? (dich erinnern an)
uniform	(Schul-)Uniform	
important	wichtig	
before the lesson	vor der (Unterrichts-)Stunde	**before** the lesson – **vor** der Stunde **before** you read – **bevor** du liest
Sorry. / I'm sorry.	Tut mir leid. / Entschuldigung.	
at home	zu Hause	
That isn't good.	Das ist nicht gut.	
know	wissen; kennen	It's art now. – I **know**! It's on the timetable.

p.23

Look, Adam.	Sieh mal, Adam. / Schau mal, Adam.	
look	sehen, schauen	
bad	schlecht; schlimm	**bad ◄► good**
idea	Idee	
canteen	(Schul-)Mensa, Kantine	
that's right	das stimmt, das ist richtig	
that's wrong	das stimmt nicht, das ist falsch	
people	Leute, Menschen	

five people

think	denken, meinen, glauben	
Ellie's tie	Ellies Krawatte	❗ Im Englischen steht vor dem -s am Ende des Namens ein Apostroph, wenn etwas (zu) jemandem gehört.
word	Wort	
theatre	Theater	

p.24

brochure	Broschüre, Prospekt
buy	kaufen
at MARTINS	bei MARTINS

Buy at MARTINS! % %

for	für	
pound (£)	Pfund *(britische Währung)*	❗ you write: **£**5 – you say: five **pounds**
pencil sharpener	Bleistiftanspitzer	
rubber	Radiergummi	
ruler	Lineal	
Africa	Afrika	
pen	Kugelschreiber, Stift; Füller	
pencil	Bleistift	
pencil case	Federmäppchen	

calculator	Taschenrechner	
exercise book	Schulheft, Übungsheft	
exercise	Übung, Aufgabe	
p.25 **network**	Netz; Wortnetz	
weekend	Wochenende	
Saturday	Samstag	
Sunday	Sonntag	
classroom	Klassenraum	
phrase	Ausdruck, (Rede-)Wendung	
card	Karte	
box	Box, Kasten	
in English	auf Englisch	What's 'Lineal' **in English**, please?
p.26 **speaking to friends**	mit Freunden/Freundinnen sprechen	
speak (to)	sprechen (mit)	
borrow	(aus)leihen, sich borgen	Can I **borrow** your calculator, please?
sure	sicher	The next lesson is art. – Are you **sure**? Can you help me? – **Sure**. (Sicher!/Na klar!)
Here you are.	Bitte schön./Hier, bitte.	
next	nächste(r, s)	
German	Deutsch; deutsch	
p,28 **it starts**	er/sie/es fängt an	
start	anfangen	
with	mit	
we **aren't**	wir sind nicht	
you're (= you are)	du bist, ihr seid, Sie sind	
student	Schüler/in; Student/in	
seventeen	siebzehn	
love	lieben, sehr mögen	
p.29 **prince**	Prinz	

Two pencils, please.

Here you are.

15	fifteen	20	twenty
16	sixteen	21	twenty-one
17	seventeen	22	twenty-two
18	eighteen	...	
19	nineteen	30	thirty
		31	thirty-one
		32	thirty-two
		...	

Unit 2: At home with Ellie

p.34 **with** Ellie	bei Ellie	Where's Cyril? – He's **with** Sandy.
house	Haus	
road	Straße (Landstraße zwischen Orten, aber auch in Ortschaften)	My house is **in Hill Road**.

flat	Wohnung	
street	Straße *(in Ortschaften)*	
kitchen	Küche	
room	Raum, Zimmer	
in the photo	auf dem Foto	
nice	nett, schön	
bedroom	Schlafzimmer	
garden	Garten	
living room	Wohnzimmer	
toilet	Toilette	
bathroom	Bad(ezimmer)	
mum	Mama, Mutti	
live	leben, wohnen	
she **lives**	sie lebt/wohnt	Ellie **lives** in Plymouth.
her dad	ihr Vater	**Her** friends live in Plymouth too.
dad	Papa, Vati	
p.36 **family**	Familie	
at Ellie's house	bei Ellie daheim, bei Ellie zu Hause	
upstairs	oben; nach oben	
at Eggbuckland	auf der Eggbuckland-Schule	
high school	*(GB etwa:)* Gesamtschule	
madhouse	Irrenhaus	
stepdad	Stiefvater	
stepmum	Stiefmutter	
miss	vermissen	
real	echt, wirklich	
his partner	sein Partner, seine Partnerin →	
baby	Baby	
cute	niedlich, süß	
you're lucky	du hast Glück	
I'd like (= I would like)	ich hätte gern, ich möchte (…) haben	
p.37 **family tree**	(Familien-)Stammbaum	
tree	Baum	
grandpa	Opa	
grandma	Oma	
stepsister	Stiefschwester	
stepbrother	Stiefbruder	
p.38 **problem**	Problem	

my	mein/e	**his**	sein/e
your	dein/e, euer/eure	**her**	ihr/e

happy	glücklich, froh	
unhappy	unglücklich	She's **happy.** 🙂 He's **unhappy.** 🙁
look at	anschauen	
pullover	Pullover	
shoe	Schuh	
messy	unordentlich	
bossy	herrisch	
too small	zu klein	
table	Tisch	
I do my homework	ich mache (meine) Hausaufgaben	➡ **homework** hat keinen Plural: **Homework is** important. **Hausaufgaben sind** wichtig.
place	Ort, Platz, Stelle	
noisy	laut, voller Lärm	

p.39 **cushion** — Kissen

lamp — Lampe

chair — Stuhl

bed — Bett

wardrobe — Kleiderschrank

flat-screen TV — Flachbildfernseher

My bedroom — bed, cushions, lamp, chair, wardrobe

p.40 **again**	wieder, noch einmal	
news	Nachrichten	❗ Englisch: That**'s** good **news.** Deutsch: Das **sind** gute **Nachrichten.**
tomorrow	morgen	
to	zu, nach, in	
after school	nach der Schule	**after** school ◀▶ **before** school
at the cinema	im Kino	
me	mir; mich	➡ with **me** mir for **me** mich
programme	(Fernseh-)Sendung	
in town	in der Stadt	
tired	müde	
very happy	sehr glücklich	
at a restaurant	in einem Restaurant	
It's her birthday.	Sie hat Geburtstag.	
p.41 **really**	wirklich	Our English teacher is **really** nice.
text (message)	SMS	
a **text from** mum	eine SMS von Mama	
week	Woche	
she **misses**	sie vermisst	Ellie **misses** her mum.
p.42 **write about**	schreiben über	

sentence	Satz	
page (= p.)	(Buch-, Heft-)Seite	Please look at **page** 42 = **p.** 42.
write **to**	schreiben an	
p.43 **answer**	Antwort	
work	arbeiten	
listen (to)	zuhören; (sich etwas) anhören ➡	
picture	Bild	
I forgot my homework.	Ich habe meine Hausaufgaben vergessen.	
banana skin	Bananenschale	
banana	Banane	
p.44 address	Adresse	What's your **address**? – 11 Greatfield Street.
phone number	Telefonnummer	
alphabet	Alphabet	
spell	buchstabieren	
talk about	sprechen über	
p.46 surprise	Überraschung	
often	oft	
all	alle(s)	
Don't be silly.	Sei nicht albern/dumm/blöd.	
p.47 book	Buch	
they're **fun**	es macht Spaß, mit ihnen zusammenzusein	

> **Listen**, please. (Hört zu, bitte.)
> **Listen to** Ellie. (Hört Ellie zu.)
> **Listen to** the song. (Hört euch das Lied an.)

I **often** have problems with my homework.

Unit 3: Luca's birthday

p.52 shop	Geschäft, Laden	
sometimes	manchmal	
go shopping	einkaufen gehen	
go swimming	schwimmen gehen	
ride a bike	Rad fahren	
on my birthday	an meinem Geburtstag	
p.54 market	Markt	at a **market**
afternoon	Nachmittag	
evening	Abend	
in the morning/afternoon/ evening	am Morgen/Nachmittag/ Abend	
vegetables	Gemüse	
always	immer	
meet	kennenlernen; (sich) treffen	

! Englisch: **Vegetables are** good for you.
Deutsch: **Gemüse ist** gut für dich.

p.55	**sports shop**	Sportgeschäft	
	want to buy	kaufen wollen	❗ Englisch: I **want** **to** **buy** new shoes. Deutsch: Ich **will** neue Schuhe **kaufen**.
	present	Geschenk	
	trainer	Sportschuh	
	expensive	teuer	
	hoodie	Kapuzenpullover	
	then	dann	
	terrible	schrecklich	
	shirt	Hemd	The red **trainers** are great, but the **hoodie** is too **expensive**.
p.56	**go bowling**	Bowling spielen gehen	
	stay	bleiben	Can't we **stay** at home? Can't I **stay** in bed?
	have a party	eine Party feiern	
	parents	Eltern	
	September	September	❗ Monatsnamen werden immer großgeschrieben.
	February	Februar	
	August	August	
	December	Dezember	
p.57	**January**	Januar	
	March	März	
	April	April	
	May	Mai	
	June	Juni	
	July	Juli	
	October	Oktober	
	November	November	
	second	zweite(r, s)	➡
	calendar	Kalender	
	when?	wann?	
	When's (= when is) your birthday?	Wann hast du Geburtstag?	❗ Englisch: **When** **is** your birthday? Deutsch: **Wann** **hast** du Geburtstag?
p.58	**Happy birthday!**	Herzlichen Glückwunsch zum Geburtstag!	
	do	machen, tun	
	something	etwas	
	Shut up!	Halt den Mund!	❗ Vorsicht! Viele Erwachsene finden **Shut up!** sehr unhöflich.
	concert	Konzert	

1st first 1.	**11th** eleventh 11.
2nd second 2.	**12th** twelfth 12.
3rd third 3.	**13th** thirteenth 13.
4th fourth 4,	(...)
5th fifth 5.	**20th** twentieth 20.
6th sixth 6.	**21st** twenty-first 21.
7th seventh 7.	**22nd** twenty-second 22.
8th eighth 8.	**23rd** twenty-third 23.
9th ninth 9.	(...)
10th tenth 10.	**30th** thirtieth 30.
	31st thirty-first 31.

ticket	Eintrittskarte, Fahrkarte	
zoo	Zoo	
there	da, dort; dahin, dorthin	
at work	bei der Arbeit, am Arbeitsplatz	→

at
at the cinema (im Kino)
at a restaurant (in einem Restaurant)
at school (in der Schule)
at work (bei der Arbeit)
at Ellie's house (bei Ellie daheim)

p.59 **first**	zuerst	
leg	Bein	
fall	fallen; hinfallen	
back from the hospital	aus dem Krankenhaus zurück	
hospital	Krankenhaus	
want	wollen	

! • **want sth.** I **want** a new bike.
etwas (haben) wollen
• **want to do sth.** I **want to buy** it now.
etwas tun wollen

end	Ende, Schluss	
come	(mit)kommen	
p.60 **price**	(Kauf-)Preis	
garage sale	Garagenflohmarkt *(privater Flohmarkt)*	
garage	Garage	
sale	Verkauf; Schlussverkauf	
get	bekommen, kriegen	I always **get** nice presents on my birthday.
money	Geld	
The calculator **is** £1.	Der Taschenrechner kostet 1 Pfund.	
The mobiles **are** £10.	Die Handys kosten 10 Pfund.	
British	britisch	
50p	50 Pence	
fifty	fünfzig	→

15 fifteen 60 sixty
16 sixteen 70 seventy
17 seventeen 80 eighty
18 eighteen 90 ninety
19 nineteen 100 a hundred/one hundred
20 twenty 101 a/one hundred and one
30 thirty 102 a/one hundred and two
40 forty 103 a/one hundred and three
50 fifty (...)

p.61 **activity**	Aktivität, Beschäftigung	
question	Frage	
ask	fragen	

! Englisch: Can I **ask** you a **question**?
Deutsch: Kann ich dir eine **Frage stellen**?

play	spielen	
Sounds fun.	Hört sich gut an./Klingt, als ob es Spaß macht.	
sound	klingen, sich anhören	
Are you free at one o'clock?	Hast du um ein Uhr Zeit?	
at one o'clock	um 1 Uhr/um 13 Uhr	It's **1 o'clock** now.
p.64 **home**	nach Hause	
get up	aufstehen	My sister **gets up** at 6 o'clock every morning.

early	früh	
go by bus	mit dem Bus fahren	I often **go** to school **by bus**. My brother always **goes by bike**.
walk	(zu Fuß) gehen, wandern	
have lunch	(zu) Mittag essen	
make	machen, herstellen	
breakfast	Frühstück	
firefighter	Feuerwehrmann, Feuerwehrfrau	
dinner	Abendessen	our **breakfast** table

Unit 4: Berry's farm

p.70 **lots of ...**	viel ..., viele ...	
visitor	Besucher/in, Gast	
child, *pl* **children**	Kind, Kinder	**!** one **child** – two **child**ren
ride a pony	auf einem Pony/ein Pony reiten	
pets corner	Streichelzoo	
		You can **ride** a bike, or you can **ride** a pony.
pet	Haustier	A tiger isn't a **pet**!
corner	Ecke	
everybody	jeder; alle	**Everybody** likes the beach.
donkey	Esel	
on	auf	**on** the farm **on** Monday **auf** dem Bauernhof **am** Montag
p.71 **watch**	*sich etwas* anschauen; beobachten	**look • see • watch** • **Look**! There's Cyril. • I can **see** Sandy. • I always **watch** the news on TV. Can we **watch** the monkeys?
duck	Ente	
trampoline	Trampolin	
zip wire	Seilrutsche	
cow	Kuh	
pig	Schwein	
sheep, *pl* **sheep**	Schaf, Schafe	**!** one sheep – two **sheep**
chicken	Huhn; (Brat-)Hähnchen	
it doesn't have ...	es hat kein/e ...	I **don't** like dogs. My brother **doesn't** like cats.
p.72 **from** Monday **to** Friday	von Montag bis Freitag	
wake	wecken	
other	andere(r, s)	

outside	draußen; nach draußen	The animals are **outside**. We can go **outside** too.
feed	füttern	
look after	sich kümmern um; aufpassen auf	On Saturday mornings I always **look after** my baby sister.
p.73 **What's the time?**	Wie spät ist es?	
oh	Null *(im gesprochenen Englisch)*	My phone number is three, four, six, two, **oh**, one.
clock	Uhr	„bitte"
You're welcome.	Bitte, gern geschehen./Nichts zu danken. ➔	Help me, **please.** (Hilf mir, bitte.) Thank you. – **You're welcome.** (Bitte, gern geschehen.) Two pencils, please. – **Here you are.** (Hier, bitte.)
p.74 **feel**	sich fühlen; fühlen	
when	wenn	**!** when = **1. wann**: **When**'s your birthday? **2. wenn**: I feel great **when** I do sport.
feel fed up	genervt sein, sauer sein; die Nase voll haben	
work	funktionieren	Please help me! My computer doesn't **work**.
text me	mir eine SMS schicken	
my bus **is late**	mein Bus hat Verspätung	
late	(zu) spät	**early ◄► late**
p.75 **because**	weil	I feel fed up **because** my bus is late.
the only student	der einzige Schüler/ die einzige Schülerin	Lilly is **the only** English student at our school.
wheelchair	Rollstuhl	
normal	normal	
can't (= cannot)	nicht können	
p.76 **on the bus**	im Bus	**!** Englisch: **on** the bus Deutsch: **im** Bus
chipmunk	Streifenhörnchen	
at night	nachts, in der Nacht ➔	**in** the morning **!** **at** night **in** the afternoon **in** the evening
Let's ...(= Let us ...)	Lass uns.../Lasst uns...	
us	uns	We're here. Can you see **us**?
to the country	aufs Land	
scene	Szene	
email	E-Mail	
sleepover	Schlafparty	
there's ... **there are ...**	es ist .../es gibt ...es sind .../es gibt ...	**There's** a ruler in the pencil case, but **there are** no pencils.
excited	aufgeregt, gespannt	**!** Beachte die Schreibweise: ex**c**ited
yeah (= yes)	ja	

	shoulder	Schulter	
	wet	nass	
	laugh	lachen	**!** du schreibst **laugh** – du sprichst ein langes **a**
p.77	eat	essen; fressen	
	through	durch	**!** du schreibst **through** – du sprichst ein langes **u**
	field	Feld; Weide	
	bull	Bulle	
	dangerous	gefährlich	a **dangerous** fish
	noise	Geräusch; Lärm	
	only	nur, bloß	**!** it's **only** a chicken the **only** chicken es ist **nur** ein Huhn das **einzige** Huhn
	city	(Groß-)Stadt	
	time **to** eat	Zeit zu essen	
	hear	hören	**!** **hear** = hören (können) **listen (to)** = zuhören, horchen **Listen**! Can you **hear** that noise?
p.78	sign	Schild; Zeichen	
	get the bus	den Bus nehmen	
	cafe	Café	
	left	links; nach links	˥eft
p.79	invitation (to)	Einladung (zu, nach)	Max, bring me the shoe!
	bring	bringen, mitbringen	
	5 pm	5 Uhr nachmittags/abends; 17 Uhr	
	5 am	5 Uhr morgens/vormittags	
	Dear …	Liebe … / Lieber …	*Dear Paul*
	hope	hoffen	*Plymouth is great.*
	thank you	danke (schön)	
	I'd love to come. (= I would love to come.)	Ich komme sehr gern. / Ich würde sehr gern kommen.	
	Best wishes	Viele Grüße, … (*Briefschluss*)	
	date	Datum	
	funny	lustig	
p.80	use	benutzen	
	dictionary	Wörterbuch, (alphabetisches) Wörterverzeichnis	
	poem	Gedicht	
p.82	wild	wild; wild lebend	
	line	Zeile	

Unit 5: All about Adam

p.88	**ferry**	Fähre	
	man, *pl* **men**	Mann, Männer	**!** one **man**, two **men**
	woman, *pl* **women**	Frau, Frauen	**!** one **woman**, two **women**
	boat	Boot; Schiff	
	some	einige, ein paar; etwas	
p.89	**harbour**	Hafen	
	summer	Sommer	
	France	Frankreich	
p.90	**cook**	kochen	
	never	nie, niemals →	
	wash up	abwaschen	
	of course	natürlich, selbstverständlich	
	him	ihn; ihm	Look, there's Zack. Can you see **him**? Let's help **him**.
	hard	schwer; schwierig; hart	This exercise isn't **hard**. You can do it. It's **hard** work to write a rap.
	must	müssen	**!** kein **-s** bei he/she/it: Adam **must** go.
	letter	Brief	
	phone	anrufen	
	need	brauchen	
	today	heute	
p.92	**boring**	langweilig	
	trouble	Ärger, Schwierigkeit(en)	
	dive	einen Kopfsprung machen	
	about	ungefähr	We get up at **about** 8.30 on Sundays.
	why?	warum?	
	club	Klub, Verein	
	send	schicken, senden	
	who?	wem?; wen?	**Who** do they see?
p.93	**rap**	rappen	
	drums	Schlagzeug; Trommeln	
	guitar	Gitarre	
	piano	Klavier	**!** Englisch: **play the** guitar / **the** drums / **the** piano Deutsch: **Gitarre / Schlagzeug / Klavier spielen**
	free	kostenlos	
	singer	Sänger/in	
	instrument	Instrument	
	sing	singen	

Box (adverbs of frequency):
never — sometimes — often — always

p.94	**difference**	Unterschied
	make a difference	etwas bewirken, etwas ausmachen
	it **was** Friday	es war Freitag
	they **were** on the bus	sie waren im Bus

→

I am/she is you/they are	I/she **was** you/they **were**

	face	Gesicht
	they **laughed**	sie lachten; sie haben gelacht
	he **said**	er sagte; er hat gesagt
	nothing	nichts
	minute	Minute
	angry	wütend, ärgerlich
	she **asked**	sie fragte; sie hat gefragt
	mean	gemein, fies
	life, *pl* **lives**	*(das)* Leben, *(die)* Leben

! one **life** – nine **lives**

	for example	zum Beispiel
	battle	Wettstreit, Battle *(im Rap)*
p.95	**nervous**	nervös, aufgeregt
	Well done.	Gut gemacht!
	proud (of)	stolz (auf)

Well done, Max. I'm proud of you.

	he **wasn't** (= he **was not**)	er war nicht
p.96	**food**	Essen, Lebensmittel; Futter
	drink	Getränk
	customer	Kunde, Kundin
	cheese	Käse
	chips *(pl)*	Pommes frites
	soup	Suppe
	scone	*kleines rundes Milchbrötchen, leicht süß, oft mit Rosinen*
	jam	Marmelade
	cream	Sahne
	salad	Salat *(als Gericht oder Beilage)*
	tea	Tee
	coffee	Kaffee
	juice	Saft
	water	Wasser
	Anything else?	Sonst noch etwas?

Can I help you? — Four scones, please. — Anything else? — scones

a **bottle (of …)**	eine Flasche …	
orange	Orange	
menu	Speisekarte	
p.97 **soon**	bald	
kiss	Kuss	
p.98 **under**	unter	→
in front of	vor	→
bag	Tasche	
behind	hinter	→
next to	neben	→
on the left	links, auf der linken Seite	
in the middle	in der Mitte	
on the right	rechts, auf der rechten Seite	
ball	Ball	

behind the TV **in front of** the TV

on the TV **under** the TV **next to** the TV

p.100 **Congratulations (on …)!**	Herzlichen Glückwunsch (zu …)!
prize	Preis *(Gewinn)*

! **prize** = Preis (in einem Wettbewerb)
price = (Kauf-)Preis

practise	üben
Good luck.	Viel Glück!
p.101 **village**	Dorf
difficult	schwierig

Das **DICTIONARY** besteht aus **zwei alphabetischen Wörterlisten**:
English – German (S. 174–181)   und   **German – English** (S. 182–188)

Im **English – German dictionary** kannst du nachschlagen, wenn du wissen möchtest, was ein englisches Wort bedeutet, wie man es ausspricht oder wie es geschrieben wird.

Im **Dictionary** werden folgende **Abkürzungen und Symbole** verwendet:

pl = *plural* (Mehrzahl)

° Mit diesem Kringel sind Wörter markiert, die nicht zum Lernwortschatz gehören.

Die **Fundstellenangaben** zeigen, wo ein Wort zum ersten Mal in *Highlight 1* vorkommt.
Die Ziffern in Klammern bezeichnen Seitenzahlen:

(8)   = Seite 8
1 (19) = Unit 1, Seite 19

Tipps zur Arbeit mit einem Wörterbuch findest du im Skills file auf Seite 144.

A

a [ə] ein/e (9)
about [əˈbaʊt] ungefähr 5 (92) **talk about** sprechen über 2 (44) **What about you?** Und du?/Was ist mit dir? (8) **write about** schreiben über 2 (42) °**ask about** fragen nach
°**access** [ˈækses] Zugang
°**act** [ækt] aufführen, spielen
activity [ækˈtɪvəti] Aktivität, Beschäftigung 3 (61)
°**add** [æd] hinzufügen, addieren
address [əˈdres] Adresse 2 (44)
°**adult** [ˈædʌlt] Erwachsene/r
Africa [ˈæfrɪkə] Afrika 1 (24)
after school [ɑːftə ˈskuːl] nach der Schule 2 (40)
afternoon [ɑːftəˈnuːn] Nachmittag 3 (54)
again [əˈgen] wieder, noch einmal 2 (40)
°**agree on** [əˈgriː ɒn] sich einigen auf
all [ɔːl] alle(s) 2 (46)
°**all around** [ɔːl əˈraʊnd] überall um … herum
alphabet [ˈælfəbet] Alphabet 2 (44)
°**alphabetical** [ælfəˈbetɪkl] alphabetisch
always [ˈɔːlweɪz] immer 3 (54)
am [æm] **I'm (= I am)** ich bin (8)
am [eɪˈem]: **5 am** 5 Uhr morgens/vormittags 4 (79)
°**America** [əˈmerɪkə] Amerika
an [ən] ein/e *(vor Vokalen)* (12)
and [ænd], [ənd] und (9)
angry [ˈæŋgri] wütend, ärgerlich 5 (94)

animal [ˈænɪml] Tier (12)
°**another** [əˈnʌðə] ein/e andere(r, s); noch ein/e
answer [ˈɑːnsə]:
1. Antwort 2 (43)
°**2.** antworten (auf), beantworten
Anything else? [eniθɪŋ ˈels] Sonst noch etwas? 5 (96)
°**appointment** [əˈpɔɪntmənt] Verabredung
April [ˈeɪprəl] April 3 (57)
are [ɑː]:
1. bist; seid 1 (10)
2. sind (11)
The mobiles are £ 10. Die Handys kosten 10 Pfund. 3 (60)
aren't = are not [ɑːnt], [ɑː ˈnɒt] bist nicht; seid nicht; sind nicht 1 (28)
°**around** [əˈraʊnd]:
1. um … herum
2. umher-
art [ɑːt] Kunst 1 (20)
°**as** [æz], [əz]: **as many as you can** so viele (wie) du kannst **the same as** dasselbe/das gleiche wie
ask [ɑːsk] fragen 3 (61) **she asked** sie fragte; sie hat gefragt 5 (94) °**ask about** fragen nach
at [æt], [ət]: **at Eggbuckland** auf der Eggbuckland-Schule 2 (36) **at MARTINS** bei MARTINS 1 (24) **at a restaurant** in einem Restaurant 2 (40) **at Ellie's house** bei Ellie daheim, bei Ellie zu Hause 2 (36) **at home** zu

Hause 1 (22) **at school** in der Schule 1 (16) **at the cinema** im Kino 2 (40)
August [ˈɔːgəst] August 3 (56)
away [əˈweɪ] weg, fort (14)

B

baby [ˈbeɪbi] Baby 2 (36)
babysitter [ˈbeɪbisɪtə] Babysitter 5 (89)
back [bæk]:
1. zurück 3 (59)
°**2.** Rückseite
bad [bæd] schlecht; schlimm 1 (23)
bag [bæg] Tasche 5 (88)
ball [bɔːl] Ball 5 (98)
banana [bəˈnɑːnə] Banane 2 (43)
banana skin [bəˈnɑːnə skɪn] Bananenschale 2 (43)
°**band** [bænd] Band, Musikgruppe
basketball [ˈbɑːskɪtbɔːl] Basketball 4 (75)
bathroom [ˈbɑːθruːm] Bad(ezimmer) 2 (34)
battle [ˈbætl] Wettstreit, Battle *(im Rap)* 5 (94)
be [biː] sein 2 (46)
beach [biːtʃ] Strand (9)
bear [beə] Bär (12)
°**beats per minute** [biːts pɜː ˈmɪnɪt] *(Musik)* Schläge pro Minute
because [bɪˈkɒz] weil 4 (75)
bed [bed] Bett 2 (39)
bedroom [ˈbedruːm] Schlafzimmer 2 (34)
before [bɪˈfɔː] vor *(zeitlich)* 1 (22) **before you read** bevor du liest 1 (22)
°**begin** [bɪˈgɪn] anfangen, beginnen

behind [bɪ'haɪnd] hinter 5 (98)

°**belong** [bɪ'lɒŋ] (hin)gehören

best [best] beste(r, s); am besten 1 (18) **Best wishes** Viele Grüße, … *(Briefschluss)* 4 (79)

°**better** ['betə] besser

big [bɪg] groß (13)

bike [baɪk] Fahrrad (13)

bird [bɜːd] Vogel (12)

birthday ['bɜːθdeɪ] Geburtstag 2 (40) **Happy birthday!** Herzlichen Glückwunsch zum Geburtstag! 3 (58) **It's her birthday.** Sie hat Geburtstag. 2 (40)

black [blæk] schwarz (10)

blue [bluː] blau (10)

°**board** [bɔːd] Tafel

boat [bəʊt] Boot; Schiff 5 (88)

book [bʊk]:
1. Buch 2 (47)
°2. buchen, reservieren

boring ['bɔːrɪŋ] langweilig 5 (92)

borrow ['bɒrəʊ] (aus)leihen, sich borgen 1 (26)

bossy ['bɒsi] herrisch 2 (38)

bottle ['bɒtl] Flasche 5 (96)

bowling ['bəʊlɪŋ]: **go bowling** Bowling spielen gehen 3 (56)

box [bɒks] Box, Kasten 1 (25)

boy [bɔɪ] Junge 1 (16)

break [breɪk] Pause 1 (21)

breakfast ['brekfəst] Frühstück 3 (64) °**have breakfast** frühstücken

bring [brɪŋ] bringen, mitbringen 4 (79)

British ['brɪtɪʃ] britisch 3 (60)

brochure ['brəʊʃə] Broschüre, Prospekt 1 (24)

brother ['brʌðə] Bruder 1 (18)

brown [braʊn] braun (10)

°**brush** [brʌʃ] bürsten

°**budgie** ['bʌdʒi] Wellensittich

bull [bʊl] Bulle 4 (77)

bus [bʌs] Bus 3 (64)

°**bus stop** ['bʌs stɒp] Bushaltestelle

°**busy** ['bɪzi]: **the cafe was busy** im Café war viel los

but [bʌt] aber (13)

°**butter** ['bʌtə] Butter

buy [baɪ] kaufen 1 (24)

by [baɪ]: **go by bus** mit dem Bus fahren 3 (64)

Bye. [baɪ] Tschüs. 1 (17)

C

cafe ['kæfeɪ] Café 4 (78)

°**cake** [keɪk] Kuchen

calculator ['kælkjuleɪtə] Taschenrechner 1 (24)

calendar ['kælɪndə] Kalender 3 (57)

camera ['kæmərə] Fotoapparat; Kamera (13)

can [kæn], [kən] können (9)

can't (= cannot) [kɑːnt], ['kænɒt] nicht können 4 (75)

canteen [kæn'tiːn] (Schul-)Mensa, Kantine 1 (23)

car [kɑː] Auto 1 (16)

card [kɑːd] Karte 1 (25)

°**careful** ['keəfl] vorsichtig

cat [kæt] Katze (12)

CD [siː'diː] CD 4 (79)

chair [tʃeə] Stuhl 2 (39)

°**check** [tʃek] (über)prüfen, kontrollieren

cheese [tʃiːz] Käse 5 (96)

°**chess** [tʃes] Schach

chicken ['tʃɪkɪn] Huhn; (Brat-)Hähnchen 4 (70)

child, *pl* **children** [tʃaɪld], ['tʃɪldrən] Kind, Kinder 4 (70)

chipmunk ['tʃɪpmʌŋk] Streifenhörnchen 4 (76)

chips *(pl)* [tʃɪps] Pommes frites 5 (96)

°**chocolate** ['tʃɒklət] Schokolade

°**chorus** ['kɔːrəs] Refrain *(in einem Lied)*

cinema ['sɪnəmə] Kino 2 (40)

°**circle** ['sɜːkl] Kreis, umkreisen

city ['sɪti] (Groß-)Stadt 4 (77)

class [klɑːs] (Schul-)Klasse (8)

class teacher ['klɑːs tiːtʃə] Klassenlehrer/in 1 (19)

classroom ['klɑːsruːm] Klassenraum 1 (25)

clock [klɒk] Uhr 4 (73)

°**close** [kləʊz] schließen, zumachen

°**clothes** [kləʊðz] Kleidung

club [klʌb] Klub, Verein 5 (92)

coffee ['kɒfi] Kaffee 5 (96)

°**cold** [kəʊld] kalt

°**collage** ['kɒlɑːʒ] Collage

°**collect** [kə'lekt] sammeln

°**college** ['kɒlɪdʒ] Fach(hoch)schule

colour ['kʌlə] Farbe (10)

come [kʌm] (mit)kommen 3 (59) °**come in** hereinkommen °**come to** kommen zu/nach °**the sea comes in** die Flut kommt, das Wasser steigt

°**community college** [kə'mjuːnəti kɒlɪdʒ] weiterführende Schule *(GB)*

°**complete** [kəm'pliːt] vervollständigen

computer [kəm'pjuːtə] Computer (13)

concert ['kɒnsət] Konzert 3 (58)

Congratulations (on …)! [kəngrætʃu'leɪʃnz] Herzlichen Glückwunsch (zu …)! 5 (100)

cook [kʊk] kochen 5 (90)

cool [kuːl] cool 1 (23)

°**copy** ['kɒpi] kopieren, abschreiben

corner ['kɔːnə] Ecke 4 (71)

°**correct** [kə'rekt]:
1. korrekt
2. korrigieren

°**cost** [kɒst] kosten

country ['kʌntri] Land 4 (76) °**in the country** auf dem Land

cow [kaʊ] Kuh 4 (71)

crab [kræb] Krebs (8)

cream [kriːm] Sahne 5 (96)

crocodile ['krɒkədaɪl] Krokodil (12)

cushion ['kʊʃn] Kissen 2 (39)

customer ['kʌstəmə] Kunde, Kundin 5 (96)

cute [kjuːt] niedlich, süß 2 (36)

°**cycling** ['saɪklɪŋ] Radfahren

D

dad [dæd] Papa, Vati 2 (34)

dancing ['dɑːnsɪŋ] *(das)* Tanzen (11)

dangerous ['deɪndʒərəs] gefährlich 4 (77)

date [deɪt] Datum 4 (79)

day [deɪ] Tag (14)

Dear … [dɪə] Liebe …/Lieber … 4 (79)

December [dɪ'sembə] Dezember 3 (56)

°**diagram** ['daɪəgræm] Diagramm

°**dialogue** ['daɪəlɒg] Dialog

dictionary ['dɪkʃənri] Wörterbuch, (alphabetisches) Wörterverzeichnis 4 (80)

difference ['dɪfrəns] Unterschied 5 (94) **make a difference** etwas bewirken, etwas ausmachen 5 (94)

different ['dɪfrənt] unterschiedlich, verschieden, anders (12)

difficult ['dɪfɪkəlt] schwierig 5 (101)

°**digital** ['dɪdʒɪtl] digital

dinner ['dɪnə] Abendessen 3 (64)

°**dirty** ['dɜːti] schmutzig

°**disabled** [dɪs'eɪbld] (körper)behindert

dive [daɪv]:
1. einen Kopfsprung machen 5 (92)
°2. (ein)tauchen

do [duː] machen, tun 3 (58) **I do my homework** ich mache (meine) Hausaufgaben 2 (38) **it doesn't have …** es hat kein/e … 4 (71) °**Which two things does Luca like?** Welche zwei Dinge mag Luca (gerne)?
dog [dɒg] Hund (12)
donkey ['dɒŋki] Esel 4 (70)
°door [dɔː] Tür
°dossier ['dɒsieɪ] Mappe, Dossier
°double circle [dʌbl 'sɜːkl] Doppelkreis
drama ['drɑːmə] Schauspiel, darstellende Kunst 1 (21)
°draw [drɔː] zeichnen
°drawing ['drɔːɪŋ] (das) Zeichnen
°dream house ['driːm haʊs] Traumhaus
drink [drɪŋk] Getränk 5 (96)
drums [drʌmz] Schlagzeug; Trommeln 5 (93)
duck [dʌk] Ente 4 (71)
DVD [diːviːˈdiː] DVD 4 (74)

E

°each [iːtʃ] jede(r, s) (einzelne)
°earlier ['ɜːliə] früher
early ['ɜːli] früh 3 (64)
eat [iːt] essen; fressen 4 (77)
eight [eɪt] acht (8)
elephant ['elɪfənt] Elefant (12)
eleven [ɪˈlevən] elf (8)
email ['iːmeɪl] E-Mail 4 (76)
end [end] Ende, Schluss 3 (59)
England ['ɪŋglənd] England (8)
English ['ɪŋglɪʃ] Englisch; englisch 1 (18)
°e-pal ['iːpæl] E-Mail-Freund/in
evening ['iːvnɪŋ] Abend 3 (54)
°every ['evri] jede(r, s)
everybody ['evribɒdi] jeder; alle 4 (70)
°everything ['evriθɪŋ] alles
example [ɪgˈzɑːmpl] Beispiel 5 (94) **for example** zum Beispiel 5 (94)
excited [ɪkˈsaɪtɪd] aufgeregt, gespannt 4 (76)
exercise ['eksəsaɪz] Übung, Aufgabe 1 (24)
exercise book ['eksəsaɪz bʊk] Schulheft, Übungsheft 1 (24)
expensive [ɪkˈspensɪv] teuer 3 (55)
°eye [aɪ] Auge

F

face [feɪs] Gesicht 5 (94)
fall [fɔːl] fallen; hinfallen 3 (59)

°false [fɔːls] falsch, unrichtig
°fame [feɪm] Ruhm
family ['fæməli] Familie 2 (36) **family tree** (Familien-)Stammbaum 2 (37)
farm [fɑːm] Bauernhof 4 (70)
°fast [fɑːst] schnell
favourite ['feɪvərɪt] Lieblings- (13) **favourite thing** Lieblingssache (13)
February ['februəri] Februar 3 (56)
fed up [fed ʌp]: **feel fed up** genervt sein, sauer sein; die Nase voll haben 4 (74)
feed [fiːd] füttern 4 (72)
feel [fiːl] sich fühlen; fühlen 4 (74)
ferry ['feri] Fähre 5 (88)
field [fiːld] Feld; Weide 4 (77)
fifty ['fɪfti] fünfzig 3 (60)
film [fɪlm] Film 3 (61)
°find [faɪnd] finden **find out** herausfinden
fine [faɪn] gut, schön 1 (17) **I'm fine.** Es geht mir gut. 1 (17)
°finish ['fɪnɪʃ]:
1. beenden, enden
2. Ende, Ziel
firefighter ['faɪəfaɪtə] Feuerwehrmann, Feuerwehrfrau 3 (64)
°fireworks (show) ['faɪəwɜːks] Feuerwerk
first [fɜːst] zuerst 3 (59) **first (= 1st)** erste, erster, erstes 1 (17)
fish [fɪʃ] Fisch(e) (12)
five [faɪv] fünf (8)
flat [flæt] Wohnung 2 (34)
flat-screen TV ['flæt skriːn tiː viː] Flachbildfernseher 2 (39)
°flavour ['fleɪvə] Geschmack(srichtung)
°focus ['fəʊkəs] Schwerpunkt **focus on language** (etwa) Schwerpunkt: Sprache
food [fuːd] Essen, Lebensmittel; Futter 5 (96)
football ['fʊtbɔːl] Fußball (11) **playing football** Fußballspielen (11)
for [fɔː], [fə] für 1 (24) °**for one minute** eine Minute lang
forgot [fəˈgɒt]: **I forgot my homework.** Ich habe meine Hausaufgaben vergessen. 2 (43)
°form [fɔːm] Form
four [fɔː] vier (8)
fourteen [fɔːˈtiːn] vierzehn (8)
France [frɑːns] Frankreich 5 (89)
free [friː] kostenlos 5 (93) **Are you free at one o'clock?** Hast du um

ein Uhr Zeit? 3 (61) °**for free** kostenlos
French [frentʃ] Französisch; französisch 1 (21)
Friday ['fraɪdeɪ], ['fraɪdi] Freitag 1 (21)
friend [frend] Freund/in 1 (18)
°friendly ['frendli] freundlich, nett
from [frɒm] aus (8) **from Monday to Friday** von Montag bis Freitag 4 (72) **a text from mum** eine SMS von Mama 2 (41)
front: in front of [ɪn ˈfrʌnt əv] vor 5 (98)
°fruit [fruːt] Obst
°full [fʊl]: **in full sentences** in ganzen Sätzen
fun [fʌn]: **they're fun** es macht Spaß, mit ihnen zusammenzusein 2 (47) °**… is fun** … macht Spaß
funny ['fʌni] lustig 4 (79)
°fur [fɜː] Fell (Tiere)
°fuss [fʌs]: **make a fuss** Theater/Wirbel machen

G

game [geɪm] Spiel (9)
garage ['gærɑːʒ] Garage 3 (60) **garage sale** Garagenflohmarkt (privater Flohmarkt) 3 (60)
garden ['gɑːdn] Garten 2 (34)
geography [dʒiˈɒgrəfi] Geografie, Erdkunde 1 (20)
German ['dʒɜːmən] Deutsch; deutsch 1 (26)
Germany ['dʒɜːməni] Deutschland (8)
get [get] bekommen, kriegen 3 (60) **get the bus** den Bus nehmen 4 (78) **get up** aufstehen 3 (64) °**get out** aussteigen
girl [gɜːl] Mädchen 1 (16)
°give [gɪv] geben
go [gəʊ] gehen; fahren (14) **go away** weggehen (14)
°goat [gəʊt] Ziege
°goldfish ['gəʊldfɪʃ] Goldfisch(e)
good [gʊd] gut 1 (17) **Good luck.** Viel Glück! 5 (100) **Good morning.** Guten Morgen. 1 (18) **Have a good day.** Ich wünsche dir einen schönen Tag./Schönen Tag noch. 1 (17) °**good at reading** gut im Lesen
goodbye [gʊdˈbaɪ] auf Wiedersehen (14)
grandma ['grænmɑː] Oma 2 (37)
grandpa ['grænpɑː] Opa 2 (37)

°**grass** [grɑːs] Gras
great [greɪt] großartig, toll (13)
green [griːn] grün (10)
group [gruːp] Gruppe (13) **group work** Gruppenarbeit (13)
°**guess** [ges] (er)raten
°**guinea pig** ['gɪni pɪg] Meerschweinchen
guitar [gɪ'tɑː] Gitarre 5 (93)
°**guys** [gaɪz] Leute (als Anrede verwendet)

H

hamster ['hæmstə] Hamster (12)
°**hand** [hænd] Hand
happy ['hæpi] glücklich, froh 2 (38) **Happy birthday!** Herzlichen Glückwunsch zum Geburtstag! 3 (58)
harbour ['hɑːbə] Hafen 5 (89)
hard [hɑːd] schwer; schwierig; hart 5 (90)
has [hæz] , [həz] hat 1 (22)
have [hæv] haben (12) **Have a good day.** Ich wünsche dir einen schönen Tag./Schönen Tag noch. 1 (17)
he [hiː] er 1 (18) **he's (= he is)** er ist 1 (18)
hear [hɪə] hören 4 (77)
Hello. [hə'ləʊ] Hallo. (14)
help [help]:
  1. helfen (14/158)
  2. Hilfe (14)
her [hɜː]: **her dad** ihr Vater 2 (34) °**for her** für sie (weibliche Person) °**with her** mit ihr
here [hɪə] hier; hierher 1 (20) **Here you are.** Bitte schön./Hier, bitte. 1 (26) °**here's (= here is)** hier ist
Hi! [haɪ] Hallo. (8)
°**hide** [haɪd] sich verstecken
high school ['haɪ skuːl] (GB etwa:) Gesamtschule 2 (36)
°**highlight** ['haɪlaɪt] Höhepunkt, Schlaglicht
him [hɪm] ihn; ihm 5 (90)
hip hop ['hɪp hɒp] Hip-Hop 5 (100)
his [hɪz]: **his partner** sein Partner, seine Partnerin 2 (36)
history ['hɪstri] Geschichte 1 (21)
hobby ['hɒbi] Hobby (11)
holidays ['hɒlədeɪz] Ferien (14)
home [həʊm] nach Hause 3 (64) **at home** zu Hause 1 (22)
homework ['həʊmwɜːk] Hausaufgabe/n 2 (38) **I forgot my homework.** Ich habe meine Hausaufgaben vergessen. 2 (43)
hoodie ['hʊdi] Kapuzenpullover 3 (55)
hope [həʊp] hoffen 4 (79)
°**horse** [hɔːs] Pferd
hospital ['hɒspɪtl] Krankenhaus 3 (59)
°**hot** [hɒt] heiß, warm
house [haʊs] Haus 2 (34)
how [haʊ] wie 1 (17) **How are you?** Wie geht's?/Wie geht es dir/euch? 1 (17)
hundred ['hʌndrəd]: **a hundred, one hundred** (ein)hundert 3 (60)
°**hungry** ['hʌŋgri]: **I'm hungry.** Ich habe Hunger.

I

I [aɪ] ich (8) **I'm (= I am)** ich bin (8)
°**ice cream** [aɪs 'kriːm] (Speise-)Eis
ICT (information and communication technology) [aɪ siː 'tiː], [ɪnfəmeɪʃn ənd kəmjuːnɪkeɪʃn tek'nɒlədʒi] Informations- und Kommunikationstechnologie 1 (20)
idea [aɪ'dɪə] Idee 1 (23)
important [ɪm'pɔːtənt] wichtig 1 (22)
in [ɪn] in (8) **in English** auf Englisch 1 (25) **in the morning/afternoon/evening** am Morgen/Nachmittag/Abend 3 (54) °**in the country** auf dem Land
instrument ['ɪnstrəmənt] Instrument 5 (93)
°**interesting** ['ɪntrəstɪŋ] interessant
interview ['ɪntəvjuː] Interview 1 (26)
°**into** ['ɪntu], ['ɪntə] in (… hinein)
invitation (to) [ɪnvɪ'teɪʃn] Einladung (zu, nach) 4 (79)
is [ɪz] ist (8) **he/she/it isn't (= is not)** er/sie/es ist nicht 1 (20) **The calculator is £ 1.** Der Taschenrechner kostet 1 Pfund. 3 (60)
it [ɪt] es, (bei Dingen und Tieren) er, sie (13) **it's (= it is)** es ist (bei Dingen und Tieren auch: er ist, sie ist) (13)

J

jam [dʒæm] Marmelade 5 (96)
January ['dʒænjuəri] Januar 3 (57)
jeans [dʒiːnz] Jeans 3 (55)
°**join** [dʒɔɪn] mitmachen (bei)
juice [dʒuːs] Saft 5 (96)

July [dʒu'laɪ] Juli 3 (57)
June [dʒuːn] Juni 3 (57)

K

kid [kɪd] Kind, Jugendliche/r 5 (94)
kiss [kɪs] Kuss 5 (97)
kitchen ['kɪtʃɪn] Küche 2 (34)
°**kitten** ['kɪtn] Kätzchen, Katzenbaby
know [nəʊ] wissen; kennen 1 (22)

L

°**label** ['leɪbl] Etikett, Schild(chen)
lamp [læmp] Lampe 2 (39)
°**language** ['læŋgwɪdʒ] Sprache **language file** Anhang zum Thema Sprache
laptop ['læptɒp] Laptop 1 (24)
last [lɑːst] letzte(r, s) (14)
late [leɪt] (zu) spät 4 (74) **my bus is late** mein Bus hat Verspätung 4 (74)
°**later** ['leɪtə] später
laugh [lɑːf] lachen 4 (76) **they laughed** sie lachten; sie haben gelacht 5 (94)
°**learn** [lɜːn] lernen **learning words** Wörter lernen
°**learner log** [lɜːnə 'lɒg] Lern-Tagebuch
°**leave** [liːv] (jemanden) verlassen; weggehen
left [left] links; nach links 4 (78) **on the left** links, auf der linken Seite 5 (98)
leg [leg] Bein 3 (59)
lesson ['lesn] (Unterrichts-)Stunde 1 (20)
let's (= let us) [lets], ['let əs] lass(t) uns 4 (76)
letter ['letə]:
  1. Brief 5 (91)
  °**2.** Buchstabe
life, pl lives [laɪf], [laɪvz] (das) Leben, (die) Leben 5 (94)
like [laɪk] mögen (10) **I don't like …** ich mag … nicht (10) **I'd like (= I would like)** ich hätte gern, ich möchte (…) haben 2 (36) °**he likes …** er mag …
°**like** [laɪk] wie **like this** so, auf diese Art
line [laɪn] Zeile 4 (82)
°**list** [lɪst] Liste
listen ['lɪsn] zuhören 2 (43) **listen to** (sich etwas) anhören 2 (43)
°**listening** (das) Zuhören
live [lɪv] leben, wohnen 2 (34) **she lives** sie lebt/wohnt 2 (34)

°**live** [laɪv] live

living room [ˈlɪvɪŋ ruːm] Wohn-zimmer 2 (34)

°**llama** [ˈlɑːmə] Lama

look [lʊk]:

1. sehen, schauen 1 (23)

°**2.** aussehen

look after sich kümmern um; aufpassen auf 4 (72) **look at** anschauen 2 (38)

lots of [ˈlɒts əv] viel(e) 4 (70)

love [lʌv] lieben, sehr mögen 1 (28) **I'd love to come. (= I would love to come.)** Ich komme sehr gern. / Ich würde sehr gern kommen. 4 (79)

luck [lʌk]: **Good luck.** Viel Glück! 5 (100)

lucky [ˈlʌki]: **you're lucky** du hast Glück 2 (36)

lunch [lʌntʃ] Mittagessen 1 (21) **have lunch** (zu) Mittag essen 3 (64)

M

madhouse [ˈmædhaʊs] Irren-haus 2 (36)

°**magazine** [mægəˈziːn] Zeitschrift

make [meɪk] machen, herstel-len 3 (64) °**Do they make good pets?** Eignen sie sich gut als Haustiere? °**I make her purr** ich bringe sie zum Schnurren

man, pl men [mæn], [men] Mann, Männer 5 (98)

°**many** [ˈmeni] viele **how many?** wie viele?

March [mɑːtʃ] März 3 (57)

market [ˈmɑːkɪt] Markt 3 (54)

°**match with** [ˈmætʃ wɪð] zuordnen

maths [mæθs] Mathematik 1 (20)

May [meɪ] Mai 3 (57)

me [mi] mir; mich 2 (40) **it's me** ich bin's (14)

mean [miːn] gemein, fies 5 (94)

°**mean** [miːn] bedeuten

°**meat** [miːt] Fleisch

°**mediation** [miːdiˈeɪʃn] Vermitt-lung, Sprachmittlung

meet [miːt] kennenlernen; (sich) treffen 3 (54)

men [men] Männer 5 (98)

menu [ˈmenjuː] Speisekarte 5 (96)

°**message** [ˈmesɪdʒ] Nachricht

messy [ˈmesi] unordentlich 2 (38)

middle [ˈmɪdl] Mitte 5 (98) **in the middle** in der Mitte 5 (98)

°**milk** [mɪlk] Milch

minute [ˈmɪnɪt] Minute 5 (94)

miss [mɪs] vermissen 2 (36)

Miss [mɪs]: **Miss Borowski** Frau Borowski 1 (22)

mobile (phone) [məʊbaɪl ˈfəʊn] Handy (13)

Monday [ˈmʌndeɪ], [ˈmʌndi] Montag 1 (21)

money [ˈmʌni] Geld 3 (60)

monkey [ˈmʌŋki] Affe (12)

°**month** [mʌnθ] Monat

°**more** [mɔː] mehr, weitere **six more** noch sechs

morning [ˈmɔːnɪŋ] Mor-gen 1 (18) **Good morning.** Guten Morgen. 1 (18)

Mr [ˈmɪstə]: **Mr Smith** Herr Smith 1 (19)

Mrs [ˈmɪsɪz]: **Mrs Smith** Frau Smith 1 (19)

Ms [mɪz]: **Ms Lee** Frau Lee 1 (18)

°**much** [mʌtʃ] viel

mum [mʌm] Mama, Mutti 2 (34)

music [ˈmjuːzɪk] Musik 1 (21)

°**musician** [mjuˈzɪʃn] Musiker/in

must [mʌst] müssen 5 (90)

my [maɪ] mein/e (13)

N

name [neɪm] Name (8)

°**narrator** [nəˈreɪtə] Erzähler/in

°**near** [nɪə] in der Nähe von, nahe (bei)

°**need** [niːd] brauchen 5 (91)

nervous [ˈnɜːvəs] nervös, aufge-regt 5 (95)

network [ˈnetwɜːk] Netz; Wort-netz 1 (25)

never [ˈnevə] nie, niemals 5 (90)

new [njuː] neu (13)

news [njuːz] Nachrichten 2 (40)

next [nekst] nächste(r, s) 1 (26) **next to** neben 5 (98)

nice [naɪs] nett, schön 2 (34)

night [naɪt]: **at night** nachts, in der Nacht 4 (76)

nine [naɪn] neun (8)

no [nəʊ] kein/e 1 (18) °**no more …** kein/e … mehr

no [nəʊ] nein (14)

°**nobody** [ˈnəʊbədi] niemand

noise [nɔɪz] Geräusch; Lärm 4 (77)

noisy [ˈnɔɪzi] laut, voller Lärm 2 (38)

normal [ˈnɔːml] normal 4 (75)

not [nɒt] nicht; kein/e 1 (20)

°**note** [nəʊt] notieren

°**notes** [nəʊts] Notizen

nothing [ˈnʌθɪŋ] nichts 5 (94)

November [nəʊˈvembə] Novem-ber 3 (57)

now [naʊ] nun, jetzt 1 (20)

number [ˈnʌmbə] Nummer 2 (44)

O

o'clock [əˈklɒk]: **at one o'clock** um 1 Uhr / um 13 Uhr 3 (61)

October [ɒkˈtəʊbə] Oktober 3 (57)

°**odd word out** [ɒd wɜːd ˈaʊt] Wort, das nicht zu den anderen passt

of [ɒv], [əv]: **the last day of the holidays** der letzte Tag der Ferien (14)

of course [əv ˈkɔːs] natürlich, selbstverständlich 5 (90)

often [ˈɒfn], [ˈɒftən] oft 2 (46)

oh [əʊ] Null *(im gesprochenen Englisch)* 4 (73)

OK [əʊˈkeɪ]: **I'm OK.** Es geht mir gut. 1 (17) °**OK at words** ganz gut bei Vokabeln

old [əʊld] alt (13)

on [ɒn] auf 4 (71) **on Monday** am Montag 1 (21) **on my birthday** an meinem Geburtstag 3 (52) **on the bus** im Bus 4 (76) °**on the phone** am Telefon

one [wʌn] eins (8)

only [ˈəʊnli] nur, bloß 4 (77) **the only student** der einzige Schü-ler / die einzige Schülerin 4 (75)

°**open** [ˈəʊpən] offen, geöffnet **opening times** Öffnungszeiten

or [ɔː] oder 1 (19)

orange [ˈɒrɪndʒ]:

1. orange (10)

2. Orange 5 (96)

°**order** [ˈɔːdə] Reihenfolge

°**organize** [ˈɔːgənaɪz] organisieren

other [ˈʌðə] andere(r, s) 4 (72)

our [ˈaʊə], [ɑː] unser/e 1 (16)

outside [aʊtˈsaɪd] draußen; nach draußen 4 (72)

P

p [piː]: **50p** 50 Pence 3 (60)

page (= p.) [peɪdʒ] (Buch-, Heft-) Seite 2 (42)

°**pair** [peə] Paar

°**paper** [ˈpeɪpə] Papier **piece of paper** Stück Papier, Zettel

parents [ˈpeərənts] Eltern 3 (56)

park [pɑːk] Park 3 (52)

°**parrot** [ˈpærət] Papagei

°**part** [pɑːt] Teil

partner [ˈpɑːtnə] Partner/in (8) **partner work** Partnerarbeit (12)

party [ˈpɑːti] Party 3 (56) **have a party** eine Party feiern 3 (56)

PE (physical education) [piː ˈiː], [ˈfɪzɪkl edʒuˈkeɪʃn] (Schul-)Sport 1 (20)

°**peahen** [ˈpiːhen] Pfauhenne, weiblicher Pfau

pen [pen] Kugelschreiber, Stift; Füller 1 (24)

pencil [ˈpensl] Bleistift 1 (24)

pencil case [ˈpensl keɪs] Federmäppchen 1 (24)

pencil sharpener [ˈpensl ʃɑːpnə] Bleistiftanspitzer 1 (24)

people [ˈpiːpl] Leute, Menschen 1 (23)

pet [pet] Haustier 4 (70) **pets corner** Streichelzoo 4 (70)

phone [fəʊn]:
1. anrufen 5 (91)
2. Telefon 2 (44)

°**phone code** [ˈfəʊn kəʊd] Vorwahlnummer

phone number [ˈfəʊn nʌmbə] Telefonnummer 2 (44)

photo [ˈfəʊtəʊ] Foto 2 (34)

phrase [freɪz] Ausdruck, (Rede-)Wendung 1 (25)

piano [piˈænəʊ] Klavier 5 (93)

°**pick** [pɪk] (aus)wählen **pick up** aufheben

°**picnic** [ˈpɪknɪk] Picknick

picture [ˈpɪktʃə] Bild 2 (43)

°**piece of paper** [piːs əv ˈpeɪpə] Stück Papier, Zettel

pig [pɪg] Schwein 4 (71)

°**pinch** [pɪntʃ] zwicken

pink [pɪŋk] rosa (10)

place [pleɪs] Ort, Platz, Stelle 2 (38)

play [pleɪ] spielen 3 (61) **playing football** Fußballspielen (11) **playing games** Spiele spielen (11)

please [pliːz] bitte 1 (22)

pm [piːˈem]: **5 pm** 5 Uhr nachmittags/abends/17 Uhr 4 (79)

poem [ˈpəʊɪm] Gedicht 4 (80)

°**point at** [ˈpɔɪnt ət] zeigen auf

pony [ˈpəʊni] Pony (12)

°**pool** [puːl] Schwimmbad

°**poor** [pɔː], [pʊə] arm

°**pop (music)** [ˈpɒp mjuːzɪk] Pop(musik)

poster [ˈpəʊstə] Poster (11)

pound (£) [paʊnd] Pfund (britische Währung) 1 (24)

°**practice** [ˈpræktɪs] Übung(en)

practise [ˈpræktɪs] üben 5 (100)

present [ˈpreznt] Geschenk 3 (55)

°**pretty** [ˈprɪti] hübsch

price [praɪs] (Kauf-)Preis 3 (60)

prince [prɪns] Prinz 1 (29)

principal [ˈprɪnsəpl] Schulleiter/in 1 (22)

prize [praɪz] Preis (Gewinn) 5 (100)

problem [ˈprɒbləm] Problem 2 (38)

programme [ˈprəʊgræm] (Fernseh-)Sendung 2 (40)

°**progress** [ˈprəʊgres] Fortschritt(e)

proud (of) [praʊd] stolz (auf) 5 (95)

pullover [ˈpʊləʊvə] Pullover 2 (38)

°**puppy** [ˈpʌpi] (Hunde-)Welpe

°**purr** [pɜː] schnurren (Katze)

°**put** [pʊt] stellen, legen, etwas wohin tun **put in** einsetzen

Q

question [ˈkwestʃən] Frage 3 (61)

quiz [kwɪz] Quiz 1 (28)

R

rabbit [ˈræbɪt] Kaninchen (12)

rap [ræp]:
1. Rap 1 (21)
2. rappen 5 (93)

°**rapper** [ˈræpə] Rapper/in

rat [ræt] Ratte (12)

read [riːd] lesen 1 (22) **reading** (das) Lesen (11)

real [rɪəl] echt, wirklich 2 (36)

really nice [ˈrɪəli] wirklich nett 2 (41)

red [red] rot (10)

remember [rɪˈmembə] daran denken, nicht vergessen; sich erinnern an 1 (22)

°**repeat** [rɪˈpiːt] wiederholen

°**reporter** [rɪˈpɔːtə] Reporter/in

restaurant [ˈrestrɒnt] Restaurant 2 (40)

ride [raɪd]: **ride a pony** auf einem Pony/ein Pony reiten 4 (70) **ride a bike** Rad fahren 3 (52) **riding** (das) Reiten (11)

right [raɪt] richtig 1 (21) **that's right** das stimmt, das ist richtig 1 (23)

right [raɪt] rechts 5 (98) **on the right** rechts, auf der rechten Seite 5 (98)

road [rəʊd] Straße (Landstraße zwischen Orten, aber auch in Ortschaften) 2 (34)

rock (music) [ˈrɒk mjuːzɪk] Rock(musik) 5 (100)

°**role** [rəʊl] Rolle (Theater, Rollenspiel)

room [ruːm] Raum, Zimmer 2 (34)

rubber [ˈrʌbə] Radiergummi 1 (24)

°**rule** [ruːl] Regel

ruler [ˈruːlə] Lineal 1 (24)

°**run** [rʌn] rennen

S

said [sed]: **he said** er sagte; er hat gesagt 5 (94)

salad [ˈsæləd] Salat (als Gericht oder Beilage) 5 (96)

sale [seɪl] Verkauf; Schlussverkauf 3 (60)

°**same** [seɪm]: **the same as** dasselbe/das gleiche wie **the same words** dieselben/die gleichen Wörter

°**sand** [sænd] Sand

sandwich [ˈsænwɪtʃ] Sandwich 5 (96)

Saturday [ˈsætədeɪ], [ˈsætədi] Samstag 1 (25)

say [seɪ] sagen (10) **Ellie says** Ellie sagt (10) **he said** er sagte; er hat gesagt 5 (94)

scene [siːn] Szene 4 (76)

school [skuːl] Schule 1 (16)

science [ˈsaɪəns] Naturwissenschaft 1 (20)

scone [skɒn] kleines rundes Milchbrötchen, leicht süß, oft mit Rosinen 5 (96)

°**sea** [siː] Meer, (die) See

second [ˈsekənd] zweite(r, s) 3 (57)

see [siː] sehen (9) **See you.** Bis dann./Tschüs. 1 (17)

send [send] schicken, senden 5 (92)

sentence [ˈsentəns] Satz 2 (42)

September [sepˈtembə] September 3 (56)

seven [ˈsevn] sieben (8)

seventeen [sevnˈtiːn] siebzehn 1 (28)

°**share** [ʃeə] teilen; austauschen

sharpener [ˈʃɑːpnə] Anspitzer 1 (24)

she [ʃiː] sie (weibliche Person) 1 (18) **she's (= she is)** sie ist 1 (18)

sheep [ʃiːp] Schaf(e) 4 (71)

shirt [ʃɜːt] Hemd 3 (55)

shoe [ʃuː] Schuh 2 (38)

shop [ʃɒp] Geschäft, Laden 3 (52)

shopping [ˈʃɒpɪŋ]: **go shopping** einkaufen gehen 3 (52)

°**shopping list** [ˈʃɒpɪŋ lɪst] Einkaufsliste

shoulder [ˈʃəʊldə] Schulter 4 (76)

show [ʃəʊ]:
1. Show, Vorführung, Aufführung 3 (62)
°**2.** zeigen

Shut up! [ʃʌt ˈʌp] Halt den Mund! 3 (58)

sign [saɪn] Schild; Zeichen 4 (78)

silly [ˈsɪli] albern, dumm, blöd 2 (46)

sing [sɪŋ] singen 5 (93)

singer [ˈsɪŋə] Sänger/in 5 (93)

sister [ˈsɪstə] Schwester 1 (18)

six [sɪks] sechs (8)

skateboarding [ˈskeɪtbɔːdɪŋ] (das) Skateboardfahren (11)

°**skill** [skɪl] Fähigkeit, Fertigkeit; Lern- und Arbeitstechnik **skills file** Anhang mit Lern- und Arbeitstechniken

sleepover [ˈsliːpəʊvə] Schlafparty 4 (76)

small [smɔːl] klein (13)

°**SMS stop code** [es em es ˈstɒp kəʊd] *Code für Bushaltestellen, mit dem man per SMS die Abfahrtszeiten der Busse erfragen kann*

°**smuggler** [ˈsmʌglə] Schmuggler/in

snack [snæk] Snack, kleine Mahlzeit 4 (72)

snake [sneɪk] Schlange (12)

so [səʊ]: **not so good** nicht so gut 2 (50)

some [sʌm], [səm] einige, ein paar; etwas 5 (94)

something [ˈsʌmθɪŋ] etwas 3 (58)

sometimes [ˈsʌmtaɪmz] manchmal 3 (52)

song [sɒŋ] Lied (9)

soon [suːn] bald 5 (97)

°**sore** [sɔː] schmerzhaft **I have a sore leg.** Mein Bein tut weh.

Sorry. / I'm sorry. [ˈsɒri] Tut mir leid. / Entschuldigung. 1 (22)

sound [saʊnd] klingen, sich anhören 3 (61) **Sounds fun.** Hört sich gut an. / Klingt, als ob es Spaß macht. 3 (61)

soup [suːp] Suppe 5 (96)

speak [spiːk]: **speak (to)** sprechen (mit) 1 (26) **speaking to friends** mit Freunden/Freundinnen sprechen 1 (26)

°**special** [ˈspeʃl] besondere(r, s) **special offer** Sonderangebot

spell [spel] buchstabieren 2 (44)

sport [spɔːt] Sport; Sportart (11) **sports shop** Sportgeschäft 3 (55)

°**stage** [steɪdʒ] Bühne

start [stɑːt]:
1. anfangen 1 (28)
°**2.** Anfang, Start
it starts er/sie/es fängt an 1 (28)

stay [steɪ] bleiben 3 (56)

°**step** [step] Schritt, Stufe

stepbrother [ˈstepbrʌðə] Stiefbruder 2 (37)

stepdad [ˈstepdæd] Stiefvater 2 (36)

stepmum [ˈstepmʌm] Stiefmutter 2 (36/163)

stepsister [ˈstepsɪstə] Stiefschwester 2 (37)

°**stick insect** [ˈstɪk ɪnsekt] Stabheuschrecke

°**stoat** [stəʊt] Hermelin

°**stop** [stɒp] anhalten; stehen bleiben; aufhören (mit)

story [ˈstɔːri] Geschichte (14)

street [striːt] Straße (in Ortschaften) 2 (34)

student [ˈstjuːdnt] Schüler/in; Student/in 1 (28)

°**studio** [ˈstjuːdiəʊ] Studio

stupid [ˈstjuːpɪd] dumm, blöd; albern (14)

summer [ˈsʌmə] Sommer 5 (89)

Sunday [ˈsʌndeɪ], [ˈsʌndi] Sonntag 1 (25)

°**supported by** [səˈpɔːtɪd baɪ] unterstützt von

sure [ʃʊə] sicher 1 (26)

surprise [səˈpraɪz] Überraschung 2 (46)

°**swap** [swɒp] tauschen

°**sweet** [swiːt] süß

sweets [swiːts] Bonbons, Süßigkeiten (10)

°**swim** [swɪm] schwimmen **swimming** (das) Schwimmen (11) **go swimming** schwimmen gehen 3 (52)

°**symbol** [ˈsɪmbl] Symbol

T

table [ˈteɪbl]:
1. Tisch 2 (38)
°**2.** Tabelle

°**table tennis** [ˈteɪbl tenɪs] Tischtennis

°**tae kwon do** [taɪ kwɒn ˈdəʊ] Taekwondo

°**take** [teɪk]: **take the dog out** mit dem Hund rausgehen

talk [tɔːk]: **talk about** sprechen über 2 (44) °**talk (to)** sprechen (mit) °**talking to friends** mit Freunden sprechen

tea [tiː] Tee 5 (96)

teacher [ˈtiːtʃə] Lehrer/in 1 (16)

technology [tekˈnɒlədʒi] Technik, Technologie 1 (21)

teenager [ˈtiːneɪdʒə] Teenager 4 (75)

°**tell** [tel] erzählen, sagen

ten [ten] zehn (8)

terrible [ˈterəbl] schrecklich 3 (55)

°**test** [test] testen

text [tekst]:
1. eine SMS schicken 4 (74)
°**2.** Text
text (message) SMS 2 (41)

thank you [ˈθæŋk juː] danke (schön) 4 (79)

thanks [θæŋks] danke 1 (17)

that [ðæt]:
1. das (da) 1 (22)
°**2.** der, die, das (Relativpronomen)

the [ðə] der, die, das (8)

theatre [ˈθɪətə] Theater 1 (23)

°**their** [ðeə] ihr/e (Mehrzahl)

°**them** [ðem], [ðəm] sie, ihnen (Mehrzahl)

°**theme** [θiːm] Thema

then [ðen] dann 3 (55)

there [ðeə] da, dort; dahin, dorthin 3 (58) **there are …** es sind …/ es gibt … 4 (76) **there's** es ist …/ es gibt … 4 (76)

°**these (people)** [ðiːz] diese (Menschen) hier

they [ðeɪ] sie (Mehrzahl) 1 (18) **they're (= they are)** sie sind 1 (18)

thing [θɪŋ] Ding, Sache (13)

think [θɪŋk] denken, meinen, glauben 1 (23)

third [θɜːd] dritte(r, s) 3 (57)

thirteen [θɜːˈtiːn] dreizehn (8)

this [ðɪs] diese(r, s) (14) **This is …** Dies ist … / Das ist … (14)

three [θriː] drei (8)

through [θruː] durch 4 (77)

°**throw** [θrəʊ] werfen

Thursday [ˈθɜːzdeɪ], [ˈθɜːzdi] Donnerstag 1 (21)

°**tick** [tɪk] mit einem Häkchen versehen, ankreuzen

ticket [ˈtɪkɪt] Eintrittskarte, Fahrkarte 3 (58)

tie [taɪ] Krawatte 1 (22)

tiger [ˈtaɪgə] Tiger (12)

time [taɪm] Zeit; Uhrzeit 1 (21) **What's the time?** Wie spät ist es? 4 (73)

timetable [ˈtaɪmteɪbl] Stundenplan 1 (21)

tired [ˈtaɪəd] müde 2 (40)

to [tu], [tə] zu, nach, in 2 (40) **to the country** aufs Land 4 (76) **write to** schreiben an 2 (42) **from Monday to Friday** von Montag bis Freitag 4 (72) **go to dad's flat** in Papas Wohnung gehen 2 (40) **time to eat** Zeit zu essen 4 (77)

today [tə'deɪ] heute 5 (91)

°**together** [tə'geðə] zusammen

toilet ['tɔɪlət] Toilette 2 (34)

tomorrow [tə'mɒrəʊ] morgen 2 (40)

too [tuː] auch (11)

too small [tuː] zu klein 2 (38)

town [taʊn] Stadt 2 (40) **in town** in der Stadt 2 (40)

°**tractor** ['træktə] Traktor

trainer ['treɪnə] Sportschuh 3 (55)

°**training** ['treɪnɪŋ] Training

trampoline ['træmpəliːn] Trampolin 4 (71)

tree [triː] Baum 2 (37)

°**trip** [trɪp] Fahrt, Ausflug

trouble ['trʌbl] Ärger, Schwierigkeit(en) 5 (92)

°**true** [truː] wahr

T-shirt ['tiːʃɜːt] T-Shirt 2 (47)

Tuesday ['tjuːzdeɪ], ['tjuːzdi] Dienstag 1 (21)

°**Turkey** ['tɜːki] Türkei

TV [tiːˈviː] Fernseher (11)

twelve [twelv] zwölf (8)

two [tuː] zwei (8)

U

under ['ʌndə] unter 5 (98)

°**understand** [ʌndə'stænd] verstehen

unhappy [ʌn'hæpi] unglücklich 2 (38/164)

uniform ['juːnɪfɔːm] (Schul-)Uniform 1 (22)

unit ['juːnɪt] Unit 1 (28) **unit quiz** Unit-Quiz 1 (28)

upstairs [ʌp'steəz] oben; nach oben 2 (36)

us [ʌs], [əs] uns 4 (76)

use [juːz] benutzen 4 (80)

V

vegetables ['vedʒtəblz] Gemüse 3 (54)

°**verse** [vɜːs] Vers, Strophe (Lied)

very ['veri] sehr 2 (40)

°**viewing** ['vjuːɪŋ] (das) Fernsehen, (das) Betrachten von DVDs, Filmen usw.

village ['vɪlɪdʒ] Dorf 5 (101)

visitor ['vɪzɪtə] Besucher/in, Gast 4 (70)

°**vocabulary** [və'kæbjələri] Vokabelverzeichnis

W

°**wait for** ['weɪt fə] warten auf

wake [weɪk] wecken 4 (72)

walk [wɔːk] (zu Fuß) gehen, wandern 3 (64) °**walk around** umhergehen

°**wall** [wɔːl] Wand, Mauer

want [wɒnt] wollen 3 (59) **want to buy** kaufen wollen 3 (55)

wardrobe ['wɔːdrəʊb] Kleiderschrank 2 (39)

was [wɒz], [wəz] war 5 (94) **he wasn't (= he was not)** er war nicht 5 (95)

wash up [wɒʃ 'ʌp] abwaschen 5 (90)

watch [wɒtʃ] sich etwas anschauen; beobachten 4 (71) **watching TV** Fernsehen (11)

water ['wɔːtə] Wasser 5 (96)

we [wiː] wir 1 (18) **we're (= we are)** wir sind 1 (18)

Wednesday ['wenzdeɪ], ['wenzdi] Mittwoch 1 (21)

week [wiːk] Woche 2 (41)

weekday ['wiːkdeɪ] Werktag, Wochentag 5 (90)

weekend [wiːk'end] Wochenende 1 (25)

welcome ['welkəm]: **Welcome to Plymouth.** Willkommen in Plymouth! (10) **You're welcome.** Bitte, gern geschehen. / Nichts zu danken. 4 (73)

well [wel]: **Well done.** [wel 'dʌn] Gut gemacht! 5 (95) °**Well, ...** Nun, ... / Also, ...

were [wɜː], [wə] waren 5 (94)

wet [wet] nass 4 (76)

what [wɒt]:
1. was (8)
2. welche(r, s) (11)
What about you? Und du? / Was ist mit dir? (8) **What's ...? (= What is ...?)** Was ist ...? (8) °**What's your name?** Wie heißt du? (8)

wheelchair ['wiːltʃeə] Rollstuhl 4 (75)

when [wen]:
1. wann 3 (57)
2. wenn 4 (74)
When's (= when is) your birthday? Wann hast du Geburtstag? 3 (57)

where [weə] wo(hin) 1 (20)

°**which** [wɪtʃ] welche(r, s)

white [waɪt] weiß (10)

who? [huː]:
1. wem?; wen? 5 (92)
2. wer? 1 (18)
Who are you? Wer bist du? /

Wer seid ihr? 1 (18) °**who's (= who is)** wer ist

why? [waɪ] warum? 5 (92)

wild [waɪld] wild; wild lebend 4 (82)

will [wɪl] werden 5 (92) **I'll phone (= I will phone) ...** ich werde ... anrufen 5 (92)

wish [wɪʃ]: **Best wishes** Viele Grüße, ... (Briefschluss) 4 (79)

with [wɪð] mit 1 (28) **with Ellie** bei Ellie 2 (34)

woman, pl **women** ['wʊmən], ['wɪmɪn] Frau, Frauen 5 (98)

word [wɜːd] Wort 1 (23)

°**wordbank** ['wɜːdbæŋk] Wortbank (Sammlung von Wörtern zu einem Thema)

work [wɜːk]:
1. Arbeit (13)
2. arbeiten 2 (43)
3. funktionieren 4 (74)
at work bei der Arbeit, am Arbeitsplatz 3 (58) °**work hard** hart arbeiten

°**workshop** ['wɜːkʃɒp] Workshop (Kurs)

would [wʊd]: **I'd love to come. (= I would love to come.)** Ich komme sehr gern. / Ich würde sehr gern kommen. 4 (79) **I'd like (= I would like)** ich hätte gern, ich möchte (...) haben 2 (36)

write [raɪt] schreiben 2 (42)

°**writing** (das) Schreiben

wrong [rɒŋ] falsch 1 (21) **that's wrong** das stimmt nicht, das ist falsch 1 (23/161)

Y

yeah (= yes) [jeə] ja 4 (76)

°**year** [jɪə] Jahr

yellow ['jeləʊ] gelb (10)

yes [jes] ja (14/158)

yippee [jɪ'piː] hurra (15)

you [juː]:
1. dich; dir; euch; Sie; Ihnen (8)
2. du; ihr; Sie (8)
you're (= you are) du bist, ihr seid, Sie sind 1 (28)

°**young** [jʌŋ] jung

your [jɔː] dein/e, euer/eure (8)

°**yourself** [jə'self] du/dir/dich selbst

Z

zip wire ['zɪp waɪə] Seilrutsche 4 (71)

zoo [zuː] Zoo 3 (58)

Das **German – English dictionary** enthält den **Lernwortschatz** von *Highlight 1*.
Es kann dir eine erste Hilfe sein, wenn du vergessen hast, wie etwas auf Englisch heißt.

Wenn du wissen möchtest, wo das englische Wort zum ersten Mal in *Highlight 1* vorkommt,
dann kannst du im **English – German dictionary** (S. 174–181) nachschlagen.

Es werden folgende **Abkürzungen** und **Symbole** verwendet:

pl = plural (Mehrzahl)

A

Abend evening ['iːvnɪŋ]
Abendessen dinner ['dɪnə]
aber but [bʌt]
abwaschen wash up [wɒʃ 'ʌp]
acht eight [eɪt]
Adresse address [ə'dres]
Affe monkey ['mʌŋki]
Afrika Africa ['æfrɪkə]
Aktivität activity [æk'tɪvəti]
albern silly ['sɪli]; stupid ['stjuːpɪd]
alle everybody ['evrɪbɒdi] **alle(s)** all [ɔːl]
Alphabet alphabet ['ælfəbət]
alphabetisches Wörterverzeichnis dictionary ['dɪkʃənri]
alt old [əʊld]
am: am Arbeitsplatz at work [wɜːk] **am besten** best [best] **am Montag** on Monday [ɒn 'mʌndeɪ] **am Morgen/Nachmittag/Abend** in the morning/afternoon/evening
an: an meinem Geburtstag on my birthday **schreiben an** write to [tu], [tə]
andere(r, s) other ['ʌðə]
anders different ['dɪfrənt]
anfangen start [stɑːt] **er/sie/es fängt an** it starts [ɪt 'stɑːts]
anhören: (sich etwas) anhören listen to ['lɪsn tʊ], ['lɪsn tə] **Hört sich gut an.** Sounds fun. [fʌn] **sich anhören** sound [saʊnd]
anrufen phone [fəʊn]
anschauen look at ['lʊk ət] **sich etwas anschauen** watch [wɒtʃ]
Anspitzer sharpener ['ʃɑːpnə]
Antwort answer ['ɑːnsə]
April April ['eɪprəl]
Arbeit work [wɜːk]
arbeiten work [wɜːk]
Arbeitsplatz: am Arbeitsplatz at work [wɜːk]
Ärger trouble ['trʌbl]
ärgerlich angry ['æŋgri]
auch too [tuː]

auf on [ɒn] **auf dem Foto** in the photo [ɪn ðə 'fəʊtəʊ] **auf der Eggbuckland-Schule** at Eggbuckland [æt], [ət] **auf Englisch** in English [ɪn 'ɪŋglɪʃ] **auf Wiedersehen** goodbye [gʊd'baɪ] **aufs Land** to the country
Aufgabe exercise ['eksəsaɪz]
aufgeregt *(gespannt)* excited [ɪk'saɪtɪd]; *(nervös)* nervous ['nɜːvəs]
aufpassen auf look after [lʊk 'ɑːftə]
aufstehen get up [get 'ʌp]
August August ['ɔːgəst]
aus from [frɒm]
Ausdruck phrase [freɪz]
ausleihen: sich (aus)leihen borrow ['bɒrəʊ]
ausmachen: etwas ausmachen make a difference [meɪk ə 'dɪfrəns]
Auto car [kɑː]

B

Baby baby ['beɪbi]
Bad(ezimmer) bathroom ['bɑːθruːm]
bald soon [suːn]
Ball ball [bɔːl]
Banane banana [bə'nɑːnə]
Bananenschale banana skin [bə'nɑːnə skɪn]
Bär bear [beə]
Battle (im Rap) battle ['bætl]
Baum tree [triː]
bei with [wɪð] **bei der Arbeit** at work [wɜːk] **bei Ellie daheim/zu Hause** at Ellie's house [æt], [ət] **bei MARTINS** at MARTINS
Bein leg [leg]
Beispiel example [ɪg'zɑːmpl] **zum Beispiel** for example
bekommen get [get]
benutzen use [juːz]
beobachten watch [wɒtʃ]
Beschäftigung activity [æk'tɪvəti]
beste(r, s), am besten best [best]

Besucher/in visitor ['vɪzɪtə]
Bett bed [bed]
bevor before [bɪ'fɔː]
bewirken: etwas bewirken make a difference [meɪk ə 'dɪfrəns]
Bild picture ['pɪktʃə]
bis: Bis dann. See you. ['siː juː] **von Montag bis Freitag** from Monday to Friday
bist are [ɑː] **bist nicht** aren't = are not [ɑːnt], [ɑː 'nɒt]
bitte *in Fragen und Aufforderungen* please [pliːz] **Bitte schön./Hier, bitte.** Here you are. [hɪə juː 'ɑː] **Bitte, gern geschehen.** You're welcome. ['welkʌm]
blau blue [bluː]
bleiben stay [steɪ]
Bleistift pencil ['pensl]
Bleistiftanspitzer pencil sharpener ['pensl ʃɑːpnə]
blöd silly ['sɪli]; stupid ['stjuːpɪd]
bloß only ['əʊnli]
Bonbon sweet [swiːt]
Boot boat [bəʊt]
borgen: sich borgen borrow ['bɒrəʊ]
Bowling spielen gehen go bowling ['bəʊlɪŋ]
Box box [bɒks]
Brathähnchen chicken ['tʃɪkɪn]
brauchen need [niːd]
braun brown [braʊn]
Brief letter ['letə]
bringen bring [brɪŋ]
britisch British ['brɪtɪʃ]
Broschüre brochure ['brəʊʃə]
Bruder brother ['brʌðə]
Buch book [bʊk]
Buchseite page [peɪdʒ]
buchstabieren spell [spel]
Bulle bull [bʊl]
Bus bus [bʌs] **den Bus nehmen** get the bus **im Bus** on the bus

C

Café cafe ['kæfeɪ]

D

da(hin) there [ðeə]
daheim: bei Ellie daheim at Ellie's house [æt], [ət]
danke thanks [θæŋks] **danke (schön)** thank you ['θæŋk juː]
danken: Nichts zu danken. *(Gern geschehen.)* You're welcome. ['welkʌm]
dann then [ðen]
darstellende Kunst drama ['drɑːmə]
das the [ðə] **das (da)** that [ðæt] **Das ist …** This is … ['ðɪs ɪz]
Datum date [deɪt]
dein/e your [jɔː]
denken think [θɪŋk] **daran denken** remember [rɪ'membə]
der the [ðə]
Deutsch; deutsch German ['dʒɜːmən]
Deutschland Germany ['dʒɜːməni]
Dezember December [dɪ'sembə]
dich you [juː]
die the [ðə]
Dienstag Tuesday ['tjuːzdeɪ], ['tjuːzdi]
Dies ist … This is … ['ðɪs ɪz]
diese(r, s) this [ðɪs]
Ding thing [θɪŋ]
dir you [juː]
Donnerstag Thursday ['θɜːzdeɪ], ['θɜːzdi]
Dorf village ['vɪlɪdʒ]
dort(hin) there [ðeə]
draußen, nach draußen outside [aʊt'saɪd]
drei three [θriː]
dreizehn thirteen [θɜː'tiːn]
dritte(r, s) third [θɜːd]
du you [juː] **du bist** you're = you are [jʊə], [ju 'ɑː]
dumm silly ['sɪli]; stupid ['stjuːpɪd]
durch through [θruː]

E

echt real [rɪəl]
Ecke corner ['kɔːnə]
ein/e a [ə]; *(vor Vokalen)* an [ən]
einhundert a hundred, one hundred ['hʌndrəd]
einige some [sʌm], [səm]
einkaufen gehen go shopping ['ʃɒpɪŋ]

Einladung (zu, nach) invitation (to) [ɪnvɪ'teɪʃn]
eins one [wʌn]
Eintrittskarte ticket ['tɪkɪt]
einzige(r, s) only ['əʊnli]
Elefant elephant ['elɪfənt]
elf eleven [ɪ'levən]
Eltern parents ['peərənts]
E-Mail email ['iːmeɪl]
Ende end [end]
England England ['ɪŋglənd]
Englisch; englisch English ['ɪŋglɪʃ]
Ente duck [dʌk]
Entschuldigung. Sorry. / I'm sorry. ['sɒri]
er he [hiː]; *(bei Dingen und Tieren)* it [ɪt] **er ist** he's (= he is) [hiːz], [hi 'ɪz]
Erdkunde geography [dʒi'ɒgrəfi]
erinnern: sich erinnern an remember [rɪ'membə]
erste(r, s) first (= 1st) [fɜːst]
es it [ɪt]
Esel donkey ['dɒŋki]
Essen food [fuːd]
essen eat [iːt]
etwas something ['sʌmθɪŋ]; *(ein bisschen)* some [sʌm], [səm] **Sonst noch etwas?** Anything else? [eniθɪŋ 'els]
euch you [juː]
euer/eure your [jɔː]

F

Fähre ferry ['feri]
fahren go [gəʊ]
Fahrkarte ticket ['tɪkɪt]
Fahrrad bike [baɪk]
fallen fall [fɔːl]
falsch wrong [rɒŋ] **das ist falsch** that's wrong [ðæts 'rɒŋ]
Familie family ['fæməli]
Familienstammbaum family tree [fæməli 'triː]
Farbe colour ['kʌlə]
Februar February ['februəri]
Federmäppchen pencil case ['pensl keɪs]
feiern: eine Party feiern have a party ['pɑːti]
Feld field [fiːld]
Ferien holidays ['hɒlədeɪz]
Fernsehen watching TV [wɒtʃɪŋ tiː'viː]
Fernseher TV [tiː'viː]
Fernsehsendung programme ['prəʊgræm]

Feuerwehrfrau firefighter ['faɪəfaɪtə]
Feuerwehrmann firefighter ['faɪəfaɪtə]
fies mean [miːn]
Fisch(e) fish [fɪʃ]
Flachbildfernseher flat-screen TV ['flæt skriːn tiː viː]
Flasche bottle ['bɒtl]
fort away [ə'weɪ]
Foto photo ['fəʊtəʊ]
Fotoapparat camera ['kæmərə]
Frage question ['kwestʃən]
fragen ask [ɑːsk] **sie fragte; sie hat gefragt** she asked [ɑːskt]
Frankreich France [frɑːns]
Französisch; französisch French [frentʃ]
Frau woman, *pl* women ['wʊmən], ['wɪmɪn]; *(allgemeine Anrede für Frauen)* Ms … [mɪz], [məz]; *(Anrede für verheiratete Frauen)* Mrs … ['mɪsɪz]; *(Anrede für unverheiratete Frauen)* Miss … [mɪs]
Freitag Friday ['fraɪdeɪ], ['fraɪdi]
fressen eat [iːt]
Freund/in friend [frend]
froh happy ['hæpi]
früh early ['ɜːli]
Frühstück breakfast ['brekfəst]
fühlen, sich fühlen feel [fiːl]
Füller pen [pen]
fünf five [faɪv]
fünfzig fifty ['fɪfti]
funktionieren work [wɜːk]
für for [fɔː], [fə]
Fußball football ['fʊtbɔːl]
Fußballspielen playing football [pleɪɪŋ 'fʊtbɔːl]
Futter food [fuːd]
füttern feed [fiːd]

G

Garage garage ['gærɑːʒ]
Garagenflohmarkt *(privater Flohmarkt)* garage sale ['gærɑːʒ seɪl]
Garten garden ['gɑːdn]
Gast visitor ['vɪzɪtə]
geben: es gibt there are … ['ðeər ɑː]; there's [ðeəz]
Geburtstag birthday ['bɜːθdeɪ] **Herzlichen Glückwunsch zum Geburtstag!** Happy birthday! [hæpi 'bɜːθdeɪ] **Sie hat Geburtstag.** It's her birthday. **Wann hast du Geburtstag?** When's (= when is) your birthday?
Gedicht poem ['pəʊɪm]

gefährlich dangerous ['deɪndʒərəs]
gehen go [gəʊ] **(zu Fuß) gehen**
walk [wɔːk] **Wie geht's?/Wie
geht es dir/euch?** How are you?
[haʊ 'ɑː juː]
gelb yellow ['jeləʊ]
Geld money ['mʌni]
gemein mean [miːn]
Gemüse vegetables ['vedʒtəblz]
genervt sein feel fed up [fed 'ʌp]
Geografie geography [dʒi'ɒgrəfi]
Geräusch noise [nɔɪz]
gern: ich hätte gern I'd like
(= I would like) [aɪd laɪk] **Ich
komme sehr gern./Ich würde
sehr gern kommen.** I'd love to
come. (= I would love to come.)
[wʊd]
Gesamtschule (GB) high school
['haɪ skuːl]
Geschäft shop [ʃɒp]
**geschehen: Bitte, gern gesche-
hen.** You're welcome. ['welkʌm]
Geschenk present ['preznt]
Geschichte (Erzählung) story
['stɔːri]; (vergangene Zeiten) history ['hɪstri]
Gesicht face [feɪs]
gespannt excited [ɪk'saɪtɪd]
Getränk drink [drɪŋk]
Gitarre guitar [gɪ'tɑː]
glauben think [θɪŋk]
Glück: du hast Glück you're
lucky ['lʌki] **Viel Glück!** Good
luck. [lʌk]
glücklich happy ['hæpi]
**Glückwunsch: Herzlichen Glück-
wunsch (zu …)!** Congratulations
(on …)! [kəngrætʃu'leɪʃnz]
**Herzlichen Glückwunsch zum
Geburtstag!** Happy birthday!
[hæpi 'bɜːθdeɪ]
groß big [bɪg]
großartig great [greɪt]
Großstadt city ['sɪti]
grün green [griːn]
Gruppe group [gruːp]
Gruppenarbeit group work
['gruːp wɜːk]
Grüße: Viele Grüße, … (Briefschluss) Best wishes ['wɪʃɪz]
gut fine [faɪn]; good [gʊd] **Guten
Morgen.** Good morning. [gʊd
'mɔːnɪŋ] **Es geht mir gut.** I'm
fine. [aɪm 'faɪn]; I'm OK.
[əʊ'keɪ] **Hört sich gut an.**
Sounds fun. [fʌn]
Gut gemacht! Well done.
[wel 'dʌn]

H

haben have [hæv] **es hat kein/e
… ** it doesn't have … ['dʌznt]
Hafen harbour ['hɑːbə]
Hähnchen chicken ['tʃɪkɪn]
Hallo. Hello. [hə'ləʊ]; Hi! [haɪ]
Halt den Mund! Shut up! [ʃʌt
'ʌp]
Hamster hamster ['hæmstə]
Handy mobile (phone) [məʊbaɪl
'fəʊn]
hart hard [hɑːd]
hat has [hæz], [həz]
Haus house [haʊs] **nach Hause**
home [həʊm]
Hausaufgabe/n homework
['həʊmwɜːk] **ich mache (meine)
Hausaufgaben** I do my homework
Haustier pet [pet]
Heftseite page [peɪdʒ]
heißen: Wie heißt du? What's
your name? [wɒts jɔː 'neɪm]
helfen help [help]
Hemd shirt [ʃɜːt]
Herr Smith Mr Smith ['mɪstə]
herrisch bossy ['bɒsi]
herstellen make [meɪk]
Herzlichen Glückwunsch (zu …)!
Congratulations (on …)!
[kəngrætʃu'leɪʃnz]
**Herzlichen Glückwunsch zum
Geburtstag!** Happy birthday!
[hæpi 'bɜːθdeɪ]
heute today [tə'deɪ]
hier here [hɪə] **Hier, bitte.** Here
you are. [hɪə ju 'ɑː]
hierher here [hɪə]
Hilfe help [help]
hinfallen fall [fɔːl]
hinter behind [bɪ'haɪnd]
Hobby hobby ['hɒbi]
hoffen hope [həʊp]
hören hear [hɪə]
Huhn chicken ['tʃɪkɪn]
Hund dog [dɒg]
hundert a hundred, one hundred
['hʌndrəd]
hurra yippee [jɪ'piː]

I

ich I [aɪ] **ich bin** I'm (= I am)
[aɪm], [aɪ 'æm] **ich bin's** it's me
[ɪts 'miː]
Idee idea [aɪ'dɪə]
ihm him [hɪm]
ihn him [hɪm]

ihr (Mehrzahl von „du") you
[juː] **ihr seid** you're = you are
[jʊə], [ju 'ɑː]
ihr/e (besitzanzeigend zu „she")
her [hɜː]
im: im Bus on the bus **im Kino** at
the cinema ['sɪnəmə]
immer always ['ɔːlweɪz]
in: in der Schule at school [ət
'skuːl] **in der Stadt** in town
[taʊn] **in einem Restaurant** at a
restaurant ['restrɒnt] **in England**
in England [ɪn] **in Papas Wohnung gehen** go to dad's flat [tu],
[tə]
**Informations- und Kommunika-
tionstechnologie** ICT (information and communication technology) [aɪ siː 'tiː], [ɪnfəmeɪʃn ənd
kəmjuːnɪkeɪʃn tek'nɒlədʒi]
Instrument instrument
['ɪnstrəmənt]
Irrenhaus madhouse ['mædhaʊs]
ist is [ɪz] **ist nicht** isn't (= is not)
['ɪznt], [ɪz 'nɒt] **es ist (vorhanden)**
there's [ðeəz]

J

ja yes [jes]; yeah (= yes) [jeə]
Januar January ['dʒænjuəri]
jeder everybody ['evribɒdi]
jetzt now [naʊ]
Juli July [dʒu'laɪ]
Junge boy [bɔɪ]
Juni June [dʒuːn]

K

Kaffee coffee ['kɒfi]
Kalender calendar ['kælɪndə]
Kamera camera ['kæmərə]
Kaninchen rabbit ['ræbɪt]
Kantine canteen [kæn'tiːn]
Kapuzenpullover hoodie ['hʊdi]
Karte card [kɑːd]
Käse cheese [tʃiːz]
Kasten box [bɒks]
Katze cat [kæt]
kaufen buy [baɪ]
Kaufpreis price [praɪs]
kein/e no [nəʊ] **Ich bin kein
Junge.** I'm not a boy. [nɒt]
kennen know [nəʊ]
kennenlernen meet [miːt]
Kind child, pl children [tʃaɪld],
['tʃɪldrən]
Kino cinema ['sɪnəmə]
Kissen cushion ['kʊʃn]
Klasse class [klɑːs]

Klassenraum classroom
['klɑːsruːm]
Klavier piano [pi'ænəʊ]
Kleiderschrank wardrobe
['wɔːdrəʊb]
klein small [smɔːl]
klingen sound [saʊnd] **Klingt, als
ob es Spaß macht.** Sounds fun.
[fʌn]
Klub club [klʌb]
kochen cook [kʊk]
kommen come [kʌm] **Ich komme
sehr gern./Ich würde sehr gern
kommen.** I'd love to come.
(= I would love to come.) [wʊd]
können can [kæn], [kən] **nicht
können** can't (= cannot) [kɑːnt],
['kænɒt]
Konzert concert ['kɒnsət]
**Kopfsprung: einen Kopfsprung
machen** dive [daɪv]
**kosten: Der Taschenrechner
kostet 1 Pfund.** The calculator
is £1. **Die Handys kosten
10 Pfund.** The mobiles are £10.
kostenlos free [friː]
Krankenhaus hospital ['hɒspɪtl]
Krawatte tie [taɪ]
Krebs crab [kræb]
kriegen get [get]
Krokodil crocodile ['krɒkədaɪl]
Küche kitchen ['kɪtʃɪn]
Kugelschreiber pen [pen]
Kuh cow [kaʊ]
kümmern: sich kümmern um
look after [lʊk 'ɑːftə]
Kunde, Kundin customer
['kʌstəmə]
Kunst art [ɑːt]
Kuss kiss [kɪs]

L

lachen laugh [lɑːf] **sie lachten;
sie haben gelacht** they laughed
[lɑːft]
Laden shop [ʃɒp]
Lampe lamp [læmp]
Land country ['kʌntri] **aufs Land
to the country**
langweilig boring ['bɔːrɪŋ]
Lärm noise [nɔɪz] **voller Lärm**
noisy ['nɔɪzi]
lass(t) uns let's (= let us) [lets],
['let əs]
laut noisy ['nɔɪzi]
Leben life, pl lives [laɪf]
leben live [lɪv] **sie lebt/wohnt**
she lives [lɪvz]
Lebensmittel food [fuːd]

Lehrer/in teacher ['tiːtʃə]
leidtun: Tut mir leid. Sorry./I'm
sorry. ['sɒri]
leihen: sich (aus)leihen borrow
['bɒrəʊ]
lesen read [riːd]; (das) **Lesen**
reading ['riːdɪŋ]
letzte(r, s) last [lɑːst]
Leute people ['piːpl]
Liebe/r … Dear … [dɪə]
lieben love [lʌv]
Lieblings- favourite ['feɪvərɪt]
Lieblingssache favourite thing
[feɪvərɪt 'θɪŋ]
Lied song [sɒŋ]
Lineal ruler ['ruːlə]
links left [left] **auf der linken
Seite** on the left [ɒn ðə
'left] **nach links** left [left]
lustig funny ['fʌni]

M

machen do [duː]; make [meɪk]
**ich mache (meine) Hausauf-
gaben** I do my homework
['həʊmwɜːk]
Mädchen girl [gɜːl]
Mai May [meɪ]
Mama mum [mʌm]
manchmal sometimes ['sʌmtaɪmz]
Mann man, pl men [mæn], [men]
Markt market ['mɑːkɪt]
Marmelade jam [dʒæm]
März March [mɑːtʃ]
Mathematik maths [mæθs]
mein/e (vor Nomen) my [maɪ]
meinen (denken, glauben) think
[θɪŋk]
Mensa canteen [kæn'tiːn]
Menschen people ['piːpl]
mich me [mi]
Milchbrötchen (leicht süß, oft mit
Rosinen) scone [skɒn]
Minute minute ['mɪnɪt]
mir me [mi]
mit with [wɪð] **mit dem Bus
fahren** go by bus [baɪ 'bʌs]
mitbringen bring [brɪŋ]
mitkommen come [kʌm]
Mittag essen have lunch [həv
'lʌntʃ]
Mittagessen lunch [lʌntʃ]
Mitte middle ['mɪdl] **in der Mitte
in the middle**
Mittwoch Wednesday ['wenzdeɪ],
['wenzdi]
möchten: ich möchte (…) haben
I'd like (= I would like) [aɪd laɪk]

mögen like [laɪk] **ich
mag … nicht** I don't like …
[ai 'dəʊnt laɪk] **sehr mögen**
love [lʌv]
Montag Monday ['mʌndeɪ],
['mʌndi]
Morgen morning ['mɔːnɪŋ]
morgen tomorrow [tə'mɒrəʊ]
müde tired ['taɪəd]
Mund: Halt den Mund! Shut up!
[ʃʌt 'ʌp]
Musik music ['mjuːzɪk]
müssen must [mʌst]
Mutti mum [mʌm]

N

nach (örtlich) to [tu], [tə]; (zeitlich) after ['ɑːftə] **nach Hause**
home [həʊm]
Nachmittag afternoon [ɑːftə'nuːn]
Nachrichten news [njuːz]
nächste(r, s) next [nekst]
Nacht night [naɪt] **in der Nacht**
at night [ət 'naɪt]
nachts at night [ət 'naɪt]
Name name [neɪm]
Nase: die Nase voll haben feel
fed up [fed 'ʌp]
nass wet [wet]
natürlich of course [əv 'kɔːs]
Naturwissenschaft science
['saɪəns]
neben next to ['nekst tə]
nehmen: den Bus nehmen get
the bus [bʌs]
nein no [nəʊ]
nervös nervous ['nɜːvəs]
nett nice [naɪs]
Netz network ['netwɜːk]
neu new [njuː]
neun nine [naɪn]
nicht not [nɒt]
nicht können can't (= cannot)
[kɑːnt], ['kænɒt]
nichts nothing ['nʌθɪŋ]
nie(mals) never ['nevə]
niedlich cute [kjuːt]
noch einmal again [ə'gen]
normal normal ['nɔːml]
November November [nəʊ'vembə]
Null (im gesprochenen Englisch)
oh [əʊ]
Nummer number ['nʌmbə]
nun now [naʊ]
nur only ['əʊnli]

O

oben, nach oben upstairs
[ʌp'steəz]

oder or [ɔ:]
oft often ['ɒfn], ['ɒftən]
Oktober October [ɒk'təʊbə]
Oma grandma ['grænmɑ:]
Opa grandpa ['grænpɑ:]
Orange orange ['ɒrɪndʒ]
orange orange ['ɒrɪndʒ]
Ort place [pleɪs]

P

paar: ein paar some [sʌm], [səm]
Papa dad [dæd]
Partner/in partner ['pɑ:tnə]
Partnerarbeit partner work ['pɑ:tnə wɜ:k]
Party party ['pɑ:ti] **eine Party feiern** have a party
Pause break [breɪk]
Pence: 50 Pence 50p [pi:]
Pfund (britische Währung) pound (£) [paʊnd]
Platz place [pleɪs]
Pommes frites chips (pl) [tʃɪps]
Pony pony ['pəʊni]
Preis (Gewinn) prize [praɪz]; (Kaufpreis) price [praɪs]
Prinz prince [prɪns]
Problem problem ['prɒbləm]
Prospekt brochure ['brəʊʃə]
Pullover pullover ['pʊləʊvə]

R

Rad fahren ride a bike [raɪd ə 'baɪk]
Radiergummi rubber ['rʌbə]
rappen rap [ræp]
Ratte rat [ræt]
Raum room [ru:m]
rechte(r, s): auf der rechten Seite on the right [ɒn ðə 'raɪt]
rechts on the right [ɒn ðə 'raɪt]; right [raɪt]
Redewendung phrase [freɪz]
reiten (das) Reiten riding ['raɪdɪŋ] **auf einem Pony/ein Pony reiten** ride a pony [raɪd]
Restaurant restaurant ['restrɒnt]
richtig right [raɪt] **das ist richtig** that's right [ðæts 'raɪt]
Rollstuhl wheelchair ['wi:ltʃeə]
rosa pink [pɪŋk]
rot red [red]
Rundgang (durch) tour (of) [tʊə]

S

Sache thing [θɪŋ]
Saft juice [dʒu:s]

sagen say [seɪ] **Ellie sagt** Ellie says ['eli sez] **er sagte; er hat gesagt** he said [sed]
Sahne cream [kri:m]
Salat (als Gericht oder Beilage) salad ['sæləd]
Samstag Saturday ['sætədeɪ], ['sætədi]
Sänger/in singer ['sɪŋə]
Satz sentence ['sentəns]
sauer sein feel fed up [fed 'ʌp]
Schaf(e) sheep [ʃi:p]
schauen look [lʊk]
Schauspiel drama ['drɑ:mə]
schicken send [send]
Schiff boat [bəʊt]
Schild sign [saɪn]
Schlafparty sleepover ['sli:pəʊvə]
Schlafzimmer bedroom ['bedru:m]
Schlagzeug drums [drʌmz]
Schlange snake [sneɪk]
schlecht bad [bæd]
schlimm bad [bæd]
Schluss end [end]
Schlussverkauf sale [seɪl]
schön fine [faɪn]; nice [naɪs] **Ich wünsche dir einen schönen Tag./Schönen Tag noch.** Have a good day. [hæv ə gʊd 'deɪ]
schrecklich terrible ['terəbl]
schreiben write [raɪt] **schreiben an** write to [tu], [tə] **schreiben über** write about ['raɪt əbaʊt]
Schuh shoe [ʃu:]
Schule school [sku:l]
Schüler/in student ['stju:dnt]
Schulheft exercise book ['eksəsaɪz bʊk]
Schulklasse class [klɑ:s]
Schulleiter/in principal ['prɪnsəpl]
Schulmensa canteen [kæn'ti:n]
Schulsport PE (physical education) [pi: 'i:], [fɪzɪkl edʒu'keɪʃn]
Schulter shoulder ['ʃəʊldə]
Schuluniform uniform ['ju:nɪfɔ:m]
schwarz black [blæk]
Schwein pig [pɪg]
schwer hard [hɑ:d]
Schwester sister ['sɪstə]
schwierig difficult ['dɪfɪkəlt]; hard [hɑ:d]
Schwierigkeiten trouble ['trʌbl]
schwimmen (das) Schwimmen swimming ['swɪmɪŋ] **schwimmen gehen** go swimming [gəʊ 'swɪmɪŋ]
sechs six [sɪks]

sehen see [si:] **Sieh mal, Adam.** Look, Adam. [lʊk]
sehr very ['veri]
seid are [ɑ:] **seid nicht** aren't = are not [ɑ:nt], [ɑ: 'nɒt]
Seilrutsche zip wire ['zɪp waɪə]
sein be [bi:]
sein/e (besitzanzeigend zu „he") his [hɪz]
Seite page [peɪdʒ]
selbstverständlich of course [əv 'kɔ:s]
senden send [send]
Sendung programme ['prəʊgræm]
September September [sep'tembə]
sicher sure [ʃʊə]
sie (bei Dingen und Tieren) it [ɪt]
Sie (höfliche Anrede) you [ju:] **Sie sind** you're = you are [jʊə], [ju 'ɑ:]
sie (Mehrzahl) they [ðeɪ] **sie sind** they're (= they are) [ðeə], [ðeɪ 'ɑ:]
sie (weibliche Person) she [ʃi:] **sie ist** she's (= she is) [ʃi:z], [ʃi 'ɪz]
sieben seven ['sevn]
siebzehn seventeen [sevn'ti:n]
sind are [ɑ:] **sind nicht** aren't = are not [ɑ:nt], [ɑ: 'nɒt] **es sind (vorhanden)** there are … ['ðeər ɑ:]
singen sing [sɪŋ]
Skateboardfahren skateboarding ['skeɪtbɔ:dɪŋ]
SMS text (message) ['tekst mesɪdʒ] **eine SMS schicken** text [tekst]
so so [səʊ]
Sommer summer ['sʌmə]
Sonntag Sunday ['sʌndeɪ], ['sʌndi]
Sonst noch etwas? Anything else? [eniθɪŋ 'els]
Spaß: es macht Spaß, mit ihnen zusammenzusein they're fun [fʌn] **Klingt, als ob es Spaß macht.** Sounds fun.
spät late [leɪt] **Wie spät ist es?** What's the time? [wɒts ðə 'taɪm]
Speisekarte menu ['menju:]
Spiel game [geɪm] **Spiele spielen** playing games [pleɪɪŋ 'geɪmz]
spielen play [pleɪ]
Sport sport [spɔ:t]; (in der Schule) PE (physical education) [pi: 'i:], [fɪzɪkl edʒu'keɪʃn]
Sportart sport [spɔ:t]
Sportgeschäft sports shop ['spɔ:ts ʃɒp]
Sportschuh trainer ['treɪnə]

sprechen: sprechen (mit) speak (to) ['spi:k] **sprechen über** talk about [tɔ:k] **mit Freunden/Freundinnen sprechen** speaking to friends [spi:kɪŋ tə 'frendz]
Stadt (*Großstadt*) city ['sɪti]; (*Kleinstadt*) town [taʊn]
Stammbaum (*der Familie*) family tree [fæməli 'tri:]
Stelle place [pleɪs]
Stiefbruder stepbrother ['stepbrʌðə]
Stiefmutter stepmum ['stepmʌm]
Stiefschwester stepsister ['stepsɪstə]
Stiefvater stepdad ['stepdæd]
Stift pen [pen]
stimmen: das stimmt that's right [ðæts 'raɪt] **das stimmt nicht** that's wrong [ðæts 'rɒŋ]
stolz (auf) proud (of) [praʊd]
Strand beach [bi:tʃ]
Straße (*in Ortschaften*) street [stri:t]; (*Landstraße zwischen Orten, aber auch in Ortschaften*) road [rəʊd]
Streichelzoo pets corner ['kɔ:nə]
Streifenhörnchen chipmunk ['tʃɪpmʌŋk]
Student/in student ['stju:dnt]
Stuhl chair [tʃeə]
Stunde lesson ['lesn]
Stundenplan timetable ['taɪmteɪbl]
Suppe soup [su:p]
süß cute [kju:t]
Süßigkeiten sweets [swi:ts]
Szene scene [si:n]

T

Tag day [deɪ]
Tanzen dancing ['dɑ:nsɪŋ]
Tasche bag [bæg]
Taschenrechner calculator ['kælkjuleɪtə]
Technik technology [tek'nɒlədʒi]
Technologie technology [tek'nɒlədʒi]
Tee tea [ti:]
Telefon phone [fəʊn]
Telefonnummer phone number ['fəʊn nʌmbə]
teuer expensive [ɪk'spensɪv]
Theater theatre ['θɪətə]
Tier animal ['ænɪml]
Tiger tiger ['taɪgə]
Tisch table ['teɪbl]
Toilette toilet ['tɔɪlət]
toll great [greɪt]

Trampolin trampoline ['træmpəli:n]
treffen, sich treffen meet [mi:t]
Trommeln drums [drʌmz]
Tschüs. Bye. [baɪ]; See you. ['si: ju]
tun do [du:] **Tut mir leid.** Sorry./I'm sorry. ['sɒri]

U

üben practise ['præktɪs]
über: schreiben über write about [ə'baʊt]
Überraschung surprise [sə'praɪz]
Übung exercise ['eksəsaɪz]
Übungsheft exercise book ['eksəsaɪz bʊk]
Uhr clock [klɒk] **5 Uhr morgens/vormittags** 5 am [eɪ'em] **5 Uhr nachmittags/abends/17 Uhr** 5 pm [pi:'em] **um 1 Uhr/um 13 Uhr** at one o'clock [ə'klɒk]
Uhrzeit time [taɪm]
und and [ænd], [ənd] **Und du?** What about you? [wɒt əbaʊt 'ju:]
ungefähr about [ə'baʊt]
unglücklich unhappy [ʌn'hæpi]
Uniform uniform ['ju:nɪfɔ:m]
unordentlich messy ['mesi]
uns us [ʌs], [əs]
unser/e our ['aʊə], [ɑ:]
unter under ['ʌndə]
Unterrichtsstunde lesson ['lesn]
Unterschied difference ['dɪfrəns]
unterschiedlich different ['dɪfrənt]

V

Vati dad [dæd]
Verein club [klʌb]
vergessen: Ich habe meine Hausaufgaben vergessen. I forgot my homework. [fə'gɒt] **nicht vergessen** remember [rɪ'membə]
Verkauf sale [seɪl]
vermissen miss [mɪs]
verschieden different ['dɪfrənt]
Verspätung: mein Bus hat Verspätung my bus is late [leɪt]
viel(e) lots of ['lɒts əv] **Viel Glück!** Good luck. [lʌk] **Viele Grüße, ...** Best wishes ['wɪʃɪz]
vier four [fɔ:]
vierzehn fourteen [fɔ:'ti:n]
Vogel bird [bɜ:d]
von: von den Ferien of the holidays [ɒv], [əv] **von Montag bis Freitag** from Monday to Fri-

day **eine SMS von Mama** a text from mum [frɒm]
vor in front of [ɪn 'frʌnt əv]; (*zeitlich*) before [bɪ'fɔ:]

W

wandern walk [wɔ:k]
wann? when? [wen] **Wann hast du Geburtstag?** When's (= when is) your birthday?
war was [wɒz], [wəz] **er war nicht** he wasn't (= he was not) ['wɒznt], [wəz 'nɒt]
waren were [wɜ:], [wə]
warum? why? [waɪ]
was? what? [wɒt] **Was ist mit dir?** What about you? [wɒt əbaʊt 'ju:] **Was ist ...?** What's ...? (= What is ...?) [wɒts], ['wɒt ɪz]
Wasser water ['wɔ:tə]
wecken wake [weɪk]
weg away [ə'weɪ]
weggehen go away [gəʊ ə'weɪ]
Weide field [fi:ld]
weil because [bɪ'kɒz]
weiß white [waɪt]
welche(r, s) what [wɒt] **Welche(s) sind ...?** What are ...? ['wɒt ɑ:]
wem? who? [hu:]
wen? who? [hu:]
wenn when [wen]
wer? who? [hu:]
werden will [wɪl] **ich werde ... anrufen** I'll phone (= I will phone) ... [aɪl], [aɪ 'wɪl]
Wettstreit (im Rap) battle ['bætl]
wichtig important [ɪm'pɔ:tənt]
wie? how? [haʊ] **Wie spät ist es?** What's the time? [wɒts ðə 'taɪm]
wieder again [ə'gen]
Wiedersehen: auf Wiedersehen goodbye [gʊd'baɪ]
wild (lebend) wild [waɪld]
Willkommen in Plymouth! Welcome to Plymouth. ['welkəm]
wir we [wi:] **wir sind** we're (= we are) [wɪə], [wi 'ɑ:]
wirklich real [rɪəl] **wirklich nett** really nice ['rɪəli]
wissen know [nəʊ]
wo(hin)? where? [weə]
Woche week [wi:k]
Wochenende weekend [wi:k'end]
wohnen live [lɪv] **sie lebt/wohnt** she lives [lɪvz]
Wohnung flat [flæt]
Wohnzimmer living room ['lɪvɪŋ ru:m]

wollen want [wɒnt] **kaufen**
  wollen want to buy
Wort word [wɜːd]
Wörterbuch dictionary ['dɪkʃənri]
Wörterverzeichnis: alpha-
  betisches Wörterverzeichnis
  dictionary ['dɪkʃənri]
Wortnetz network ['netwɜːk]
wütend angry ['æŋgri]

Z

zehn ten [ten]
Zeichen sign [saɪn]
Zeile line [laɪn]
Zeit time [taɪm] **Hast du um ein**
  Uhr Zeit? Are you free at one
  o'clock? [friː]
Zimmer room [ruːm]
Zoo zoo [zuː]
zu *(örtlich)* to [tu], [tə] **zu klein**
  too small [tuː] **zu spät** late [leɪt]
zu Hause at home [ət 'həʊm] **bei**
  Ellie zu Hause at Ellie's house
  [æt], [ət] **Zeit zu essen** time to eat
zuerst first [fɜːst]
zuhören listen ['lɪsn]
zum Beispiel for example
  [ɪg'zɑːmpl]
zurück back [bæk]
zwei two [tuː]
zweite(r, s) second ['sekənd]
zwölf twelve [twelv]

English sounds

[iː]	green, he, tea	[b]	bike, table, crab
[ɑː]	ask, class, car, park	[p]	pen, stupid, shop
[ɔː]	or, ball, four, morning	[d]	day, idea, good
[uː]	ruler, blue, too, two, you	[t]	ten, letter, at
[ɜː]	early, her, girl, work, T-shirt	[g]	go, again, bag
[ɪ]	in, big, expensive	[k]	kitchen, car, black
[e]	yes, bed, again, breakfast	[m]	man, remember, mum
[æ]	animal, Africa, black, cat	[n]	no, one, ten
[ʌ]	mum, bus, colour	[ŋ]	wrong, young, thanks
[ɒ]	song, on, dog, what	[l]	like, old, small
[ʊ]	book, good, pullover	[r]	ruler, friend, sorry
[ə]	again, today, a sister	[w]	we, where, one
[i]	happy, monkey	[j]	yes, you, uniform
		[f]	family, after, laugh
[eɪ]	name, eight, play, great	[v]	very, seven, have
[aɪ]	I, time, right, my	[s]	six, poster, yes
[ɔɪ]	boy, toilet, noise	[z]	zoo, quiz, his, music, please
[əʊ]	old, no, road, yellow	[ʃ]	she, brochure, English
[aʊ]	now, house	[ʒ]	garage
[eə]	where, chair, bear	[tʃ]	child, teacher, watch
[ʊə]	tour	[dʒ]	German, orange
[ɪə]	here, dear	[θ]	thing, three, bathroom, both
		[ð]	the, brother, with
		[h]	house, who, behind

The English alphabet

a	[eɪ]	h	[eɪtʃ]	o	[əʊ]	v	[viː]
b	[biː]	i	[aɪ]	p	[piː]	w	[ˈdʌbljuː]
c	[siː]	j	[dʒeɪ]	q	[kjuː]	x	[eks]
d	[diː]	k	[keɪ]	r	[ɑː]	y	[waɪ]
e	[iː]	l	[el]	s	[es]	z	[zed]
f	[ef]	m	[em]	t	[tiː]		
g	[dʒiː]	n	[en]	u	[juː]		

NUMBERS

English numbers

0 **oh, zero, nil** [əʊ, ˈzɪərəʊ, nɪl]
1 **one** [wʌn]
2 **two** [tuː]
3 **three** [θriː]
4 **four** [fɔː]
5 **five** [faɪv]
6 **six** [sɪks]
7 **seven** [ˈsevn]
8 **eight** [eɪt]
9 **nine** [naɪn]
10 **ten** [ten]

11 **eleven** [ɪˈlevn]
12 **twelve** [twelv]
13 **thirteen** [θɜːˈtiːn]
14 **fourteen** [fɔːˈtiːn]
15 **fifteen** [fɪfˈtiːn]
16 **sixteen** [sɪksˈtiːn]
17 **seventeen** [sevnˈtiːn]
18 **eighteen** [eɪˈtiːn]
19 **nineteen** [naɪnˈtiːn]
20 **twenty** [ˈtwenti]

21 **twenty-one** [twentiˈwʌn]
22 **twenty-two** [twentiˈtuː]
23 **twenty-three** [twentiˈθriː]
...

30 **thirty** [ˈθɜːti]
40 **forty** [ˈfɔːti]
50 **fifty** [ˈfɪfti]
60 **sixty** [ˈsɪksti]
70 **seventy** [ˈsevnti]
80 **eighty** [ˈeɪti]
90 **ninety** [ˈnaɪnti]
100 **a / one hundred**
[ə / wʌn ˈhʌndrəd]

101 **one hundred and one**
102 **one hundred and two**
...

1st **first** [fɜːst]
2nd **second** [ˈsekənd]
3rd **third** [θɜːd]
4th **fourth** [fɔːθ]
5th **fifth** [fɪfθ]
6th **sixth** [sɪksθ]
7th **seventh** [ˈsevnθ]
8th **eighth** [eɪtθ]
9th **ninth** [naɪnθ]
10th **tenth** [tenθ]

11th **eleventh** [ɪˈlevnθ]
12th **twelfth** [twelfθ]
13th **thirteenth** [θɜːˈtiːnθ]
14th **fourteenth** [fɔːˈtiːnθ]
15th **fifteenth** [fɪfˈtiːnθ]
16th **sixteenth** [sɪksˈtiːnθ]
17th **seventeenth** [sevnˈtiːnθ]
18th **eighteenth** [eɪˈtiːnθ]
19th **nineteenth** [naɪnˈtiːnθ]
20th **twentieth** [ˈtwentiəθ]

21st **twenty-first** [twentiˈfɜːst]
22nd **twenty-second** [twentiˈsekənd]
23rd **twenty-third** [twentiˈθɜːd]
...

30th **thirtieth** [ˈθɜːtiəθ]
40th **fortieth** [ˈfɔːtiəθ]
50th **fiftieth** [ˈfɪftiəθ]
60th **sixtieth** [ˈsɪkstiəθ]
70th **seventieth** [ˈsevntiəθ]
80th **eightieth** [ˈeɪtiəθ]
90th **ninetieth** [ˈnaɪntiəθ]
100th **hundredth** [ˈhʌndrədθ]

101st **hundred and first**
102nd **hundred and second**
...

190 one hundred and ninety

GRAMMATICAL TERMS

answer	Antwort(satz)
negative statement	verneinte Aussage
noun	Nomen, Hauptwort, Substantiv
personal pronoun	Personalpronomen (persönliches Fürwort)
plural	Plural, Mehrzahl
positive statement	bejahte Aussage
present	Gegenwart
present progressive	Verlaufsform der Gegenwart
pronoun	Pronomen, Fürwort
question	Frage(satz)
question word	Fragewort
short answer	Kurzantwort
simple present	einfache Form der Gegenwart
singular	Singular, Einzahl
statement	Aussage(satz)
verb	Verb

First names (Vornamen)
Boys

Adam ['ædəm]
Alex ['ælɪks]
Ben [ben]
Benny ['beni]
Casper ['kæspə]
Charlie ['tʃɑːli]
Chris [krɪs]
Conor ['kɒnə]
Cyril ['sɪrɪl]
Dan [dæn]
Daniel ['dænjəl]
Finn [fɪn]
Harry ['hæri]
Jack [dʒæk]
Jake [dʒeɪk]
Kevin ['kevɪn]
Luca ['luːkə]
Mike [maɪk]
Paul [pɔːl]
Pete [piːt]
Peter ['piːtə]
Sam [sæm]
Steve [stiːv]
Thomas ['tɒməs]
Tim [tɪm]
Timothy ['tɪməθi]
Tom [tɒm]
William ['wɪljəm]
Zack [zæk]

First names (Vornamen)
Girls

Alisha [ə'lɪʃə]
Amanda [ə'mændə]
Amy ['eɪmi]
Anna ['ænə]
Babe [beɪb]
Berry ['beri]
Charlotte ['ʃɑːlət]
Connie ['kɒni]
Ellie ['eli]
Emily ['eməli]
Emma ['emə]
Grace [greɪs]
Hannah ['hænə]
Jackie ['dʒæki]
Josie ['dʒəʊsi]
Lulu ['luːluː]
Mara ['mɑːrə]
Moona ['muːnə]
Ruby ['ruːbi]
Sandy ['sændi]
Sarah ['seərə]
Susan ['suːzən]
Tamara [tə'mɑːrə]
Zainab ['zeɪnæb]
Zoe ['zəʊi]

Family names/Surnames
(Familiennamen)

Boateng ['bwɑːteŋ]
Borowski [bə'rɒvski]
Brown [braʊn]
Cole [kəʊl]
Dixon ['dɪksən]
Donovan ['dɒnəvən]
Finden ['fɪndən]
Ford [fɔːd]
Gray [greɪ]
Johnson ['dʒɒnsn]
Jones [dʒəʊnz]
Lee [liː]
Newton ['njuːtən]
Osmanovic [ɒz'mænəvɪtʃ]
Potter ['pɒtə]
Rooney ['ruːni]
Smith [smɪθ]
Victor ['vɪktə]
Young [jʌŋ]

Place names
(Ortsnamen)

Berlin [bɜː'lɪn]
Borough Road
   [bʌrə 'rəʊd]
Cawsand ['kɔːsænd]
Central Park
   [sentrəl 'pɑːk]
Charles Street
   ['tʃɑːlz striːt]
Cook Street
   ['kʊk striːt]
Drake Circus
   [dreɪk 'sɜːkəs]
Exeter ['eksɪtə]
Fore Street ['fɔː striːt]
George Street
   ['dʒɔːdʒ striːt]
Ghana ['gɑːnə]
Gratefeld
Street ['greɪtfeld striːt]
Great Field Road
   [greɪt fiːld 'rəʊd]
Greatfield
Street ['greɪtfiːld striːt]
Harbour Road
   [hɑːbə 'rəʊd]
Hill Road [hɪl 'rəʊd]
Kingsand ['kɪŋsænd]
Leeds [liːdz]
Liverpool ['lɪvəpuːl]
London ['lʌndən]
Malaysia [mə'leɪʒə]
Martins ['mɑːtɪnz]
Merryweather
Farm [meriweðə 'fɑːm]
Paignton ['peɪntən]
Plymouth ['plɪməθ]
Plymouth Barbican
   [plɪməθ 'bɑːbɪkən]
Plymouth Cinema
   [plɪməθ 'sɪnəmə]
Plymouth Hoe (the Hoe)
   [plɪməθ 'həʊ]
Raglan Road
   [ræglən 'rəʊd]
Reel Cinema [riːl 'sɪnəmə]
Saltash ['sɔːltæʃ]
Theatre Royal
   [θɪətə 'rɔɪəl]
Tinside Lido
   [tɪnsaɪd 'laɪdəʊ]
Tinside Park
   [tɪnsaɪd 'pɑːk]
Tinside Pool
   [tɪnsaɪd 'puːl]
Windsor Street
   ['wɪnzə striːt]
Woolwell ['wʊlwel]
York [jɔːk]

Other names
(Andere Namen)

Big Bash [bɪg 'bæʃ]
Digicomp ['dɪdʒikɒmp]
Dreamrooms ['driːmruːmz]
Eggbuckland Community College
   [eg'bʌklənd kə'mjuːnəti kɒlɪdʒ]
Eggy ['egi]
Francis and the Drakes ['frɑːnsɪs ənd ðə 'dreɪks]
Jam Band ['dʒæm bænd]
Kaiser Chiefs ['kaɪsə tʃiːfs]
Manchester United ['mæntʃɪstə ju'naɪtɪd]
Phones 4U [fəʊnz fə 'juː]
Plymouth Argyle [plɪməθ ɑː'gaɪl]
Plymouth High School [plɪməθ 'haɪ skuːl]
PMZ (Plymouth Music Zone)
   [piː əm 'zed], [plɪməθ 'mjuːzɪk zəʊn]
Roof Raisers ['ruːf reɪzəz]
Streetbeatz ['striːtbiːts]
Travelline ['trævəlaɪn]
www.plymouthmusiczone.org.uk [dʌblju: dʌblju:
dʌblju: plɪməθ'mjuːzɪkzəʊn dɒt ɔːg dɒt juː'keɪ]

Answers to TEST AND CHECK

Unit 1, page 33

1 WORDS School, hobbies, colours, …
a) 1 tie 2 Monday 3 canteen 4 lesson 5 brother 6 art   `6 points`
b) One answer is OK.
1 pencil case, pencil sharpener, ruler, exercise book, calculator, …
2 PE, history, geography, technology, English, German, ICT, drama, art, music, …
3 riding, skateboarding, …
4 blue, green, white, pink, red, orange, …
5 teacher, principal, uniform, tie, …
6 one, two, three, four, five, six, seven, eight, nine, ten, eleven, …   `6 points`
c) One answer is OK.
1 My favourite school day is Monday / Tuesday / Wednesday / Thursday / Friday.
2 My favourite lesson is English / German / maths / PE / …   `2 points`

2 WORDS Talking to friends
1 How 2 good 3 to 4 you 5 your 6 class 7 She's 8 lesson   `8 points`

3 LANGUAGE Pictures on Ellie's mobile
a) Look, this is Eggy. It's my new school.
Here are two teachers. They're OK.
This is Ms Lee. No, she isn't my PE teacher
– she's my English teacher.   `4 points`

b) Here's Adam. He's OK. And here are my
friends, Ruby and Charlie. But they aren't in
my class. They're in 7X.
I'm not in 7X – I'm in 7Y!   `5 points`

4 WRITING Tamara – a new student
Put Tamara's sentences in the right order and write the dialogue.

Berry	Tamara
– Hi, I'm Berry. What's your name?	– Hi, I'm Tamara.
– Are you from Plymouth?	– No, I'm from London. What about you?
– I'm from Woolwell. I'm in class 7Y. What about you?	– I'm in class 7X. What's your favourite lesson?
– I like science. What about you?	– I like history.
– See you, Tamara.	– OK. Bye!

`5 points`

Für jede richtige Antwort bekommst du einen Punkt. Dann zähle alle Punkte zusammen.

36–32 points	31–19 points	18–0 points
☺	😐	☹
Very good!	OK, but you can do better. Which test is difficult?	You should do more practice. Ask your teacher for help.

Answers to TEST AND CHECK

1 WORDS

family: dad, stepsister
house: kitchen, wardrobe, bedroom, chair. **6 points**

2 WORDS   Talking about friends

1 Tim is tired.
2 Lilly is happy.
3 Anna is unhappy.
4 Jan is noisy.
5 Utku is messy.
6 Sarah is bossy. **6 points**

3 LANGUAGE   On the phone

1 Hi, Luca. Are you at home? – No, I'm not.
2 Are you in town? – Yes, I am.
3 Are your friends with you? – Yes, they are.
4 Are you in a shop? – Yes, we are.
5 Are Adam and Charlie with you? – No, they aren't.
6 Is Ellie with you? – Yes, she is.
Good! Can I talk to her? **6 points**

4 WRITING   Jake – a new friend

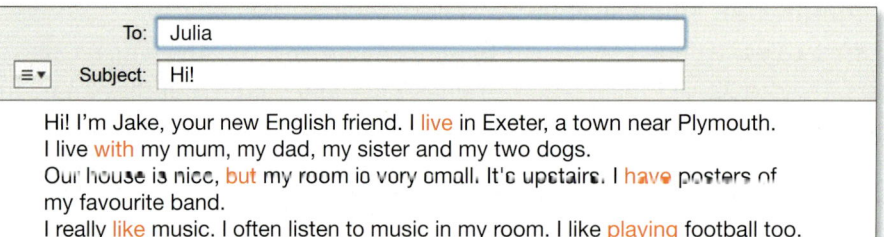

To:	Julia
Subject:	Hi!

Hi! I'm Jake, your new English friend. I live in Exeter, a town near Plymouth.
I live with my mum, my dad, my sister and my two dogs.
Our house is nice, but my room is very small. It's upstairs. I have posters of my favourite band.
I really like music. I often listen to music in my room. I like playing football too.
Is your family big or small? Is your house in town?
Jake

6 points

5 SPEAKING   A dialogue

Emma	Sam
Can I see you tomorrow?	– Yes, I'm at home tomorrow.
What's your phone number?	– 921 690.
And what's your address?	– 26 Borough Road.
Can you spell that, please?	– B-O-R-O-U-G-H.
B O R O U G H?	– Yes, that's right.
Great! Thanks, Sam. Bye.	– See you.

6 points

Für jede richtige Antwort bekommst du einen Punkt. Dann zähle alle Punkte zusammen.

30–27 points	26–16 points	15–0 points
☺	☺	☹
Very good!	OK, but you can do better. Which test is difficult?	You should do more practice. Ask your teacher for help.

Unit 3, page 69

1 WORDS

March – May – June – July – October – December   `6 points`

2 WORDS   In a shop

1 The hoodies are eighteen pounds.
2 The sweets are thirty-five p.
3 The shoes are sixteen pounds.

4 The trainers are forty-five pounds.
5 The bikes are ninety-nine pounds.
6 The shirts are six pounds ninety-nine.   `6 points`

3 LANGUAGE   At the weekend

a) Pick the right verb.

1 At the weekend I often meet my friends in town.
2 We sometimes buy sweets there.
3 But my dad stays at home.

b) Find the right form of the verb.

1 On Saturday my mum goes to work.
2 I often go to town.
3 My two sisters go swimming.   `6 points`

4 SPEAKING   Birthdays

Daniel When's your birthday, Sarah?
Sarah Friday 11th June.
Daniel And what are your favourite activities on your birthday?
Sarah We often play games. And we sometimes watch a film.
Daniel Sounds fun. Thanks, Sarah.   `6 points`

5 WRITING

My Sunday
In the morning I get up at 11 o'clock. I have breakfast with my family.
In the afternoon I often meet my friends or ride my bike. In July and August I go swimming.
In the evening I watch TV or play games with my brother.   `12 points`

Tests 1–4: Für jede richtige Antwort bekommst du einen Punkt.

Test 5: Für jeden korrekten Satz gibt es zwei Punkte.

Dann zähle alle Punkte zusammen.

36–32 points	31–19 points	18–0 points
☺	😐	☹
Very good!	OK, but you can do better. Which test is difficult?	You should do more practice. Ask your teacher for help.

Answers to TEST AND CHECK

Unit 4, page 87

1 WORDS Activities

1 Dad wakes mum in the morning.
2 First he feeds all the animals.
3 He often goes shopping.
4 Then he works on the farm.
5 He has a snack when Berry comes home.
6 He has dinner with Berry. **6 points**

2 LANGUAGE What's the time?

1 D   2 B   3 A   4 E   5 C   6 F   **6 points**

3 LANGUAGE Family and animals

1 I don't like hamsters.
2 My sister doesn't like bulls.
3 My parents don't like rats.
4 My grandma doesn't like pets.
5 My dad doesn't like zoos.
6 We all don't like snakes.   **6 points**

4 READING

1 C   2 E   3 B   4 F   5 A   6 D   **6 points**

5 WRITING

Dear Anna,
Please come to my sleepover.
It's on Saturday, 15th June.
It's at my house: 25a Gartengasse.
It's from 6.00 pm to 10.30 am.
I want to ride bikes and listen to music.
Please bring trainers, a pullover, your bike and your favourite CD.
I hope you can come.
Lukas   **12 points**

Tests 1–4: Für jede richtige Lösung bekommst du einen Punkt.

Test 5: Für jeden korrekten Satz gibt es zwei Punkte.

36–32 points	31–19 points	18–0 points
☺	☺	☹
Very good!	OK, but you can do better. Which test is difficult?	You should do more practice. Ask your teacher for help.

Unit 5, page 105

1 WORDS New words in Unit 5

1 Instruments: guitar, drums, piano.
2 Food: cheese, chicken, scone.
3 Drinks: juice, tea, water.
4 How you feel: angry, excited, nervous.

6 points

2 WORDS What's in the picture?

There's a harbour / cafe / boy / girl / ...
There are two men / boats / birds / tables /
chairs / customers / ...

10 points

3 LANGUAGE An English friend

1 Do you watch sport on TV?
2 Does your house have a garden?
3 Do you live near a school?
4 Do your parents like rap?
5 Do you have lots of homework?
6 Does your town have a good cinema?

6 points

4 MEDIATION Help your friend.

Bist du in der Schule? Wir haben heute keine Schule
und keine Hausaufgaben, es ist toll.
Bis später.
Chris

3 points

5 WRITING and SPEAKING In the Harbour Cafe

Man:
– Hello. Can I help you ?
– OK. Anything else?
– Here you are.
  Anything else?
– That's £ 4.25.
– Thanks.

Customer:
– Hello. Yes, please. A cheese sandwich, please.
– Yes, an orange juice, please.
– No thanks. That's all.
  OK. Here you are.

8 points

Test 1: Für jedes richtige Wort bekommst du einen halben Punkt.

Tests 2–5: Für jeden korrekten Satz gibt es einen Punkt.

33–29 points	28–17 points	16–0 points
☺		
Very good!	OK, but you can do better. Which test is difficult?	You should do more practice. Ask your teacher for help.

Illustrationen

Roland Beier, Berlin (Umschlaginnenseite Karte Ireland castle icon (M)); **Carlos Borrell**, Berlin (Umschlaginnenseite Karte (M)); **Cornelsen Bildarchiv** (S. 101 unten: Arnold); **Christian Görke**, Berlin (S. 52/53 Karte); **Jeongsook Lee**, Heidelberg (Umschlaginnenseite alle Icons außer Ireland castle; S. 140 (u. 159); S. 141 oben; S. 142; S. 144; S. 146 oben; S. 155; S. 156; S. 157; S. 158; S. 159; S. 161; S. 162; S. 163; S. 164; S. 165; S. 166; S. 168; S. 169; S. 170; S. 172; S. 173; S. 200; Umschlaginnenseite 3); **David Norman**, Meerbusch (S. 70; S. 72; S. 84; S. 87 Bild 1–6; S. 123; S. 128; S. 132 oben u. unten; S. 133; S. 134; S. 136–138); **Elwood H. Smith**, Rhinebeck, New York (S. 17 Sandy; S. 21; S. 24 Africa pencil case; S. 28; S. 29; S. 30; S. 31 Bild A–D; S. 44; S. 46; S. 48 oben, Nr. 3 li. u. re.; S. 52; S. 65; S. 66 unten li. u. re.; S. 82; S. 86; S. 98; S. 100; S. 101 oben; S. 102 Bild 1–5; S. 105 oben; S. 113; S. 121; S. 122; S. 130–131; S. 146 unten; S. 147; S. 148; S. 149); **Steffen Wolff**, Brohl-Lützing (S. 6; S. 8/9; S. 14–15; S. 16; S. 18; S. 31 Bild 1–10; S. 36; S. 38; S. 39; S. 40–41; S. 42; S. 43; S. 47; S. 48 Nr. 1 u. 2 li. u. re.; S. 50; S. 54; S. 55; S. 56; S. 57; S. 60 oben; S. 64; S. 66 Bild A–H; S. 67; S. 69; S. 76; S. 77 oben u. Mitte; S. 83 (u. 125); S. 90; S. 92; S. 94 oben, Mitte li. u. unten li.; S. 95 oben li.; S. 106–108; S. 110; S. 111; S. 114; S. 119; S. 145; S. 152)

Bildquellen

Susan Abbey & Frank Donoghue, Nenagh (S. 78 Bild A–D); **Alamy**, Abingdon (S. 7: Brian Mitchell; S. 8: Picture Partners; S. 11 Bild 6: image100; S. 12 crocodile: moodboard, hamster: Wildlife GmbH; S. 19 scarf: kris Mercer; S. 34 Bild 5: Elizabeth Whiting & Associates/ewastock kitchens; S. 35 Bild 3: Ivan Barta, Bild 7 kitchen (M): Andrew Butterton, Bild 8: Brian Hoffman; S. 44 oben: sharpstock; S. 46 unten: Richard Newton; S. 51 Bild 1: Woodystock, Bild 2: Cultura Creative, Bild 3: JJ pixs, Bild 5: Bubbles Photolibrary, Bild 6: Clearviewstock; S. 52 Bild 1 dad, Grace (M): Golden Pixels LLC/Kablonk! RF; S. 53 Bild 5: Benjamin Volant; S. 58 Bild 1 u. 2. dad, Grace. Golden Pixels LLC/Kablonk! RF, S. 63 market. Marc Hill; S. 65 dad: Golden Pixels LLC/Kablonk! RF; S. 67 bed: Art Directors&trip, TV: LJS photography; S. 69 sweets: Studiomode; S. 70 pony riding: The Photolibrary Wales/Rex Moreton; S. 71 Mitte li.: John James, Mitte re.: Mark Boulton; S. 73 Bild A: Stephen Bardens; S. 88 Bild A ferry (M): Marc Hill; S. 108 oben: ian woolcock; S. 112 Bild 1: Gareth Byrne; S. 114: Profimedia International s.r.o; S. 117 oben: ISP Photography, unten: Nina Kissell; S. 135 helmet: Photodisc (RF); S. 151 cap: Art Directors & TRIP, friendship bracelet: Image Source, game console: mediablitzimages (uk) Limited, biology: fSTop/Adam Burn, chemistry: Juice Images/Juice Images242, homework club: MasKot, home economics: MBI/Stockbroker, physics: Images Source/IE371; S. 152 dad (M): F1 online digitale Bildagentur GmbH, family (M): Big Cheese Photo LLC; S. 153 musical chairs: image 100, fancy dress party: Angela Hampton Picture Library; S. 154 sleep: Maximilian Weinzierl); **Bigstock.com** (S. 11 swimming (unten): Heidi's photos, skateboarding (unten): goldenangel; S. 39 bed: llandrea; S. 55 shirt: catsmeow); **Trevor Burrows Photography**, Plymouth (S. 4; S. 5 unten; S. 6; S. 10 Bild 1–4; S. 11 Bild 1; S. 12 oben li.; S. 13 unten; S. 16 Bild A (M, ohne Hund), Bild B; S. 17 Bild C, Bild D; S. 18; S. 20; S. 22 Bild 1–4; S. 23 Bild 5–6; S. 26; S. 28; S. 33 Ellie (M), Ms Lee (M); S. 34 Bild 1 u. 2; S. 37 Zoe, Conor, Ellie; S. 44 unten; S. 46 oben; S. 52 Bild 1 (M), 4, 6; S. 53 Bild 2; S. 55 Bild C; S. 58 Bild 1 u. 2 Luca, Jack, mom (M), Bild 3; S. 59 Bild 4 Jack, Luca (M), Bild 5–7; S. 65 Luca; S. 67 oben; S. 70 oben li. u. unten li.; S. 71 unten; S. 74 oben; S. 75 Bild A–D, Bild E Berry (M); S. 78 Bild E; S. 82; S. 88 Bild A dad (M), Bild B; S. 89 Bild D; S. 90 oben; S. 91 unten; S. 100; S. 103; S. 104 Bild 1–7; S. 112 Bild 2, 4, 5, 6, 7); **ClipDealer**, München (S. 151 card collection:

Lasse Kristensen); **Corbis**, Düsseldorf (S. 62 Bild C: India Picture; S. 135 Mitte li.: Corbis Sports/Tim de Waele); **Cornelsen Bildarchiv**, Berlin (S. 10 hand: Griebel; S. 16/17 Hintergrund: Zieschang; S. 27; S. 45; S. 60: Catania/used with permission of The Royal Mint/Bank of England); S. 63 oben, Bild 1–4, Hoe, Lido, shopping centre, aquarium, S. 63 cinema: Bensmann; S. 81; S. 89 Bild C: Bensmann; S. 99 Sarah, Paul, Anna, Mitte, Bild 1–3; S. 109 oben, Bild A–D, unten; S. 139 Bild A–H: Bensmann); **Drake Circus Shopping Centre**, Plymouth (S. 53 Bild 3); **Eggbuckland Community College**, Plymouth (S. 91 oben logo); **Fotolia.com** (S. 150 in-line skating: Kathin39); **Getty Images**, München (S. 5 oben. (u. 35 Bild 4): Bob Stevens; S. 11 Bild 4: Image Source (RF), Bild 5: Sean Justice, Bild 8: Chris Ryan (RF), reading (unten): Nick Dolding; S. 134 unten (M): Fresh Food Images/Tony Robbins; S. 135 unten: Getty Images Sport/Bryn Lennon; S. 150 canoeing: Flickr/An Lumatic image (RF)); **iStockphoto.com** (S. 11 Bild 2: Michael Braun, Bild 7: Hedda Gjerpen; S. 12 bird: Mr_Jamsey, elephant: Peter Malsbury, snake: VMJones, rabbit: Nikola Spasenoski; S. 13 mobile phone: Baris Simsek; S. 19 sisters: knape; S. 22 oben: andres alcazar; S. 24 pencils (2x): mahesh14, exercise book: Nikolaas Boden; S. 32 oben (u. 110): Cliff Parnell; S. 37 Alisha: Kelly Cline, Finn: manley099; S. 49 tae kwon do outfit: tarras79, football, tennis golf: Jamie Parker; S. 55 Bild D: Jitalia17, hoodie: Fabio Cecconello; S. 67 calendar: Marko Kovacevic; S. 84 Bild F: Elena Dobrova, Bild G: Mehmet Salih Guler; S. 93 guitar player (M): Jamie Carroll; S. 96 Bild B: darrenwise, Bild G: Gary Radler; S. 97 Bild D (u. 128 u. 134): Amanda Rohde, unten: 77 studio; S. 112 Bild 10: Gabor Izso; S. 133 unten re.: Edward Shaw; S. 139 oben: Nikki Bidgood; S. 143 Mitte li. u. re.: i359702; S. 150 boxing: Chris Schmidt; S. 151 DVD player: mbbirdy, textile technology: Catherine Yuelet; S. 153 sports club: Chris Schmidt; S. 154 clarinet: Christopher Futcher); **Mauritius**, Mittenwald (S. 151 ethics: mauritius images/Alamy RF/Eyebyte; S. 153 youth centre: Maskot); **Okapia**, Frankfurt/Main (S. 12 rat: J-L Klein & M-L Hubert); **Photolibrary**, London (S. 11 Bild 3: pixtal images (RF), S. 133 unten li.: Fresh Food Images/Heather Brown); **Picture Alliance**, Frankfurt/Main (S. 29: empics; S. 68 Casper: AP Photo/Plymouth Herald/Amy Standford; S. 88 – 89 Hintergrund); **Plymouth Music Zone**, Plymouth (S. 93 PMZ logo); **Thomas Schulz**, Teupitz (S. 54; S. 61; S. 73 unten, S. 74 unten; S. 86, S. 121); **Shutterstock.com** (S. 10 sweets: spaxia; S. 12 cat: Irina Bondareva, bear: red-feniks, monkey: Simone van den Berg, dog oben: Eastimages, fish: Ekaterina V. Borisova, tiger: Tiago Jorge da Silva Estima, dog on playcard: Eric Isselee; S. 13 camera: taelove7, computer: Elnur, football: Luis Luoro, girl: Andrey_Popov; S. 16 Bild A dog (M): Erik Lam; S. 19 unten li.: Monkey Business Images, dog: Eric Isselée, Tim: Andrea Slatter, unhappy emoticon (u. 32 u. 68 u. 74 u. 75 u. 86 u. 104): Dawn Hudson, happy emoticon (u. 32 u. 68 u. 74 u. 75 u. 86 u. 104): In-Finity; S. 23 unten (u. 77): Alhovik; S. 24 background: Natticka, pencil sharpener: Gelpi, rubber: Chet, ruler: David Brimm, pens: Volodymyr Krasyuk, pencil case: Brooke Becker, calculator: Fotoline, laptop: Elnur; S. 25 box: Oleksii Sagitov; S. 32 light bulb: Marish; S. 34 Hintergrund: Hitdelight, Bild 6: Chertanova; S. 35 Hintergrund: Ala Alkhouskaya, Bild 7 baby bottle (M): Elena Schweitzer, high chair (M): ekipaj, Bild 9: Schaefer Elvira, Bild 10: Fekete Tibor; S. 37 grandpa Fox and grandma Fox: images.etc, grandpa Cole and grandma Cole: Pressmaster; Pete: Juriah Mosin, Jackie: Olga Sapegina, Steve: Yuri Arcurs; S. 39 cushions: Baloncici, lamp: Margo Harrison, wardrobe: terekhov igor, poster: Petrafler, table: Simon Krzic, chair: 3rdbrained; S. 49 oben: Monkey Business Images, bike: Paprikubani, rugby ball: joingate, skateboard: Igorij, snowboard: sabri deniz kizil; S. 51 Bild 4: aldegonde; S. 55 Bild A: karkas, Bild B: Serg64, tie: KULISH VICTORIIA, shoes:

Turumtaev Ildar, trainers: Ronen, pullover: Karkas; jeans: Simone Andress; S. 59 Bild 4 boy with red shirt (M): Tomasz Trojanowski; S. 62 Bild A dancer (M): Boobl, stage (M): Patricia Hofmeester, Bild B fireworks: Deymos; S. 67 breakfast: R.Legosyn, football: krasowit, lunch: Aaron Amat, bike: Senol Yaman, S. 69 blue shoes: nadi555, hoodies: Will Tilroe-Otte, shirts: Evgenia Sh., bikes: Petr Nad, trainers: Serg64; S. 70/71: Capture Light; S. 70 unten re.: Graeme Dawes; S. 71 oben li.: Keith Publicover, Bild 1: jokerpro, Bild 2: Ivonne Wierink, Bild 3: aleks.k, Bild 4: robertimages, Bild 5: Pichugin Dmitry, Bild 6: pgaborphotos, Bild 7: Geanina Bechea, Bild 8: Tom Grundy, Bild 9: Alexruss, Bild 10: Nataliia Melnychuk, Bild 11: Maslov Dmitry, Bild 12: gillmar; S. 72 clock: Slavoljub Pantelic; S. 73 Bild B: Michael Ransburg, Bild C: cynoclub, Bild D: fpolat69; S. 75 Bild E dog (M): Eric Isselée; S. 77 phone (u. 90 u. 97 u. 128): Oleksiy Mark; S. 79 balloons: Kolja; S. 80 dog: Louis D. Slyono, goldfish, hamster, snake, monkey, rabbit: Klara Viskova; llama, donkey: Albert Ziganshin; S. 83 oben: Michael Pettigrew, unten: Cynoclub; S. 84 Bild A: Roman Sigaev, Bild B: Harper, Bild C: Anthony Berenyi, Bild D: Feng Yu, Bild E: Michael Iawlor, Bild H: J. Shomo; S. 90 A: Oleksiy Mark, B: Aleksei Potov, Bild C: TT Photo, Bild D: Volodymyr Krasyvk; S. 93 DJ (M): sita ram, Bild A, B, C: k13art, Bild D: Dick Stada; S. 95 singer re.: freelanceartist; S. 96 Bild A: Thomas M Perkins, Bild C: Nayashkoya Olga, Bild D: ER_09, Bild E: jon le-bon, Bild F: Nitr, Bild H: Feng Yu, Bild I: Vlue, Bild J: ronstik, menu: BlueSunday; S. 99 dancer: sparkdesign, guitar player: AZ, singer: TEA; S. 102 crab: haveseen, seagull: Dan Costa; S. 107 parchment (u. 108): Anan Kaewkhammul; S. 109 Bild 1: nicepictures, Bild 2: Ivonne Wierink, Bild 3: Nayashkova Olga, Bild 4: Menna, Bild 5: Naturaldigital, Bild 6: vnlit, Bild 7: Roman Sigaev, Bild 8: marco mayer; S. 111: Mike Flippo; S. 112 Bild 8: marco mayer, Bild 9: Doug Matthews; S. 115: AVAVA; S. 116 Bild 1: Baksym Bondarchuk, Bild 2: marylooo, Bild 3: marekuliasz, Bild 4: Valentin Agapov, Bild 5: Becky Stares, Bild 6: Fedorov Loeksiv, Bild 7: Simon Krzic, Bild 8: ehe, Bild 9: Shkurd; S. 118 pencil: DenisNata, garden: Sandra Cunningham, homework: Quang Ho, lucky: mart, house: dslaven, teacher: qualtiero boffi, happy: Giuseppe R, baby: Vasiliy Koval, cushion: marylooo, tie: sabri deniz kizil; S. 124 Bild 1: Andrey Shadrin, Bild 2: iofoto, Bild 3: Elena Elisseeva, Bild 4: AISPIX, Bild 5: dragon fang, Bild 6: Monkey Business Images, Bild 7: CREATISTA, Bild 8: eiwhite; S. 125 li.: Dragos Iliescu, re.: Ana del Castillo; S. 132 Mitte li.: Takra, re.: aispl; S. 133 stocking: Miachel C. Gray, cracker: JCEly; S. 135 oben BMX bike: Attl Tibor, gloves: PavelSh, pads: nito, Mitte park: Jorg Hackemann, Mitte re.: Snezana Kundric; S. 140 oben: Rene Jansa, Mitte u. unten: schankz; S. 141 elephant: Talvi, monkey, bear, cat, sheep, cow: eric Isselée, guinea pig: vovan, chicken: s_oleg, rabbit: Stefan Petru Andronache, unten re.: Blend Images; S. 143 oben: Ilya Andriyanov, unten: Yayayoyo; S. 150 climbing: Frances A. Miller, cycling: archana bhartia, athletics: max blain, drawing: Jeka, ice hockey: Govorov Pavel, listening to music: Goodluz, making models: Zivica Kerkez, playing basketball: Lorraine Swanson, playing table tennis: JJpixs, snowboarding: Konstantin Shishkin, skiing: Gorilla, surfing the internet: LUCARELLI TEMISTOCLE, taking photos: Jorg Hackemann, trampolining: Sonya Etchison; S. 151 bag: Nikolay Postnikov, mp3 player: Jessmine, necklace: Gregory June, poster: kots, TV: gordana, German: V. Schlichting, RE: Glam, social studies: andresr, special needs training: oliveromg, tutor period: Monkey Business Images; S. 153 fast food restaurant: Blend Images, zoo: Glenda M. Powers, shopping centre: prim68, football stadium: Alexander Chaikin, video shop: Pavel L Photo and Video, skate park: ARENA Creative, popcorn: Alex Staroseltsev, water fight: Andy Heyward, balloons: djem, biscuits: c byatt-norman, barbecue: BlueOrange Studio, camp:

wavebreakmedia ltd., sleeping bag: photo25th, pyjamas: Dario Sabljak, fancy dress: Kruchankova Maya, torch: Petr Malyshev; S. 154 special food: Ruben Pinto, vegetables: missanzi, basket: Hannamariah, meat: Paul Krugloff, birdseed li.: dusan964, re.: Chepe Nicoli, aquarium: MattJones, cage: Thomas Skjaeveland, bark: Eric Isselée, run: Martin Valigursky, jump: Norman Chan, cello: Fotokostic, saxophone: Anton Albert, recorder, Apollofoto, violin: Brian Chase, flute: Fotokostic, trumpet: Katrina Brown, keyboard: Nicole Gordine; S. 167: Gemenacom); **Stills-Online**, Hamburg (S. 151 keyring, skateboard); **ullstein bild**, Berlin (S. 154 hutch: cuveland)

Titelbild
Trevor Burrows Photography, Plymouth

Liedquellen
S. 53 *This is my city*. Text, music and copyright: Timothy Victor/www.timothyvictor.com.

Textquelle
S. 80 *Muuuuuuummmmmmm* © Peter Dixon. From "Read me out loud: Poems to rap, chant, whisper or shout for every day of the year." Chosen by Nick Toczek and Paul Cookson, page 159–260, Macmillan Children's Books 2007

Special thanks to:
The staff and students at **Eggbuckland Community College**, Plymouth and **Canoe Tamar**; Tavistock; **The Cawsand Ferry**, Plymouth/www.cawsandferry.co.uk, **Elvira's Café**, Plymouth, **The Miniature Pony Centre**, Dartmoor/www.miniatureponycentre.com; **Plymouth Music Zone**, Plymouth, for inspiring and composing 'Music Makes a Difference'/www.plymouthmusiczone.org.uk; **The Strand Tea Rooms**, Plymouth, **The Tuck Shop**, Plymouth; **The National Marine Aquarium**, Plymouth/www.national-aquarium.co.uk; **Visit Plymouth**, Plymouth/www.visitplymouth.co.uk; **Woodlands Family Theme Park**, Totnes/www.woodlandspark.com; **Spirit of Adventure**, Yelverton/www.spirit-of-adventure.com

CLASSROOM ENGLISH

Diese Arbeitsanweisungen findest du häufig im Schülerbuch

English	Deutsch
Act the dialogue / the scenes for the class.	Spiel(t) den Dialog / die Szenen vor der Klasse.
Ask questions. / Ask different partners.	Stelle Fragen. / Frage verschiedene Partner/innen.
Answer the questions (about the story).	Beantworte die Fragen (über die Geschichte).
… as many as you can.	… so viele wie du kannst.
Before you listen / read / …	Bevor du hörst / liest …
Pick a picture / the right answer.	Wähle ein Bild / die richtige Antwort aus.
Compare with a partner.	Vergleiche mit einem Partner / einer Partnerin.
Complete the questions / the rules / the sentences.	Vervollständige die Fragen / die Regeln / die Sätze.
Copy and complete the table / your learner log.	Schreibe die Tabelle / dein Lerntagebuch ab und vervollständige sie / es.
Correct the sentences.	Berichtige die Sätze.
Fill in the table.	Fülle die Tabelle aus.
Find the right answers.	Finde die richtigen Antworten.
Finish the sentences.	Vervollständige die Sätze.
Go to page 25.	Gehe zu Seite 25.
Listen and check / repeat / write.	Hör zu und überprüfe / wiederhole / schreibe auf.
Look at the brochure / photos / pictures.	Sieh die Broschüre / Fotos / Bilder an.
Make a dialogue / a table.	Fertige einen Dialog / eine Tabelle an.
Match the sentences / titles with the pictures.	Ordne die Sätze / Titel den Bildern zu.
Pick a card / words from the box.	Nimm eine Karte / Wörter aus dem Kasten.
Point at the right picture	Zeige auf des richtige Bild.
Practise with a partner.	Übe mit einem Partner / einer Partnerin.
Put the answers in the right order.	Bringe die Antworten in die richtige Reihenfolge.
Read the text / story.	Lies den Text / die Geschichte.
Right or wrong?	Richtig oder falsch?
Swap partners.	Tausche den Partner / die Partnerin.
Talk about …	Sprich über …
Talk to different partners.	Sprich mit verschiedenen Partnern / Partnerinnen.
Tell the class.	Erzähle das der Klasse.
Use your notes / table.	Benutze deine Notizen / Tabelle.
Walk around.	Gehe herum.
Write a dialogue / sentences about you.	Schreibe einen Dialog / Sätze über dich.
You can put it in your DOSSIER.	Du kannst es in deinem Dossier abheften.